EXPERIMENTAL TIMES

EXPERIMENTAL TIMES

Startup Capitalism and Feminist Futures
in India

HEMANGINI GUPTA

UNIVERSITY OF CALIFORNIA PRESS

University of California Press
Oakland, California

© 2025 by Hemangini Gupta

Library of Congress Cataloging-in-Publication Data

Names: Gupta, Hemangini, 1980– author.
Title: Experimental times : startup capitalism and feminist futures in India /
    Hemangini Gupta.
Description: Oakland, California : University of California Press, [2025] | Includes
    bibliographical references and index.
Identifiers: LCCN 2024026869 (print) | LCCN 2024026870 (ebook) | ISBN 9780520392762
    (cloth) | ISBN 9780520392779 (paperback) | ISBN 9780520392786 (ebook)
Subjects: LCSH: New business enterprises—India—Bangalore. | Businesswomen—
    India—Bangalore. | Capitalism—Social aspects—India—Bangalore. | Feminism—
    India—Bangalore. | Technological innovations—India—Bangalore.
Classification: LCC HD62.5 .G87 2025 (print) | LCC HD62.5 (ebook) |
    DDC 658.1/10954—dc23/eng/20240809
LC record available at https://lccn.loc.gov/2024026869
LC ebook record available at https://lccn.loc.gov/2024026870

34 33 32 31 30 29 28 27 26 25
10 9 8 7 6 5 4 3 2 1

For Moyukh, for mapping the horizon and firming the ground
And my parents, "for all the sacrifice" and the continual faith

Contents

Illustrations

Acknowledgments

THIS PROJECT has shifted shape and form, at times altering slightly, at others reconfiguring tectonically. Many people placed their faith in its ability to eventually settle—at least for a while until the next movement. It began as a dissertation for my PhD, and since I started graduate school after several years as a journalist, I am always grateful to the people who helped me onto that path with my proposal and initial ideas, Lalitha Kamath, Mathew John, and Lawrence Liang.

I might not have found a place at Emory's WGSS Department without any prior gender studies classes if my adviser, Carla Freeman, had not taken a chance on me. She helped this project to stabilize with a theoretical foundation and achievable goals and introduced me to the worlds of feminist anthropology and women's, gender, and sexuality studies; the rich terrain of Marxist feminism; and the chaos and pleasures of belonging to the tribe of anthropologists. My graduate committee, Pamela Scully, Joyce Flueckiger, and Jennifer Patico, were generous with their time and inspiring with their comments. Joyce Flueckiger taught me how to listen to ethnography and to let it shape my theorizing rather than the other way around. Jennifer Patico taught an incredible class in the anthropology of consumption and material cultures at Georgia State that remains one of my favorite classes and shaped the attention to consumption and leisure in this book as well. Pamela Scully guided my dissertation toward much-needed form, coherence, meaning, and reason.

In Bangalore, Arjun Narayan and Abishek Laxminarayan let me enter their worlds of startup culture and venture capital; puzzled over ideas; and suggested sites, spaces, and people to research. The man I call Pushkar Subramaniam made this research possible with his trust in the ethnographic method and in academic enterprise. At his company, I made lifelong friends and found a rich research site. I cannot thank the individuals with whom I interacted by their real names, but they opened their lives, frailties, vulnerabilities, aspirations, and ambitions to me with generosity and great spirit. I am deeply moved and eternally grateful for their trust, time, and stories. "Naina" let me into her home and life; shared her trials and tribulations; and gamely hosted all kinds of sleepovers, lunches, dinners, and parties. Diya Nanjapa accompanied me to dance bars and catered my ethnographically inclined social events with fluency, ease, and general joie de vivre. Jiti Nichani made my friends hers. Jasmeen Patheja listened, waited, suggested, supported, and took care of my family when I was away.

Joseph Ollapally made a grand exit from this world on April 1, 2010, dying as magnificently as he lived, in a free fall from a rock ledge behind a waterfall on the Thailand-Myanmar border. His support for my dreams, writing, and adventures and his spirit remain. Minu Pani kept an open house, enlivened by good food, beer, cigarettes, and constant company. She offered me home, friendship, and company during my fieldwork, and I wish she could have lived to hear about my "findings."

In Atlanta, during graduate school, families congealed around me over coffees, study dates, sleepovers, and meals. Noemi Molitor, Sydney Silverstein, Rachel Weitzenkorn, and Sasha Klupchak made sure I graduated and that I was well cared for, healthy, and happy throughout this period—with food, drink, celebrations, kindness, and friendship. Chanel Craft made me write, revise, and redraft and showed me how; she made a home for me at the CWE with Tiffany del Valle's enthusiasm and infectious humor. My cohort, Lisa Frazier, Rachel Dudley, and Ayisha al-Sayyad, read countless drafts of my writing with patience and generosity and watched this project evolve from a hasty prospectus. Isabella Alexander, Dinah Hannaford, Mael and Stu, Sarah Franzen, Rebecca Spurrier, and Silas Allard were the book clubs, long conversations, evenings by the fire, and company that sustained me. Suyun Choi and Shunyuan Zhang engaged my work honestly and critically. Suma and Jamie enlivened my weekends and put my dissertation in perspective. Smriti, Akshay, and Maya Rao; Zoey Chen; and Aliya Firozvi reminded me that there was a world beyond my writing—and showed me how to live in it.

I formed the Bangalore Research Network with Manisha Anantharaman in 2012; it helped me find academic community and solidarity in Bangalore. Carol Upadhya helped me to contextualize my findings with her infinite knowledge of labor, class, and gender in the city. Smriti Srinivas co-organized several iterations of the annual Bangalore research Network-NAGARA workshop with me and helped me to scale and widen my analytical approaches to the study of urban phenomena.

A graduate fellowship at the Center for Women at Emory offered financial support and an incredible feminist community in my sixth year of writing. Thanks especially to Chanel Craft for living her feminism and forming the Graduation Dissertation Writing Group. My other writing group with Claire-Marie Hefner, Jenn Ortegren, and Shunyuan Zhang witnessed the carnage of terrible first drafts and sharpened my thinking. The Colonial Post-Colonial Studies group—Ajit, Navyug, Shreyas, Sydney, Shatam, Moyukh, Adeem, and Bisan—offered helpful and constructive comments on a chapter and were the social lifelines that sustained me.

A faculty fellowship in the Department of WGSS at Colby College enabled me to finish my dissertation by placing me in the company of the most engaged and thoughtful students and colleagues. Their presence was a daily reminder of why I teach and research in WGSS. In Maine, when the sky was at its bleakest, a magical community formed to push me along with hikes, films, cookouts, and long conversations: Mariola Alvarez, Vivek Freitas, Nadia El-Shaarawi, Rachel Lesser, Elana Nashelsky, and Maki Smith made a home where none seemed possible. Chris Kreider kept me cared for. In Montreal, I continued writing during a visiting fellowship at IGSF in Montreal, with thanks to the warmth and camaraderie of Alanna Thain and the late Marguerite Waller.

My postdoctoral position at the National Institute of Advanced Studies in Bangalore enabled me to continue follow-up fieldwork on my project and work with fabulous scholars who refined my thinking on capital, class, and labor; Carol Upadhya was a generous and engaged mentor, and Michael Goldman, Vinay Gidwani, Helga Leitner, and Eric Sheppard were continually inspiring with their work.

Incisive and formative comments from scholars in the field at conferences have led to pleasurable turns in my argument and unexpected detours: many thanks to Ilana Gershon, Karen Ho, Sareeta Amrute, and Rachel Heiman, who served as respondents and interlocutors at key junctions. Lilly Irani's magical work opened up a field for me that I didn't know existed, and through it I found a place of scholarly belonging. My book workshop with Kalindi Vora, Banu Subramaniam, and Sareeta Amrute was challenging but generative, and I'm so grateful for their time and attention to the manuscript in the midst of the COVID pandemic. I've especially loved audience comments that invited me to think in new and exciting directions; thanks are due to gender studies audiences at Ohio State University, Dartmouth, Bowdoin College, the

National Institute of Advanced Studies, Arizona State University, Middlebury College, and Goethe University. The engaged International Political Economy research group at the University of Edinburgh offered critical commentary on the introduction, and the Gender and Politics Research group has kept me thinking about my research through various other responsibilities—special thanks are due to Annika Bergman-Rosamond and Mihaela Mihai.

Working with fantastic feminist editors—Priti Ramamurthy, Jennifer Nash, Ashwini Tambe, Nassim Parvin, and Sareeta Amrute—has been a joy that has shaped the publications allied to this book. Helpful comments on draft articles came from the Ideas on Fire team and from Kareem Khubchandani and Dwai Banerjee, and a special thanks to Dwai who, as a true STS scholar, retrieved and salvaged my whole manuscript when it was corrupted. This book went through a protracted review process, so I should specifically thank reviewers one and three, who sent back comments and completed the process; reviewing is challenging under current conditions of work, and these reviewers enabled a two-year process to come to completion. Thanks to Caren Kaplan, who provided the vital connections that led me to the perfect publishing house, where Naomi Schneider was patient and supportive through a protracted review process and Aline Dolinh has been an absolute pleasure to work with. Thanks to Shezad Dawood for permission to use his piece *Ambiguous Relationships*, which speaks to the uncertainty, ambiguity, and play at work in this book.

The bulk of this book was written while I taught at Middlebury College, and where teaching seven new classes focused on labor, gender and sexuality, technology, globalization, and collaborative filmmaking helped me sharpen my arguments and finish this book. The humanities labs for gender, technology, and the future opened my work to debates in feminist STS, and those interdisciplinary classes (and support from Mike Roy) were an absolute dream. Thanks to Matt Martignoni for helping with curating that work and Melanie Chow for the detailed work compiling the citations. Nobody loves a precarious job, and nobody loves one through a decimated job market and COVID, but I was unbelievably supported by a department that became family. Laurie Essig fought for us, lived her principles, and kept things fun, enabling me to enjoy my most rewarding professional years so far. Carly Thomsen had deep faith in this book, read it, engaged it, put me in conversation with other generative scholars, and continues to be a favorite collaborator. Catharine Wright and Karin Hanta make the GSFS space and Chellis Resource Center a hub of support and goodwill, and I'm so grateful for three years in Vermont with them.

Middlebury gave me the vital experience of living in a small town, where you can ring someone's doorbell and know they will be home: for impromptu visits; continual socializing; and the family I needed through freezing winters, COVID, and severe depression, I am forever grateful to Nikolina Dobreva (and her magnificent family), Jenn and Ajay (and Zahi!), Kristy and Danny (and Pepper!), Eva and Julien (and Chloe and Luca!), Raquel Albarran who held so much space for me (I miss you), Febe and Boğaç, and so many special families who gathered around our son.

Finally, my family in India (the Guptas, Mukundas and Iyengars) have been curious about my work and committed to supporting it both financially and emotionally. Thanks to Kumar Iyengar and my mesho for supporting my move to Atlanta so materially. My mashi and cousins make Bangalore home. My parents-in-law and KC have been patient and supportive and have forgiven my various lapses and constraints by adopting my deadlines and stresses as their own. My parents have borne (mostly with patience) the disappearances caused by my life as a journalist and then as an academic. My mother has visited me in cramped student halls, hot and dusty top-floor apartments, condos flung up next to the highway, and rickety rural houses, in London, Mumbai, New Delhi, Atlanta, and Waterville. She gamely adopts my (mis)adventures and capricious forays into uncertainty as her own, has taught me the survival skills to thrive on my own anywhere, and has made me a better person. My father knows me better than I know myself and keeps me buoyant with his unflappable faith in my abilities. Moyukh introduced me to anthropology and philosophy and reminds me why I love what I do. He fixes what I break, smooths the edges, changes the filter and the zoom on the lens, and remembers to live the good life. He has taken over the continual labor of cooking, cleaning, parenting, and erranding through several years with (mostly) good cheer, and this book would not exist without his enthusiasm. Finally, thanks to Nikhil, who slows us down, ends our working day when it seems like it has barely begun, and keeps us on our toes and always on the move. I love you and I hope you can help build a world that is different from the one we're giving you.

INTRODUCTION

IT WAS A CHILLY September day in Bangalore, the atmosphere thick with a mix of construction-related particles, smoke, and vehicular exhaust.[1] Around me, this South Indian city of over fourteen million people slowly climbed upward. In every neighborhood my auto rickshaw passed, construction cranes stretched to the sky, and blue tarpaulin scaffolding flapped in the wind, announcing yet another collapsed bungalow that had made way for a multistory building. After an hour in the auto, I finally reached a quiet cul de sac and climbed up a stairway to meet old friends at the start of my fieldwork.

When the door was flung open, I stepped inside a spacious living room bathed in diffracted lamplight. A disco ball still oscillated wildly from the ceiling above where we had mounted it at my farewell party for graduate school, held here many years before. People were picking at the remains of the dinner laid out on the table: rice, lentils, salad, a mixed vegetable curry. Inside the room were artists, entrepreneurs, and technological innovators. A heated discussion about when it was appropriate to leave work was underway.

"I just leave when I make ten mistakes!" Nayan said.

"What if that happens right in the morning?" someone asked him.

"Then I leave right in the morning!" he replied, laughing.

Bangalore was not always a city known for such pleasurable work. Through the 1990s and early 2000s, it was associated with the long nights of the call center employee orchestrating mobile phone plans and airline ticketing, or perhaps the "project time" of the software engineer working to the rhythms of the Western clients who needed information technology (IT) infrastructure serviced.[2] "Bangalore" was also the specter of outsourced jobs, invoked by former US president Barack Obama and hailed by *New York Times* journalist Thomas Friedman. And yet something had distinctly shifted since then.

This book examines zones of "experimental time" as simultaneously productive for the fabrication of global startup capitalism and feminist future making. This time moves between the blurred boundaries of paid and unpaid work and of hypervisibilized and invisibilized work to understand what forms of labor undergird the shift to startup capitalism. In recent years, middle-class technology work in the city has been reimagined from "back-end" labor to innovation that is visibilized and celebrated. Entrepreneurs and state officials in Bangalore, India's technology hub, situate their work and city as sites of technologically driven creativity and joy; citizens are not back-end call center employees mimicking Western accents but entrepreneurs-employees in the global economy of startup and entrepreneurial work. This dream of science as modernity was mobilized by India's first prime minister, Jawaharlal Nehru, when he spoke of "dams as the temples of modern India"; for a postcolonial nation like India, science and technology were seen as the promise of an anti-imperial modernity (Prakash 1999).[3] Capital, state, and affective investments in science and technology promise change that can move Bangalore from a site of back-end tech labor—the world of the past—to an innovation center of the future. This is a form of masculine nationalism and postcolonial aspiration spurred by the vision of the entrepreneur/innovator-as-hero.

The global startup economy depends on technological innovation to rapidly scale and transform work conditions to maximize profit. Workforces need to be kept precarious, flexible, and ever replaceable by technology. These conditions of labor are met by workers in India's entrepreneurial economy—in cities like Bangalore—who work to enable their class mobility and sometimes to craft a life away from the persistent and disciplining gaze of their extended kin. Unlike the call center economy—in which several of my interviewees might have been employed—here in the office-based entrepreneurial economy, there was no nighttime work and thus none of the stigma associated with those service-sector jobs. Work is meant to be pleasurable and creative, and this promise allured workers to engage in experimental work and cocreate technological futures that rewrite the conditions of labor. My ethnographic work in Bangalore's entrepreneurial economy signals the ascent of these forms of work toward a specific form of capitalism: what I understand as *startup capitalism*.

Startup capitalism promises workers conditions of labor that are enjoyable and pleasurable: flexible work hours, the ability to shape work futures, and leisure and fun built into the daily rhythms of work rather than adjacent to them. One premise of such work is *meritocracy*, or the reassurance that a good idea can build new techno-futures and scale to global success wherever in the world you are, and whoever you might be. This vision coalesces with a postcolonial promise of global and class mobility allowing Indian workers and entrepreneurs to access and shape global markets. The promise is especially alluring given the racialized conditions of labor mobility that structure Indian workers' access to global labor markets.

But I show a third aspect of startup capitalism in addition to the promise of creative labor and postcolonial mobility. I demonstrate that these promissory notes about startup futures are premised on the feminized labor of precarious and racialized workers. Workers experiment with new systems of work and technology use, only to then be replaced or extracted by these same systems.

The story of globalization has been narrated as one propelled by the feminization of labor, in which labor is devalued, relies on deskilling to prevent mobility, and invokes the myth of docile and racialized workers having "nimble fingers."[4] Contemporary uses of the phrase "feminized labor" understand it within the terms of a globally ascendant service economy in which all work is increasingly feminized, replicating the terms of work historically coded as "women's work" (Weeks 2011). Thus, as Mezzadra and Neilson assert: "A whole set of qualities and competences historically constructed as female under patriarchal regimes of the sexual division of labor have come to define standard performances required from workers in a wide range of occupations" (2013, 104). In fact, most office-based work since the 1990s has been characterized by the need for flexibility that will ride all "waves" and secure permanent technological advantage (Boltanski and Chiapello 2007, 71). But the workforce is simultaneously feminized through the expectation of labor that is continuous and extractive and that blends spaces of work, home, and leisure so that work is performed across these sites (chapter 4), with love (chapter 5), and through invisibilized and unremunerated experimentation (chapter 6). Such unfolding of work significantly redraws relations between waged work and capital to blur the Marxist distinctions between productive labor that is formally accounted for within capitalism and reproductive labor as the unwaged labor essential for capitalism to survive but taken for granted and thus invisibilized.

This book also shows how work under startup capitalism is racialized. Elite entrepreneurs leverage their caste privilege to define desirable work as the work of creative innovation. They imagine and build their products and services by deploying imaginaries of racialized labor. When I refer in this book to the racialized labor on which startup capitalism is predicated, I am suggesting that this is not only because it is performed cheaply by brown workers in the postcolony, but also because it assigns and devalues certain forms of work as expendable and unskilled.

As entrepreneurs and technologists narrate how they approach work through the creative use of technology, they simultaneously distance themselves from what they consider "menial" and "repetitive" work. My fieldwork found that elite upper-caste entrepreneurs assemble these hierarchies through imaginaries of race and caste, thus creating an underclass of racialized labor from whom they distance themselves. The fully "human" being of the creative elite entrepreneur is sedimented through a differentiation from the "less-than-human" workers. Through these hierarchies of the human, entrepreneurs working in the service of startup capitalism produce innovation as the creative genius of the mind that is separate from devalued everyday work. These hierarchies of mind and body, and of assigned versus chosen work, are deeply rooted in race, caste, and gender-striated hierarchies.

When call center work first began to be outsourced to India, the cultural critic Harish Trivedi (2003) memorably called this the work of "cyber coolies," in reference to a centuries-long system of indentured labor through which workers were shipped to plantations in service of British empire. I am not suggesting a commensurability between indentured servitude and current-day startup labor (as Trivedi might have); instead I turn my attention to how these racialized hierarchies haunt contemporary discussions of labor, this time in global startup economies like Bangalore. Race is integral to startup economies because of how labor hierarchies determine whose work is valued, believed to be creative, and thought to contain the human capital that deserves nurturing.[5] As upper-caste male entrepreneurs celebrate their own work as innovative and creative, they obscure the forms of advantage that produced such work. As with liberal Enlightenment thought, "'the human' and 'the universal' subject of rights and entitlements assumed a highly particularized subject that is held as paradigmatic, subjugating all other conceptions of being and justice" (Jackson 2020, 28). So too with elite Indian entrepreneurs: their innovation and self-production as performing valuable "human" work that cannot be automated signals the generalization of their conditions into the sui generis figure of the entrepreneur, unmarked by upper-caste status, masculinity, and class advantage.

Startup capitalism offers us visions of the future that are hypermasculinist and nationalist, foregrounding the entrepreneur as the sine qua non figure of startup capitalism. What would it mean to decenter this figure to understand the infrastructures of care, labor, and friendship through which the everyday work of creative innovation and technological experimentation is conducted? Startup capitalism thrives on, and requires, creative world making to maintain its fiction of work as passion. It is workers who craft these projects of experimental world making through their friendship, their fun, and their creativity. The idea of the experiment appears in this book not as a controlled lab setting but rather in Rheinberger's terms (1997, 28): "Experiments are systems of manipulation designed to give unknown answers to questions that the experimenters themselves are not yet able clearly to ask."[6] It takes from feminist STS the concern with tracking which bodies are made available for global experiments in science and technology (Murphy 2017). To approach startup capitalism by centering these experimental labors is to explore a transnationalism from below, locating workers as vital to this economy. This lens is central to feminist ethnography, examining gendered processes under globalization, as Carla Freeman explains, not just by adding women's stories but analyzing how "producers, consumers, and bystanders are situated within social and economic processes and cultural meanings that are central to globalization itself" (2001, 1010).

CONTRIBUTIONS OF THIS BOOK

This book rewrites dominant fantasies around entrepreneurial work on three scales. First, I insist on the significance of place and spatial imaginary in the production of startup capitalism. Innovations happen in certain places—what entrepreneurs gloss as "ecosystems"—fueled by the efforts and aspirations of government planners, parastatal agencies, and entrepreneurs who seek to build the "startup cities" that they want to inhabit. Workers' dreams and desires around class and gender mobility are oriented by imaginaries of the city and their material spaces—the pubs, bowling alleys, and malls that signal belonging in an urban global middle class. It is through these postcolonial and gendered publics that forms of value are created and caste and class belonging are navigated. Postcolonial publics assemble through embodied and intimate acts of labor, leisure, learning, and craft that show us how people make sense of dominant forms of nationalism and capitalism. Thus the startup city, as I show in chapters 1 and 2, offer us insights into how gendered publics of leisure, fitness, and networking are all constitutive of postcolonial entrepreneurial work itself.

Second, I examine the compelling figure of the entrepreneur. IT professionals and startup entrepreneurs claim they are welcoming to all, irrespective of their "background," referring to their historical and political social location. They name this focus on merit as the ingredient that enabled India's new middle class to thrive. Yet the worlds of high technology deeply reproduce caste and engage in caste-based stratification and valuation of labor. This disjuncture between the narrative of entrepreneurial success and the material realities of difference and advantage through which certain subjects can inhabit the entrepreneurial ideal is crucial to understanding the figure of the entrepreneur. Rather than focus on [his] inventions, I show [his] constitution through forms of caste, class, and gender.[7] In other words, I show how economic value attaches itself to certain subjects by translating forms of advantage into modern market economies. This has deep implications for how success in this economy is imagined and achieved, and how everyday conditions of work are laid out as supposedly accessible and welcoming.

Third, the book shows that what is produced under neoliberal startup capitalism is more than an individualized entrepreneurial subjectivity. Current conditions of labor also produce new spaces of care, friendship, and leisure that are essential for surviving—and even thriving—in the lean entrepreneurial office. One evening, after fieldwork, I waited in the pouring rain with young women in the entrepreneurial office where I conducted most of my fieldwork. As the rain beat down relentlessly and streets began flooding, their anxiety about finding a ride home turned to anger as one of them began questioning why cab rides were not provided as some of the larger technology companies did. As she prepared to angrily call the company's director, her friends calmed her down, and they all managed to share an auto home and to placate worried parents who were continually phoning them. Similarly, during periods of office stress and long work hours, employees planned their own nights out dancing to express their creativity and cement their friendships. When the company organized an offsite trip to introduce us to white-water rafting to develop our team spirit, it was through a literal chain of bodies that we survived rapids and created intimate, embodied memories.

These vignettes of office life appear throughout the book: they speak of the friendships and desires of workers who dealt with the new consumption practices of startup life by learning how to be middle class from each other. Workers also expressed creativity and friendship both while figuring out ways to make work more efficient and after work, participating in dance troupes or enjoying post-work evenings together. As young workers living alone in a large city (of eleven million people in 2022), many of them navigated romance and marriage through the intimacies of the office, where they found and made alternate imaginings of home and kinship. Startup work is thus made possible via the infrastructures of care and friendship among its workers.

Such relations are key modes of worker regeneration through which new class practices are learned, desires are explored, and aspirations are fulfilled. Thus, reproductive labor—the work of regenerating labor power—is fundamentally transformed as affective capacities are renewed through interactions outside the heterosexual household. They are driven by the desire for momentary pleasures and unsustainable pursuits rather than oriented toward childbirth.

Even as global forms of entrepreneurship exhort us to privilege passion over work, this book recenters labor. By retaining focus on labor—visibilizing it, naming it, recognizing the work that it does even when it is obscured—we understand the material conditions under which startup capitalism takes root as an ideological orientation and shapes working conditions.[8] While sites of precarious and racialized work often segregate workers in enclosures and divide their living and working conditions by region, ethnicity, and race (see Wright 2021), the startup economy presents itself through the opposing fiction of a loving family, integrating and trivializing difference into production of meaningful work. I track labor through an approach that I call *labor as method* to insist that we address contemporary startup economies through the lens of labor.

LABOR AS METHOD

A feminist approach to understanding the current formation of startup capitalism is one that is shaped through relations of difference. As Priti Ramamurthy et al. (2022, 479) write, "Always relational, feminism is adept at thinking about gender and capital as constitutive and in relation to difference—of sexuality and sex, race and caste, disability and debility, public and private, rural and urban, human and nonhuman animal, and Global North and Global South." Such a feminist approach to capitalism asks us to interrogate the entrepreneurial invitation to imagine work as always innovative and creative even while it elides the historical and persistent differences of labor that build it.

It would not be anything new to say that capitalist lifeworlds are predicated and maintained through difference and inequality—this is key to racial capitalism. Racial capitalism is the analytic that indicates global capitalism as a system that accumulates and extracts labor and value through racial violence and colonial history (Robinson 2021; see also Danewid 2023, 6). The role of the state in aggrandizing dominant power and producing the subaltern as governable through racial and caste-based logics further emerges in India through a project of right-wing rule that has built the world's largest biometric system to govern its billion plus population and routinely develops surveillance technologies to create and manage categories of citizenship (Mertia 2020). Yet *startup capitalism* is more than a system of exploitation based on racialized difference and expropriation. In this book, I show that focusing on startup capitalism allows us to understand the ingenuity of capitalism to continually reinvent itself, this time recasting differences through management-driven projects of inclusivity that speak the language of imbricated love and labor: "work as happiness" and company as "family."[9] Thus, startup capitalism works through difference but continually fabricates itself as a project of inclusivity and equity that depends on technology to achieve these aims. In this, it joins conversations on other forms of capitalism like homocapitalism (Rao 2024) that "does not simply fraction populations along lines of race and caste but also aligns with and intensifies ideological tensions *within* racialized and oppressed caste groups over the putative merits of capitalism as a vehicle for social mobility" (Rao 2024, 90).

India's right-wing prime minister, Narendra Modi, came to power nationally in 2014 with key mandates to build a future-oriented "Startup India" program offering the possibility of work futures as experimental, innovative, and risk-taking.[10] Under its terms, an earlier national policy emphasis on creating an accessible "knowledge for all" program to address developmental issues was replaced by a focus on innovation and entrepreneurship.[11] In this nationalist imaginary, "Digital India" is the future: the symbolic production of muscular Hindu nationalism signals that the Bharatiya Janata Party (BJP) means business in "more ways than one" (Kaur 2020b).[12] Thus, a turn to startup capitalism has never been about technological change alone; it has always been embedded in a postcolonial, masculinist nationalism that foregrounds class aspiration and global mobility.

Under the new vision, entrepreneurs and state officials can persistently orient toward a speculative future in which Bangalore is imagined as an open and welcoming startup ecosphere—a center for innovation. Work will be unshackled from the tight reins of outsourced IT project assignments and the protocols of bureaucratic government work that Indians have associated with middle-class work. Innovation is encouraged through government initiatives such as the Smart India Hackathon and state funding to incubate entrepreneurs.

Such a framing of "the market" presents it as an ideology or representation disembedded from material sociocultural relationships (Mosse 2020, 7). Economics is performative, a representation that "is *made* true through a new field of practices of planning, regulation, or development management" (Mosse 2020 citing Mitchell 1998; emphasis in original). A feminist perspective reminds us that such erasure of the material conditions of gendered, racialized, and caste-based work invisibilizes the reproductive labor of *who* manifests and materializes ideas, *how* labor is erased through a focus on innovation, and *whose* jobs are kept precarious in order to enable technological experimentation.[13] In *Gens: A Feminist Manifesto for the Study of Capitalism*, the authors note that they take seriously the idea of gens as "a capacious, flexible term that references our interest in the generative powers of capitalism and the inequalities these powers create" (Bear et al. 2016). This book examines such movements between the generative aspects of capitalism and the ways in which they work in and through multiple temporalities and sociospatial relations of inequality and difference.

I understand the productive force of difference in constituting experimental work and life by developing labor as method.[14] Rather than assume that labor is contained in a particular time or place—an already constituted "research object" ready to be studied—I follow critical labor theorists to examine how it is formed (Mezzadra and Neilson 2013, 16–17). Allied with commitments to "Asia as method" and "border as method," labor as method keeps alive the indeterminacy of contemporary forms of labor and recognizes labor as a practice that exceeds the workspace to create the conditions for a livable life.[15] Thus, labor is not only a research object but an epistemic approach that allows me to understand the blurring of categorical distinctions and their proliferation (Mezzadra and Neilson 2013, x). We need this new methodological approach, as startup capitalism generates value from productive and reproductive labor, from immaterial and embodied labor, and technical and affective labor, thus muddying the distinctions between the formal realm of work and everyday forms of labor.

METHOD AT WORK

My everyday fieldwork was made possible by a chance meeting early on. I met Naina, a young entrepreneur, through mutual friends at the dinner I described at the beginning of this chapter, very soon after I moved to Bangalore. The conversation turned to the project I was embarking on. I explained that I was here to study the lives of IT workers. When I first planned my fieldwork, it was organized around IT companies, but I found it almost impossible to enter them as a researcher. After several formal letters and statements of research interest that I had submitted via friends of my father who promised to connect me to IT companies, I had given up on this sector. Software companies often have higher degrees of security owing to patented information circulating on-site, and they seemed ambivalent about the insights an ethnographer might bring. I hadn't had much luck thus far, so when one of the guests at the dinner suggested I should study entrepreneurs instead, Naina, an entrepreneur herself, said she could help me.

Through Naina, I met several other entrepreneurs who ran small businesses. She opened her networks widely and enthusiastically, listening to my research and then deciding whom I should meet next. To tune my research more finely to questions of Bangalore's refashioning, I also conducted interviews at a startup festival; at accelerator labs; and with entrepreneurs, technologists, and venture capitalists whom I met at various networking events and through friends and former classmates. The Startup Festival I attended in 2013 was a particularly rich site from which to learn about how entrepreneurs "teach" ideas of risk and passion to wider publics and to market the image and ideal of a startup entrepreneur. I discuss this festival at more length in chapters 2 and 3.

Next, I wanted to understand what it meant to work at the next stage of startups. How do startup ideologies shape entrepreneurial workplaces as they scale up? The startup economy involves not only innovation and launching a new business—the most publicized aspects of this form of enterprise—but also the more routine labor of sustaining these as lean and flexible entrepreneurial workplaces. I concentrate on one workplace that I call "Captivate," cofounded by a man I call Pushkar Subramaniam, at which I conducted in-depth everyday fieldwork for nine months. Such companies, as I was to discover, are not premised on profit but equally develop a distinctive "ethic" that embodies the principles and values of the founder(s). This is a postcolonial remaking that is important for Indian entrepreneurs as they form global companies and orient to elite markets.

My experiences of work at Captivate were refracted through my embodied experiences: I suffered the dull headaches (see Gupta 2019) from hours of screentime, the unending boredom of continuous tasks shaped my day (sorting out photographs, editing website text), and I looked forward desperately to the evenings and breaks when I would share meals in the back of the office with other women or go drinking and dancing after work. Yet I was not vulnerable in the same way that other workers were. I did not fear the loss of my job, harsh words from a manager, or feedback that my work was not good enough.

The WhatsApp messages from workers at Captivate began arriving just months after I left Bangalore to return to graduate school in Atlanta. The first was from Sukhleen, on the marketing team at Captivate. "I think I'm next," it said discreetly. "I have a meeting with Pushkar at the end of the week." A few days later, Sukhleen texted again. She had been asked to leave. More cuts ensued, across the board. Captivate had developed forms of automation that enabled much of the work of itinerary building to be performed with the help of new software. Other jobs, like Sukhleen's in marketing, were replaced by contract, project-based labor. In a reversal of dominant processes of offshoring work, her specific India-based job was "offshored" to a specialist consultant in the United States. Employees were laid off with little notice as new forms of automation replaced them or as their work was parceled out to project-based consultants.

Captivate offers us a microscopic view into how the larger discourses of technological experimentation and the move away from "back-end, routine labor" for Indian workers are experienced in the everyday world. The decision to automate at Captivate was made by the company's in-house, Bangalore-based technologist to deal with loss in revenue. By automating the work of itinerary building, several jobs could be cut. For the company's management, retrenchment was a success, thus prompting the desire for an even smaller workplace. When I returned to do follow-up fieldwork between 2017 and 2019, the lead technologist was working on further technological innovation. He was keen to "maximize human capital" or to enhance the capacity and potential to provide valuable work. In other words, by deciding what forms of labor, and indeed which kinds of workers, were the most valuable, some jobs would be cut and others would be enhanced by predictive technology that would help them cater to guests' needs. Thus one kind of automation assigns certain forms of labor as "rote labor" (what the anthropologist David Graeber [2018] called "drudge work") that can be automated. Another kind of technological intervention values particular forms of labor and seeks to further humanize interactions.

My ethnography within the larger startup world and at Captivate in particular shapes this book's concerns with the disjunctures between entrepreneurial dreams of experimentation and creative work and the effects of this on workers' lives. While startup capitalism hopes to shape work as meaningful and creative and to redraw Bangalore's place as an "outpost of the global economy" (Upadhya and Vasavi 2013), it is the entrepreneurs' own working conditions that are imagined for all workers. Technologists imagine their innovations not only as strategies to make profit for their companies but also as performative aspects of their own entrepreneurialism and belonging in a global ecosystem. My experience at Captivate showed me how employees begin work participating in the entrepreneurial promise that we can all join the company "family" and do what we love. By the end of fieldwork, I witnessed how those promises held true for some while others found meaning and joy through their own infrastructures of care and friendship, outside the terms and promises of work, but that could only be experienced through it. Imagining feminist futures in and through work might be a troublesome endeavor, as feminist theorists like Kathi Weeks (2011) show us. However, in what Sareeta Amrute and Luis Felipe Murillo (2020) term "the global majority world," work also offers possibilities for emergent socialities that work through and *beyond* distinctions of caste and class to imagine pleasure and map desire. These feminist futures emerge from within the experimental time and space of the new economy and are essential to its functioning.

BENGALURU/BANGALORE'S TECHNO-FUTURES

So far I have been referring to the city of my fieldwork as "Bangalore," although its official name is "Bengaluru," a name change prompted by a politics of language that now mandates all commercial signage in the city to be in Kannada. On my last visit to the city in 2023, I walked down the busy shopping street 8th Cross and encountered an open truck carrying a loudspeaker blasting recent Kannada movie hit songs while a group of men danced on a makeshift stage onboard. One of them brandished a loudspeaker and was shouting over the already loud music. He offered a running commentary on street signs that the truck was slowly rolling past. "Hey Manjula Stores!" he shouted in Kannada. "Why's your English signage so big and your Kannada lettering so small? Who are your customers? Are they from here or from elsewhere? Don't make us remind you to change your sign again!" Across the city that day, other commercial establishments received harsher treatment. Malls and independent stores had their signage and storefronts vandalized by members of right-wing regional chauvinist parties insisting on prominent Kannada signage. Despite the strong movement toward using Kannada names and nomenclature, in this book I use "Bangalore" as the term all my interlocutors used.

I understand visions of the futures of work that emerge from Bangalore as a racial formation, shaped by the city's past as a supplier of cheap labor; *cyber coolies* was intended to be derogatory but concealed the experimental thrust of policymaking and futures imagined by government bodies and entrepreneurial professionals. When Indian markets underwent economic liberalization in the 1990s, IT transformed and began to aggressively court foreign capital.[16]

The IT sector had already been identified as a site of growth in the earlier decade. A widespread emphasis on computing technology in India came in 1984 when the microcomputer became available in India and Prime Minister Rajiv Gandhi launched the New Computer Policy,

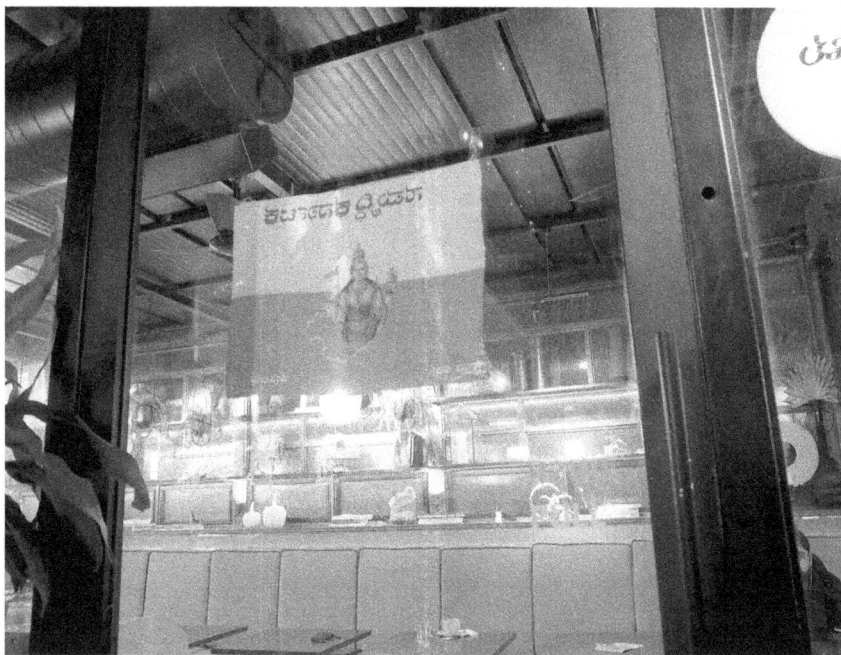

Figure 1. Local flag on coffee shop door, Bangalore, 2024. Photo by author.

liberalizing the computer sector. In 1977 Tata Burroughs was created in Bangalore as a separate unit of the national Tata Industries to serve the software requirements of the US-based Burroughs Ltd. (Heitzman 2004, 181).

Middle-class technological work in the city drew on these histories and trained workforce, cultivated in local engineering colleges and the city's past as a science city. By the early 2000s, Bangalore was one of India's premier IT cities, with over one thousand IT firms, employing more than eighty thousand IT professionals in the early 2000s (van Dijk 2003). Companies choose Bangalore as a base for its temperate climate, cheap labor, and educational resources that continually produce a large class of IT graduates with the requisite skills for global work, cosmopolitan culture, and status as the first state to develop its own technology policy (van Dijk 2003).

While currency devaluation and economic stabilization are among the short-term measures initiated with liberalization, a far more significant aspect of the 1990s is the longterm reformulation of the relationship between the state and economy, as Gupta and Sivaramakrishnan (2011) note. In Bangalore, this had the effect of transforming a work culture steeped in bureaucracy and the slow and steady work of professionals employed in the city's large public-sector units.[17] This was visible in the shift from the notion of middle class, as William Mazzarella (2005) writes, from a relatively coherent category describing a "Nehruvian civil service-oriented salariat, short on money but long on institutional perks—to a bewildering (and, to some, distasteful) array of new, often markedly entrepreneurial pretenders to the title."[18]

Software brought India an international reputation by the 1990s; in fact, economic projections as early as 1970 had suggested a substantial revenue increase if India could capture even 1 percent of the US software market (Heitzman 2004, 1819). This labor process has yielded a verb in English—*Bangalored*—to refer to outsourced work and a job loss in the United States. In addition to revenue earnings, IT performed a symbolic role in circulating the image of Indian professionals—middle-class men and women—as modern, skilled, global workers (Radhakrishnan 2011).

My family moved to Bangalore in the 1990s with the hope of pursuing the promises of this techno-future of software capitalism. My father had a job with Tata Burroughs (later Tata Unisys), an early American multinational to base its software work in Bangalore. In a wood-paneled office high up in a building on a central city street, he worked as a regional marketing manager for the company, attempting to sell B-25 computers and promoting software engineering mostly among the defense establishments that were the only big industries in the city at the time.[19]

Like many other middle-class families, we had been drawn by the promise that a new horizon of global work was now available in India. In 1999 the chief minister of Karnataka, S. M. Krishna, articulated a future for Bangalore based on planning and development models used in Singapore and rooted in public-private partnerships. The city was to be a "world city." The Bangalore Agenda Task Force (BATF) was the vehicle for this transformation, unveiled in 2000 at the Bangalore Summit and intended to marshal public-private synergy. Within the new paradigm of corporate governance, urban problems were regarded as a sign of inefficient management (see Nair 2005, 124). Neoliberalism was taken up to recast problems as nonideological and nonpolitical issues that need technical solutions to maximize intended outcomes (Ong 2006).

Examining how the ends of work are imagined and invested in from the postcolonial South allows me to inhabit a different landscape of work. Here, entry into professional work or entrepreneurial startup work is a promissory note—it might offer experiences of aspiration, pleasure, and community that offer caste or class mobility or gendered insurgences that refuse normative modes of living and loving. It holds out the promise of experimental time in which workers might be more than cogs in the wheel of global capitalism. Perhaps, finally, the thinking goes, from here in Bangalore we might build globally successful innovation or engage in meaningful and respected work. And yet we can't conflate this moment of techno-capitalist experimentation in the South with a liberatory potential, as they emerge within authoritarian regimes, moving alongside nationalist visions for Indian entrepreneurship and manufacturing prowess. At different sites across Asia, feelings of postcolonial triumphalism reign; Ravinder Kaur (2020a) describes it in *Brand India* as the utopian nationalist visions that promise tantalizing and exciting new futures for the potential investor. Kuan-Hsing Chen describes these feelings: "Wherever in Asia one is geographically positioned, a syllogism is emerging: Asia is becoming the center of the world and we are at the center of Asia, so we are the center of the world" (2010, 68). He reminds us that this moment of postcolonial triumphalism as a reaction to colonialism in fact reinscribes us within the boundaries of colonial history.[20]

As Bangalore's growth as a world city parallels its reframing as a leader in technological enterprise, the lives of technocrats and the planning of the city merge (cf. Dasgupta 2015). Technology leaders actively participate in planning the city, and central city spaces are now routinely inhabited by middle classes practicing yoga in the park, running for fitness, and strolling down newly renovated streets and boulevards. These reimaginings of the city are contested, of course: activists have criticized the erasure of public vending, the impracticality of new cobblestone streets, and the focus on overpasses to the detriment of bicyclists and pedestrians. As a city known for a large middle-class population (Nair 2005), Bangalore also shows the deeply contested nature of this class rule.

The city's technological czars run universities and nonprofits, sit on public-private urban planning committees, and have moved on to shape technological policy at the national level. Technological imaginaries shape how the city itself is imagined; through public-private partnerships, "infrastructurescapes," as Govind Gopakumar (2020) terms them, are mobilized to situate the desired citizen as the middle-class professional and consumer. Landscaped city parks and multilane highways, but also the new private spaces of startup work (WeWork and other coworking spaces), shape the city as an actor and startup spaces as sites where techno-futures are spatialized and materialized.

If India's older middle classes were associated with hierarchy and bureaucratic structure, the new middle classes have been built on an ideal of meritocracy and a privileging of the go-getting attitude.[21] Most of my interlocutors in this book would consider themselves middle class, yet some use the term as an aspirational category, some as a derogatory word referring to those not open to experimentation. I use *middle class* in this book capaciously as a category marked by both its structural position and its aspirational and performative aspects (Heiman, Freeman, and Liechty 2012). Class and its attendant spatial reformulations significantly transformed Bangalore, a city known as Pensioner's Paradise because of its slow, sleepy air and pleasant climate, home to many

Figure 2. WeWork sign on a central city location in Bangalore, seen from behind, 2022. Photo by author.

public-sector, middle-class workers. A work culture steeped in bureaucracy and the slow and steady work of professionals employed in the city's large public-sector units began to turn to neoliberal enterprise.

TEACHING ENTREPRENEURSHIP: THE STARTUP FESTIVAL

The city's inhabitants needed to learn how to inhabit these emergent landscapes of startup capitalism. One of my early introductions to Bangalore's entrepreneurial worlds came at the launch event of a startup festival held at the outdoor amphitheater of a large mall in Bangalore. The space itself was part of a larger constellation of buildings that had been inspired in design by Japanese architecture; the design team told me that they had traveled the world to find inspiration before creating this space. The Startup Festival was announced in advertisements in a local English-language newspaper and so, on a sunny day in March, I took my place amid a sparse group of people who gathered out of curiosity at the mall.

The theater was flanked by standing banners with hearts and soaring balloons announcing the festival. A mic check was going on at a low ad hoc stage set up at the venue. Vlad Dubovskiy opened the event. At the time, he was the founder of two companies and associated with Unreasonable Institute, an accelerator lab in Boulder, Colorado, that was supporting the festival. He began calling out to passersby and hailing audience members, inviting them to come on stage to perform impromptu. He started off with some quick spot games and a laughter contest, offering startup festival T-shirts as prizes.

Behind him, a light wind rippled the waters of the artificial lake that marked the mall's premises. Groups of people were milling around, tourist-like, staging photo opportunities by the lake. A couple stood smiling with the glass facades of the mall as a backdrop, its storefronts advertising Zara and Guess. A family posed awkwardly by the massive hospital across the lake, glistening blue and glass towering upward, filled with state-of-the-art technology. There were other scenic backdrops: the five-star Hilton was on one side; the Indian World Trade Center rose behind it.

On the stage, Vlad was introducing the idea of startup entrepreneurship to those gathered on the steps of the amphitheater. He was pitching a mood for this afternoon that would be carefree and fun. Several young men in the audience, no doubt buoyed by the weather and their location in this space of hypermodernity, accepted his challenge and jumped on the stage. As they performed for the audience and each other—laughing, shouting, jumping around on stage—their friends yelled encouragement from the audience. T-shirts were offered as gifts, accompanied by free passes to the festival. In front of me a small group of women from a nearby college watched, looking bored. Soon one of them stood up and suggested they move elsewhere, and then they all

Figure 3. Startup Festival launches at a mall in Bangalore, 2013. Photo by author.

did. Their departure marks a certain refusal of the promises and hyperbole of startup capitalism. Their boredom punctures the allure of the free T-shirts and branded merchandise.

The antics in the festival's inaugural stage suggest that to inhabit the startup world is to experience as pleasurable its seductive vision of the future as structured by fun and enjoyable work rather than the forms of offshore processing and colonial labor India has been known for. It was no coincidence that the launch event for the festival was at a mall—a site of leisure and consumption that marks and produces visitors as cosmopolitan.[22] To locate the festival's launch here was to integrate it in the register of what Miya Tokumitsu (2015) describes as the mantra "Do What You Love": the traveling image of hope symbolized by Steve Jobs assuring the Stanford graduating class of 1996 that they should follow their dreams. "Work that is fun, that the worker loves, that indulges the worker's individual predilections, not only generates wealth, but is also, by mere dint of being enjoyable, good" (Tokumitsu

2015, 11–12). Yet the production of the startup entrepreneur as anyone wanting to enter work as fun and pleasurable is not only part of a global Jobsian discourse. It also emerges in the context of postcolonial capitalist development and in relation to hierarchies of difference.

Kavita Philip (2016, 13–14) examines how citizenship and subjectivity are tied to technological development in ways that "do not obviate the State but alter the State's developmental interventions" and marks the entanglement of difference with the ascendant referents of technology. Taking on this relationship between technology and difference, Lilly Irani's (2019, 2) ethnography of design thinking in New Delhi shows how the ideal of entrepreneurial citizenship emerges through articulation with histories of difference and social hierarchies. Examining who becomes the innovator and who becomes the innovator's other, Irani shows how invisibilized labor, caste hierarchies, and ambiguous ideas about who can be invested in shape entrepreneurial value. My book shows how the production of the entrepreneur himself needed to be unembedded from narratives of passion in order to examine its consolidation through privileges of caste, class, and gender.

Middle-class professional work in India has thus far been studied through the lens of corporate IT companies and their workers. There is a story that Indian IT companies tell about themselves: they are meritocratic, constitutive of a new middle class, and global spaces (Upadhya 2016). Ethnographic research shows us how merit conceals systematic and inherited forms of privilege; the class, caste, and cultural capital through which IT professionals acquire their jobs by succeeding in spoken interviews and demonstrating their potential to circulate in global spaces were they to be sent abroad on a project placement (see Upadhya 2013, 2016). Analyses of caste show that caste remains as a form of discrimination right from the milieu of the elite engineering school in India to the corporate office in the US, where it stays as a form of discrimination (Subramanian 2019; Upadhya 2007; Vaghela, Jackson, and Sengers 2022).

Caste is hypervisibilized through the celebration of caste-Hindu customs and festivals, thus "outing" Dalit colleagues who do not celebrate these (Vaghela et al. 2022). Caste is also invisibilized as employees deny the many, multiple, and compounding privileges through which they acquire elite education, access networking opportunities, and succeed in professional environments both in India and abroad (Subramaniam 2019). In 2016, an Equality Labs report showed that 25 percent of Dalits surveyed in the US reported experiences of caste-based discrimination (Equality Labs 2018). Thus caste is a central logic within high-technology worlds.

I consider the imbrication of caste with other social hierarchies to show how the figure of the modern, future-oriented startup entrepreneur is produced. Following Ramesh Bairy's (2016) work, this book takes up the ability of upper castes to enter spaces of modernity (such as those of startup capitalism) through apparently "non-caste factors" like education, urban migration, and modern occupations. In India, Brahmins played key roles in naturalizing their practices as science, for instance, and Brahmin practices are not looked at askance within supposedly secular scientific institutions (Thomas 2020). In startup capitalism, I show, ideas of risk and experimentation demonstrate the naturalization of a certain Brahmin habitus as the entrepreneurial figure to whom and through whose practices entrepreneurship is mapped. Further, the privileges of upper-caste life and networks are solidified through their articulation in nonspecific and supposedly universal languages of freedom and flexibility. The production of startup capitalism's representative figure—the entrepreneur—is enabled through a mobilization of forms of individual difference but also via access to realms of knowledge and expertise that have naturalized Brahmanism.

The workers of middle-class technology worlds are also no longer upper-caste Brahmin women. In its early years in India, middle-class technology work consolidated a new middle class that was also largely a South Indian upper caste. This is the "South Indian middle-class ethos" that Smitha Radhakrishnan (2011) describes when she writes about how "IT women" perform a respectable middle-class femininity. They privilege home over family and maintain their allegiance to caste and class even when they enter professional work environments.[23] Richa Patel (2010) shows how the mobility practices of software companies consolidate class and caste practices as they delegate private taxi services to ferry women workers from the protective confines of their homes to the corporate workplace. This sheltered nature of professional IT work made it a desirable avenue for upper-caste women's employment—reproducing rather than disrupting caste and class privilege, as Sarasvati Raju (2013) notes. The entrepreneurial worlds of startup capitalism and its allied work then offer new vantage points to ask how gender, class, and caste are being reproduced and negotiated outside of the hegemonic figure of the upper-caste software engineer.

While everyone is told to find the work that they can love, we might tell the story of startup capitalism not only through those who occupied the stage of the startup festival but by those who left. The nonelite workers who inhabit and shape the experimental worlds of technocapitalism offer us a sense of other futures emerging when we think about technological change in the Global South.

FEMINIST FUTURES

Following the figures who left the stage, this book extends the scene of entrepreneurship from its lead figure to its invisibilized workers. We move to everyday life in offices of the service sector, where the workers I interacted with do not claim upper-caste and class status. Instead, amid a group of women who were often young migrants to the city from different parts of India, I was able to witness how professional work is embodied and negotiated by unruly subjects—the other to the figure of the respectable middle-class South Indian IT worker or the successful career lawyer.[24] Rather than consider work as a means to an end—a promotion, more money, a more secure middle-class life—the scenes of work in the entrepreneurial sector here are precarious ones. Workers, and indeed the nature of digital platforms themselves, transform rapidly according to technological changes. A new form of automation causes widespread job losses, as I witnessed during my own fieldwork. I move beyond a familiar feminist question of resistance to capitalist change and the nature of work itself to ask what happens when we follow labor as method to discover new forms of social life and conceptual terrain.[25]

When we shift the scene away from the Euro-American contexts that (over)determine the debates on work, we find the multiple meanings of work and time that are not limited to paid employment but are generative of important friendships, class learning and mobility, and freedom from the expectations of domestic life.[26] In the scarcely resourced entrepreneurial office, I found that workers replace material resources with care and friendship that are essential to their survival and even thriving. The experimental worlds of entrepreneurship offer important sites from which to reconceptualize how social relations are forged under conditions of precarity. These relations reproduce the worker body and her enthusiasm for work.

Recent theoretical work understands social reproduction as a form of labor and life that "encompasses the daily and long-term reproduction of the means of production, the labor power to make them work, and the social relations that hold them in place" (Norton and Katz 2017). Social reproduction thus understood is not only about labor and capitalism but also, as Vinay Gidwani and Priti Ramamurthy (2018) argue, about cultural production and the resources through which reproduction is also queered by challenging normative categories and practices. What term might we use for the regeneration of spirit and body at work? With worker replenishment and sustenance forged outside the heterosexual family and in the entrepreneurial office, our normative idea of social reproduction is queered and dislocated from the

Euro-American nuclear family ideal under startup capitalism. The fields of queer and trans Marxism, along with disability studies, have already charted the need for a theory of social reproduction that considers the essential emotional labor of surviving in community in order to survive.[27] I follow their lead to consider how sustenance and survival might be shifted outside the typical site of its theorization: the heterosexual nuclear family.

Spending important moments of work, leisure, and friendship away from their biological kin or filial relations, workers in Bangalore's entrepreneurial economy learn about—and reproduce and practice—class and professionalism in the spaces of the office. Creating rituals for religious festivals on the office floor and learning how to whitewater raft with colleagues are not only modes of worker's subjective fashioning. Importantly, they are material aspects of class and gender reproduction that communicate new ideals, values, and possibilities through the shared camaraderie and space of work. As Aihwa Ong has shown for factory workers in Malaysia, new conditions of living for migrant labor far from the reproach of parental and familial eyes realign expectations around marriage and marriageable age, leisure options, and the consumption of cosmetics (Ong 2010). A new migrant class of women are free from the responsibilities and dense networks of joint families and immerse themselves in urban leisure and consumption.[28] Under startup capitalism, forms of creative world making and care that I describe in detail in chapter 6 are essential and invisibilized forms of social relations.

Even as I conducted fieldwork, many workers at my primary field site lost their jobs to a new form of automation. Other jobs were outsourced to consultants and contract workers. In this context I examine how workers assemble relations of care amid ongoing precarity. As Sarah Sharma writes, "Temporalities do not experience a uniform time but rather a time particular to the labor that produces them. Their experience of time depends on where they are positioned within a larger economy of temporal worth" (2014, 8). When Pushkar Subramaniam, the managing director of Captivate Travels, asked me, "Why don't they [his employees] utilize development funds?" that are made available for their self-improvement through the office; perhaps the answer was that they were not interested in projects that would prepare them for neoliberal markets that demand continual skill upgrades and reinventions of the self.[29] Asiya Islam (2021) describes as "willful resignations" the intentional way in which women from a lower middle class chose to leave their jobs and used their time in search of education and skills training that would enhance their employability; thus the question of work is not linear, and an absence from the formal workforce does not mean women's full absorption into domestic work. My research found that workers could not determine the stability of their work, but their participation frequently refused the speculative and linear futures expected of neoliberal workers. Instead they invested in friendships, desires, and pleasures to fashion experimental selves and futures in keeping with the unpredictability of work.

WHAT IS A FEMINIST APPROACH
TO STARTUP CAPITALISM?

Chapter 1 excavates feminist concerns with categories of labor to understand how they are challenged and reconfigured in the current economic moment. It develops labor as method, introduces my primary field sites and interlocutors in detail, and locates my own position as an ethnographer returning to a "home" that seems unfamiliar. It shows that a methodological approach that centers labor and understands its indeterminacy opens us to the possibilities of friendship and feminist futures in the unlikely spaces of the entrepreneurial office.

In chapter 2 I show how feminist futures had been devised in Bangalore far before its signaling as a startup city. I trace these feminist publics via a small assembled archive of personal letters, poems, and festival itineraries from my own family, as well as from my ethnography. Tracking gendered movements in space from the late 1800s to the present, I offer this chapter in an experimental vein to show how feminist futures are not ever completely separate from dominant nationalist projects of modernity; neither are they subsumed by them. Instead I show that feminist futures exist adjacent to nationalist projects and create possibilities for experimentation. Some of these are sustainable, and some bring shame and failure, but tracing hopes for feminist futures through time shows us how experimental modes of life and work can be historicized.

In chapter 3 I continue a spatial analysis through a focus on the keyword *risk*. Rather than think of risk as located in the individual, I show how it is produced as a specific relation between the "public" world of startup capital and the "private" world of caste and community. When startup mentors say they need to "teach" risk to produce proper entrepreneurs, they are referencing a particular kind of subject who is not expected to be risk-taking. I show how the middle-class Brahmin is centered as the de facto and unnamed subject of entrepreneurial energy through this focus on risk-taking as a new and desirable practice. The chapter follows aspiring entrepreneurs beyond the public sites at which they pitch their companies to their homes, gated communities, and family lives. Following labor as method thus, I outline first a mode of "experimental time" that demands flexibility, mobility, and masculinized upper-caste and middle-class privileged access to startup spaces. I also show how commitments to heterosexual reproductive labor and middle-class and upper-caste domestic arrangements preclude the mobilities required from dominant modes of startup capitalism. Located within oral histories and in-depth interviews, this chapter analyzes life at the spatial and symbolic edges of Bangalore's startup economy.

While readers might expect a book on feminized labor and startup capitalism to offer suggestions for how to increase women's participation in entrepreneurship, this book has a different project. Rather than asking "How can we encourage more women to join entrepreneur-ship?," I ask, "What are the terms on which entrepreneurship is imagined so that women are seen as a latent and unproductive labor force?"[30] This book shows how contemporary directives to make women "entrepreneurial" do not challenge patriarchal structures and gendered reproductive labor. Part Two of the book moves to a particular space, the office of Captivate Travels, where I focused the second half of my fieldwork.

In chapter 4 I take up the keyword *flexibility*. First, I introduce managerial fantasies of flexibility as they unfold at Captivate Travels, locating them as a celebration of postsocialist and neoliberal modes of work. I then consider how we might read flexibility otherwise. Rather than emphasize the failure of this form to apply to others, I offer a reparative reading of my fieldwork to detail how practices of world building emerge through the everyday lives of Captivate's employees. Ideals of flexibility emerge from life histories and desires, as I show through the example of Sanjay, an employee who strives for order and proceduralism. The chapter ends with a consideration of what bodies are offered the possibilities of flexibility and how certain bodies meet the limits of such offers through exhaustion, illness, and pain. In these pages, we journey along a brief arc of entrepreneurial work cultures, from exuberance to exhaustion.

If management discourses situate the ideology of Do What You Love to offer a portal into the dream of a better future, chapter 5 asks how workers reimagine this imperative. Taking up the keyword *love*, I show how it is diffracted into the affective life of startup capitalism, showing up as care, friendship, and happiness. It is the invisible labor of gendered and racialized workers that maintains and circulates forms of care that are vital for the company's well-being. This care exceeds the for-profit expectations of employee happiness, yet the production of this care is not a process that merely depletes workers. Instead, I suggest that the fragmentation of affect beyond happiness and Do What You Love also *creates* experimental socialities and subjectivities. Thus, while startup capitalism is often associated with the production of the individualized subject, I found that it also queered the idea of the "family" and offered work as a practice of world making that transcends the self.

In chapter 6 I draw on postcolonial science and technology studies to interrogate the startup keyword *experiment*. I ask how startup capitalism reworks transnational offshoring to Asia or the work of so-called cyber coolies to instead create labor as a site of innovation and experimental consumption. Such modes of work open up nonelite access to middle-class cultural production through work as leisure and experiments in consumption. Simultaneously, startup capital looks to technological innovation to render nonelite consumption-work obsolete and to fine-tune work as leisure techno-utopias. I show how automation caused the loss of jobs for 30 percent of the workers in an entrepreneurial Bangalore office where I conducted fieldwork and analyze how the labor of raced, classed, and gendered bodies underwrites experiments in transnational technological innovation and automation.

In the conclusion, I ask: What happens to workers who lose their jobs to automation in a company where they were encouraged to Do What You Love, consume as cosmopolitan subjects, and take ownership of work? Where do they go, and how do those who stay on continue to embed themselves in the entrepreneurial embrace of loving work and being creative?

STARTUP CAPITALISM

Figure 4. Audience gathered at the Startup Festival, 2013. Photo by author.

PART ONE

STARTUP CAPITALISM

1

LABOR AS METHOD

Exploring the Space-Time of Techno-capitalism

ON THE SECOND EVENING of my fieldwork in Bangalore, I caught a ride to meet a friend at a new beer brewery. I wrapped a long *dupatta* around my hair and shoulders, carefully shrouding myself from the dust and pollution of constant construction work in the city: new flyovers, buildings, underpasses, and gated communities. We bumped and swerved at a manic pace, disturbing sand, rubble, and grit in flurries. An impossible sea of brake lights resolutely snaked to the horizon, and the auto rickshaw stalled and revved in their glow. Finally, after an hour, we had traversed the 11 kilometers (or 6.8 miles) to our destination.

Bouncers in black guarded the entrance to the brewery, swinging back its heavy doors at regular intervals to let in the constant stream of young people, usually still in office attire. My friend and I were soon seated, and we looked around us to find most tables already taken. A large group of office colleagues boisterously chatted on one side. On the other, East Asian businessmen inked a deal with two local men, signing papers and then sipping their beers, nervous laughter all around. Rock music thundered, and groups of people continued flocking in as the night wore on.

Soon a familiar figure loped across to meet me, a friend who was one of the three entrepreneurs who had opened this bar. He was a software engineer from Bangalore who had recently moved back to the city, part of the reverse transnational migration that spurs startup entrepreneurship in Bangalore. The bar was always full despite its three-level seating for four hundred people. He sat down with us and began pointing out the local favorites. "That's the woman who owns the bra company Butter Cups," he said, gesturing to a young woman seated on a barstool, chatting with the bartenders. "She's an entrepreneur and comes here to unwind after work. If you want to meet people, you should come and hang out here," he suggested. The bar is a popular choice for entrepreneurs to network and socialize, for large office groups to unwind after work, for business meetings, and for software techies who like their beer and rock music. On just my second evening I was being introduced to how Bangalore's new urban spaces extend, support, and intersect with everyday work life for the growing middle classes.

The city felt new to me, too. Unlike the Bangalore of the 1990s, when middle-class teenagers stumbled into a pub only to invariably run into family friends (and subsequent trouble), tonight the brewery was a sea of unfamiliar faces. The "opening up" of Bangalore's economy offers not only new kinds of work (small startups in fashion, design, hospitality, travel) but also spaces for these entrepreneurs to mingle, socialize, and network. Amid the surge in pubs, malls, bowling alleys, breweries, and restaurants the chance of accidentally running into familiar faces seemed less likely.

As the evening wore on, a post-beer haze settled on our table. It felt as though I had never left Bangalore, as though this was not the city of my birth—a city that always felt strangely provincial. I was returning to study a city that I could claim as my own in some ways, having lived here until I was sixteen, as what Kamala Visweswaran (1994) calls a "hyphenated-ethnographer." Yet on my return, people encountered me like a newcomer to the city. It was a strangely liberating feeling, to be somewhere that seemed at once familiar and strange. Over the next few days this feeling repeatedly crept up on me—feeling displaced when I met so many strangers, encountered entrepreneurial cultures and a landscape of new leisure. Yet it was familiar in reassuring ways: speaking local languages (Tamil and Kannada), living a half hour away from my mother's house, and reconnecting with old school friends. Many of them had returned to India after between five and ten years overseas, and almost all of them were startup entrepreneurs. I didn't realize it at first, but each of these encounters was unfolding a new aspect of urban life in Bangalore to me—if I wanted to study it.

Startup capitalism claims to operate in an inclusive and welcoming manner for all those who can innovate and show initiative. However, by following labor as method, I understand how workers enter, experience, and make sense of different sites of the startup economy. Labor as method privileges and foregrounds worker bodies as ontological mechanisms to understand the current political economy in India. Tracking workers' movements across spaces, this method captures the blurred distinctions between home and work, ethnographer and informant as I trace their various intersecting routes through the city.

My journey into fieldwork began, quite literally, with trying to find a home to live in and to travel to research from. My hunt began in the listing sections of local newspapers that I found at street corner newsstands. I called tens of real estate agencies and devotedly visited their offices. At each one a new man emerged, motorbike keys in hand, and I would ride pillion, gingerly clinging onto the side of faded leather seats as real estate agents took me on bumpy rides through inner neighborhood streets looking for rentals. We often entered the grand gate of a spacious bungalow only to make an abrupt turn and head around to the back of the building. There, narrow staircases arranged behind tangles of clothing lines led to dimly lit, single rooms. Dogs howled, and neighbors' eyes seemed everywhere. Landlords asked me persistent questions: What hours would I keep? Would I be home late? Would I have male visitors? What was my research about? How old was I? What did my parents do? I needed to be located, tied down, and contextualized against a social fabric with the appropriate configurations of caste, class, and profession, and only then would I be allowed to stay.

Elsewhere, reading phone numbers on the photocopied signs stating "Ladies Hostels," I entered a thriving economy of small homes turned into living arrangements. Each room was lined with single beds. Three or four women shared these rooms, which all tunneled into each other, ending with a single bathroom that was always in use. These were for less affluent women, often employed in office jobs in smaller firms, who had moved from smaller towns and cities across India to work in this technology hub. As I found out later, these women performed accountant work, secretarial work, and back-end office work in small, local private firms across the city. Their jobs were usually support oriented and did not involve any interaction with people outside their office or require them to be fluent in English.

My male cousin, hunting for an apartment just months before I was, quickly found an independent room and attached bathroom. I, on the other hand, toured neighborhoods and agents unsuccessfully. For women, hostels only offered densely packed rooms. Wary of accommodating single women, hostel owners instead distributed what they considered their risk of housing such a demographic by offering space to groups of working women. Stuck between the inquisitive landlord and the controlling hostel owner, I realized my limited options for mobility and freedom as a single woman.

Some months later Naina, mentioned in the introduction as the startup entrepreneur a sports company, called to follow up on her offer that I move in with her. I packed up my things immediately. I had first

Figure 5. One of many frequently seen signs for ladies hostels, in this case on a bus stop pillar, 2012. Photo by author.

met Naina just a few months before through common friends, and we had made promises to keep in touch and hang out. Naina had a work background in public relations and ran the company, which provided media support and strategizing, planned events, advised sports celebrities, and ran campaigns.

Until her spare room became free, though, we did not know each other very well. We ended up living together throughout my fieldwork, Naina the startup entrepreneur and I, the ethnographer of startup capitalism. We lived the life of two single women in a spacious and airy apartment off Bangalore's central boulevard. One street away, pubs discharged air conditioning blasts suffused with cigarette smoke, and students hung out on bikes and scooters, gossiping after college. Our street was at the beginning of a residential neighborhood; large leafy trees shrouded the sky, vigilant security guards manned the building, and domestic help walked their employers' yapping dogs in the late afternoons.

I had no field site established when I first moved in with Naina. I walked out of my room every morning to find her alert and awake, hunched over her iPhone at the breakfast table, typically dressed in a sleeveless T-shirt and tights, having returned from a nearby gym. She would hastily sip a tumbler of South Indian filter coffee, simultaneously trawling Facebook and Twitter (now known as X). She generally offered me a running news feed of what her sports clients had said (her sports publicity firm employed between five and ten people), what latest shocking thing the right-wing BJP had done, and updates on friends and events in the city. Once she was done giving me a dense rundown of events, people, and the challenges that faced her as an entrepreneur that day, she would look at me. "And you? What's your plan today?" I had just begun fieldwork and was still hunting for a field site, so my response was usually vague and abstract. Naina began taking me around with her, and from there my fieldwork analyzing startup capitalism and its diverse labor practices began.

THE DISPERSED SITES OF STARTUP CAPITALISM

Naina was twenty-nine years old when I moved in with her. An energetic and driven entrepreneur, she had recently moved back to Bangalore from Singapore and lived in an apartment one floor above her mother and sister. Rather than join the nursery school that they had launched and worked at together, she chose to run her own business. She often commanded me to write down what she thought people should know about women startup entrepreneurs: "Tell them how hard it is to be the boss and command a team!" she would say one day. On another, "Dude, tell them how sexist the sports business is!" On a third: "You know the main problem? I literally don't know where the money to pay salaries is going to come from! I can't give those kids [her employees] late pay—they pay rent every month! You know I can't sleep at night worrying about money? Why do clients pay so late?! Should I break my financial bonds? Please write about this!"

Living with her enabled me to understand how varied each working day was from the next. In the morning we might rent a cab and be driven miles away to a hospice for end-of-life cancer patients where she sat in on a meeting advising volunteers on how to rope in a sports celebrity for a donation drive. In the afternoon I could be persuaded to photograph a football league she was introducing to Bangalore; the team posed as I organized a shoot at Bangalore Club. The late afternoons could be meetings with her employees, scrunched up at narrow desks behind a wall that separated us from the office foosball table. In the evenings Naina might meet a client for a drink, demanding that I accompany her—"Wait, 'client?' Which client is this? Is this a date?! I'm not accompanying you on a date, Naina!"—or she might make a day trip to another city to handle publicity at an event.

I learned by accompanying her and watching her, living with her, and sharing her life that there was no central workplace that anchored her. Every day was different for her. Her sites of work were displaced across the city—volunteer meeting, office, club event, bar—as was the notion of "work" itself. She drew on her work clients to enrich her service to the cancer hospice, building goodwill with both the charity organization that ran it and her sports client, but which part was work? She met a client for drinks in the evening: Was this a casual business drink or a date? Sites of work and the notion of work are fluid and diffuse and seep into each other. Most significantly, they are also spread across the city and take place in a range of different environments.

Events and networking opportunities often occurred in the late evenings, and Bangalore's unpredictable traffic meant the city emerged in my fieldwork as an actor that shaped how people enter entrepreneurial worlds and indeed, who enters at all. While Naina often jumped into a cab (Uber in India had just launched at the time of my fieldwork), I did not have a smartphone and took autos late at night despite being told it was unsafe. Through my fieldwork I met entrepreneurs who had to be home by dinner time to meet their families and others who lived far away from event venues in middle-class, gated communities. Movements across space and time presented the frictions to startup capitalism's celebratory account of enabling flexible business for all.

Crafting my research design, I knew that to understand startup capitalism I would have to attempt to practice Naina's mobility and flexibility, traveling to different sites and spaces, threading together the varied practices that loosely categorize contemporary "work." Labor as method is one conceptual approach to meet this fragmentation. It serves as a political commitment to naming and following as labor a set of apparently discrete practices to show their interrelatedness. This insistence on labor is especially significant within a public discourse that promises work as love and creativity. Adopting the frame of labor as method allows me to understand how entrepreneurial innovations are forms of labor even though they distance themselves from any references to work through a focus on creativity and genius. By studying how people can *enter* labor—be present at meetings, evening networking, and late office work hours—and extend labor beyond a single workspace, labor as method allows me to additionally understand what friendships and solidarities count as labor and make it possible.

Through this book, and following Kathi Weeks, I understand work as "productive cooperation organized around, but not necessarily confined to, the privileged model of waged labor" (Weeks 2011, 14). Yet as Naina demonstrates, entrepreneurial and startup work exceeds any model of waged labor. Labor then is the more expansive category:

"The human capacity for labor may be hobbled by the organization of waged work, but as a collective creative potential, can also exceed them" (Weeks 2011, 15). My understanding of feminized and racialized labor as also world making, creative, and experimental comes from this expansive understanding of labor as more than the stipulated conditions of waged work.

Naina introduced me to her friends and to young women whom she mentored. Additionally, through common introductions I met a group of entrepreneurial women who gathered every few Fridays to network and socialize and build a stronger community of support for each other. I visited the workplaces of these entrepreneurs—startups in travel, events, and image consulting—and volunteered my labor, writing skills, and time.

Some months into this fragmented fieldwork, I noticed a large advertisement in the city's leading English-language newspaper advertising the Startup Festival. Registration was open to "all" (but required a registration fee of Rs. 2,500 or roughly $37), and over four days, four different neighborhoods in the city would open startup offices to the public. We would be able to meet entrepreneurs, interact with them, learn their stories, and ask them questions. There were sessions with venture capitalists and angel investors, with "pitching sessions" allowing aspiring entrepreneurs to acquire seed funding. Startups in yoga, fitness, dating, and hospitality opened their doors for participants to train their bodies, learn fitness techniques, and sample new spaces to network at.

THE BROAD LANDSCAPE OF STARTUP CULTURE

Living with Naina had shown me what the everyday life of an entrepreneur looks and feels like, but at the Startup Festival I would be "taught" how to become one. As I describe in the next chapter, this learning is not limited to the logics of business alone, such as how to draw up a plan, how to scale a startup. It was focused on how to cultivate the figure of the startup entrepreneur; as a pedagogical instruction it offered direction about the everyday rhythms, modes of self-making, forms of love and passion, and mobile practices that produce the startup entrepreneur. It struck me at the very first startup event that I attended that this kind of entrepreneurship was ontologically premised on masculine ways of interacting in public, comporting oneself, and dressing. Startup entrepreneurship produced an upper-caste and middle-class masculinity as risk-taking and desirable, worthy of funding.

I attended several events at the Startup Festival and demonstrate in the next chapter how individuals were taught about what it means to be a startup entrepreneur in Bangalore. People I spent time with influenced my experience of the event: typically, women who drifted to me or found me. Gathering from these women's experiences that there are gendered challenges to entering the ostensible "public" of startup capitalism, I set out to explore what these are and how they manifest. At networking sessions, pitching sessions, and the various public and semipublic events at which entrepreneurs sold their innovations, I found that they also sold themselves as sites of human potential, inviting speculative investment into what future value they might generate.

There is no way to know how valuable a startup is when it is being conceptualized; efforts to assign value are largely speculative. At the kinds of pitch sessions I attended, funders had to assess the potential of a company based not only on the product or service they were hearing about but also on the potential of the entrepreneur to be or become properly *entrepreneurial*. I found that in the early stages of a company, this required entrepreneurs to show single-minded dedication to their business idea and an ability to commit all their time to it. They had to show that they could sever domestic responsibilities and care duties to work around the clock and travel around the city to meet people when necessary. Conducting this fieldwork well before COVID meant that I encountered an economy that was premised on the value of face-to-face meetings and social interactions. The ability of aspiring entrepreneurs to appear unattached to anything but their business was a sign to investors that the startup founder would stay focused on exponential growth and scale the business, rather than just produce a "lifestyle company" (which I came to understand as gloss for a company making a modest profit). Thus the early stages of startup growth require a control and mastery over one's own mobility: commuting across the city both in the day and the evening, staying immersed in entrepreneurial networks, and signaling orientation toward business (not home) and toward growth and expansion rather than small-scale home enterprise. Each of these facets of startup labor is both gendered and classed, premised on a secondary system of labor that (invisibly) enables the mobile, aspirational startup founder.

The world's dominant startup sector in Silicon Valley is male dominated for some of these very reasons: men's training in technology and their ability to immerse themselves in formal work. Michael Kimmel (2015) explains how the masculine figure of the internet entrepreneur reproduces narratives of the "self-made man" so dominant in turn-of-the-century America. I turned entrepreneurial ethnographer myself, handing out business cards and starting to network to gain more startup contacts. I negotiated the continual stress of hunting for formal clothes to wear at professional meetings, sweating in them while taking autos and buses to meetings and navigating the different expectations of decorum in public transport and in meetings at five-star hotels. Gradually I began to build a "database" of people and to start to understand how entrepreneurs are expected to move in and out of dispersed and diverse sites including local accelerator labs, incubation centers, and networking events. I found that their access to these sites, their participation, and their hopes for interactions were all shaped by how closely they could adjust their ability to move across sites and master the desired presentation at each one.

The first six months of my research were spent dropping in and out of various entrepreneurial sites, reassembling the social and economic world of startups. As Bruno Latour explains, social scientists can no longer expect actors to conform to the behavior of some well-known "types"; instead we have to "'follow the actors themselves,' that is try to catch up with their often wild innovations in order to learn from them what the collective existence has become in their hands, which methods they have elaborated to make it fit together, which accounts could best define the new associations that they have been forced to accomplish" (2005, 12). I spent the first phase of my research following entrepreneurial actors in the early stages of their companies' growth.

I spent days and sometimes weeks at startups in sports media, event planning, and travel consultancy, interviewing women who launched a range of startups (including human resource matching companies, educational resources, technology startups, and children's products). Women entrepreneurs who had left corporate jobs started or headed these companies, and each had between one and six employees. They were various ages (from twenty-five to forty-five), and their life stages, religion, caste, and class background determined their approach to work. For young and unmarried women, work expanded to fill their days—yet there were caveats. For instance, a Muslim entrepreneur from a family that she herself termed "conservative" was dissuaded from running her own business and presented with almost daily stresses by way of phone calls, visits to her single mother, and admonitions about her choice of life by her extended family. The married women enjoyed far more freedom; as Perveez Mody (2008) explains, when Indian women pass from their father's family to their husband's care through marriage, the responsibility for their actions and movements also passes on to the marital household. For women married to men who supported their business, marriage could be a far more enabling and supportive experience than one's own natal home and kin. I explain gendered relationships with startup work culture and expectations in detail in chapter 3.

I offered to help with everyday work at these startup companies and organized events, planned website development, and sat in on meetings and office work. As mentioned previously, employees at these companies were young, usually between twenty-one and twenty-five, and right out of college. They were being paid around Rs. 10,000 (or $150) a month or less, and worked from 9:00 a.m. to late evening depending on the events and schedule for the day. I draw on my fieldwork with them in more detail in chapter 3.

ENCOUNTERING MY MAIN FIELD SITE: CAPTIVATE

I wanted to understand what it meant to work at the next stage of startups. How do startup ideologies shape entrepreneurial workplaces as they scale up? After all, startup capitalism involves not only innovation and launching a new business—the most publicized aspects of this form of enterprise—but also the more routine labor of sustaining these as lean and flexible entrepreneurial workplaces.

During my second phase of fieldwork (March–December 2013) I concentrated on one workplace, studying it in-depth over nine months. I was able to understand how young migrant women bear the burden of individualistic entrepreneurial narratives of risk-taking by drawing on gendered ideals of duty, giving, and family life and also create new social formations and fictive kin ties to enter professional work worlds.

Like many encounters in the startup world, my entry into this field site was not planned. Six months into my fieldwork, I found myself at an incubation lab, waiting to hear how aspiring entrepreneurs pitch their products to a venture capitalist (VC). When the VC walked in, he turned out to be an acquaintance, known through common friends, and was curious about my research. He suggested I contact his brother's company; it had been funded by my acquaintance as a startup and it had now grown into a midsize entrepreneurial workplace. Anant, the venture capitalist, sent me an email introducing me to his brother, Pushkar, the company's managing director. We fixed a time to chat on the phone since Pushkar was leaving for South America the next day.

Pushkar called me exactly on time. This was unusual by Bangalore's laid-back standards for other fields in which I had previously worked in 2004 and 2007 (like media and education). However, the startup economy has many return migrants from the US, like Pushkar himself, for whom rigidly adhering to time schedules is one way of maintaining a distinction from the local workforce. Pushkar's questions were precise and brief, occasionally interspersed with instructions to his children, who were shouting in the background. He told me a little bit about Captivate and then asked me about my research and requirements.

I offered a general explanation for my research—that I was interested in studying the everyday work world of entrepreneurial companies and its gendered and classed experiences. In exchange for being at the office every day, I offered my unpaid labor. Pushkar said he could think of a few possible roles for me in the company, but for now he would put me in touch with the marketing team, where I would be "on trial" for two months. Following this period, we would check in with each other to see how things were working before committing to a longer fieldwork period. I agreed immediately. This site eventually became my main fieldwork site: the lens through which I understand how entrepreneurial imperatives of risk-taking and flexibility are experienced in the long term by those who enter the company's work environment and lifeworlds and become shaped by it, even as they shape and enable its expansion, growth, and profit.

I call this company Captivate; as mentioned previously, it was launched in 2006 by an Indian man (Pushkar) and a German man and began in two small home offices in Bangalore and Munich. In 2013 when I began fieldwork here, it had scaled up to a company with over one hundred employees in Africa, Asia, Europe, and North and South America, but it still valued and celebrated its entrepreneurial roots. Employees who had been in the company since its inception spoke to me proudly of the long hours that they put in and the ways they had learned how to nurture the company when it was a fledgling entity.

The head office is in Bangalore, and when I was first introduced to the company, it had over fifty employees in this office, around 75 percent of whom were women. Six employees were foreign nationals and two of Indian descent, but the rest were Spanish, Scots, and English. Several languages were heard in the office: mostly Kannada, English (the primary medium of communication), Tamil, and Spanish. Captivate's position in the travel sector, as a startup company that had scaled up, and its employee base of both middle-class, well-traveled professionals and young migrant women who were the first generation of professionals in their families, made it an ideal fieldwork site, as I explain later.

Pushkar put me in touch with his marketing team before he left on his travels, and presently I received a phone call from a Captivate employee named Susan. She was Scottish and spoke rapidly, with an accent that I could not place immediately at the time. I later discovered that she had lived in Kenya (and spoke some Swahili) and had now moved to Bangalore, where she was learning some Kannada. She gave me directions to the office and invited me over for a chat to meet the team.

The office was in Indiranagar, Bangalore's so-called startup neighborhood, and I set off on a warm March afternoon for my first meeting there. Its main street—colloquially referred to as "Hundred Feet Road"—was filled with restaurants, cafés, bars, and small offices. The Café Coffee Day nearby invariably hosted startup entrepreneurs sitting in meetings: laptops open, discussing ideas and plans. I finally found the office on the second floor of a nondescript white building, with a cell phone store and a sari store at its base. A rack of motorbikes and a small cabin for a security guard lined the side of the building.

This was a vastly different landscape from the gated communities of IT offices that comprise the dominant image of middle-class professional life in Bangalore. Not only was it smaller, but there was also little that distinguished it from neighborhood commerce and consumption spaces. Squeezing past the bikes, I entered the building to face a tiled wall with a tiny alcove in which a statue of the Hindu

Figure 6. Lounge at Captivate Travels, 2013. Photo by author.

god, Ganesha—the pot-bellied elephant god of prosperity—had been recently worshipped with flowers and a lit incense stick. A cramped elevator for about three people took me to the second floor.

Entry to Captivate Travels was through a glass door requiring a swipe card. The card was amended to record time during my nine months at Captivate. Official work hours were 9:00 a.m. to 6:00 p.m. but—depending on the team you were on—hours were flexible. Unlike many travel agencies that hosted walk-in customers making inquiries, all of Captivate's business was conducted online. This was a back-end office.

The main Captivate office comprised many open cubicles, separators between desks running to around four feet in height. Teams sat within the same cubicle and swiveled their chairs around to confer with each other. The layout of the open office reflected what Henry Braverman (1974) understands as the rationalization and disciplining of office work: employees didn't have to move to interact with others on the same team, and their computer screens were visible to passersby,

Figure 7. Midmorning chat at Captivate Travels, 2013. Photo by author.

including senior management, who let them know if they had been seen surfing social media sites. The office opened on both sides of an entrance from the lounge area; in the center was a glass-walled conference room. Trees, sky, and neighboring buildings were visible through walls made of massive glass panes. In one corner the marketing team sat by one of these sheets of glass, and an employee, Jyothi, looked out onto dense tree cover that she called her "private garden."

The CEO sat in a private glass-walled cabin, but his was the only permanent workspace with a door. A few small rooms allowed employees the privacy to make phone calls to guests and clients. There were two tiny restrooms and a small snack area where employees ate lunch and where, every afternoon—I found out later—a man who rolled up in an auto rickshaw brought large steel tiffin carriers of homemade Indian food.

Presently Susan and Jyothi from the marketing team came out to meet me. They were both warm and friendly and welcomed me into a little conference room. Susan was a bustling figure in a knee-length, teal-colored dress with a shrug over her shoulders and large earrings and a necklace. Jyothi seemed self-contained; as a middle-class woman from a North Indian family with a business background, she had developed an interest in German and won scholarships through all levels of training until she became a qualified teacher at the Goethe Institut in New Delhi and simultaneously worked with Captivate there for many years before moving to Bangalore. She was dressed modestly in a simple salwar kameez with a dupatta and had long hair tied into a low, no-nonsense bun.

They sat on either side of me in the conference room and began to explain their work. As part of a four-member marketing team, Susan and Jyothi were responsible for writing website content, soliciting guest blog posts after or during their travels, and enlivening the websites for all Captivate's destinations with enticing photographs and perfectly grammatical (and alluring!) text. Susan also established lengthy email communication with guests after their stay. She organized and conducted guest events in London to meet past and prospective guests over hosted dinners and presentations of Captivate's plans. These long emails, along with the spontaneous gestures that Susan organized (a surprise bottle of wine, a suite upgrade), personalized relationships and offered a unique advantage to traveling with Captivate; not surprisingly, many guests had traveled with Captivate more than once and recommended it to friends.

As I came to see, these emails performed an important affective function. They were especially valuable for Captivate's primary clientele, who were elderly, affluent residents in the Global North, often living alone or away from their families. Susan's long and warm emails to them described her everyday life in Bangalore; guests in turn responded with their own news and travel reminiscences. Guests sometimes organized "viewing parties" of photographs from their Captivate travel, with Indian takeaway food, for friends and neighbors upon their return home from a trip, and Susan inquired with care about these as well, offering suggestions for Indian movies to watch during the gathering. Guests were invited to write blogs about their recent trips, resembling the postcards that might have been sent by traveling British colonial officers and their families to relatives and friends back home that captured glimpses of worlds away from the metropole (see also Stevenson 2023). Jyothi did not undertake this kind of intensive communication with guests; it required someone from the milieu of the guests themselves, like Susan. Captivate—as a former two-person firm that had since scaled up—positioned itself to accrue the most competitive advantage from its workforce. Thus middle-class women, typically foreign nationals, were employed in guest interface roles, known as travel consultants. These jobs drew from the company's existing cultural capital, expecting them to "naturally" know how to interact with elite clients in the North.

Jyothi, however, offered value in her dedication to the company and her commitment to what she understood as its values. Her labor included the emotional work of forming attachments and sentimental bonds; she took on large amounts of work, battled her body as it collapsed under neurological stress, and averred her commitment to the company. Her role resembled that of the trip advisers to whom work was sent (I describe their work below). While Captivate offered several opportunities for individuals to acquire familiarity with speaking English; visit the offered destinations in India on "test trips"; and experiment with new food, leisure activities, and adventure sports, these largely functioned as staged encounters with the new middle-class startup worlds. There were only one or two employees who had moved from a back-end role to a guest interface one.

Susan and Jyothi represent two distinct groups of employees at Captivate. The visible difference between the groups was obvious at first glance: middle-class and elite women often wore pants, dresses, and shirts to work, whereas the back-end workers more typically wore *salwar kameezes* or dressed like college students in skinny jeans, dressy tops (with puffed sleeves, decorations, or synthetic material), and makeup. In other words, people's aesthetic tastes were distinctions, as Pierre Bourdieu (1986) argues, made in relation to other classes to consolidate how one's class status was publicly managed and read.

The travel consultants (women like Susan, who was a travel consultant before taking on her role in marketing) were typically foreign nationals—referred to as "expatriates" rather than immigrants, signaling their adjacency to whiteness and their class status—as well as upper middle-class Indians, who sold travel packages and interfaced with guests on the phone. They were between thirty and forty years old, with prior work histories in corporate finance or communications and a rich history of personal travel for pleasure. They often came to the office in auto rickshaws, drove their own cars, or used chauffeured cars—vastly different from the scooter commute or two-bus journeys that women in back-end jobs frequently undertook. Commuting time was short for them, fifteen minutes to half an hour. The three Indians in this group had all worked in major metropolitan cities before (Mumbai and New Delhi) and were already well-established, middle-class professional women leading teams and in positions of authority before they moved to Captivate.

Although the company did not offer more than their former pay or even match it, these women worked there because they loved travel, wanted a less stressful job, desired to move to India and experience something different from before, and so on. Writing about traveling theory in "Questions of Travel," Caren Kaplan notes the fantasies of escape that relentlessly gendered expatriation as a masculine phenomenon participating in imperialist nostalgia and marked by "the melancholic quest for substance while erasing or violating the object of concern" (2000, 45). When Pushkar described his expat employees on the phone to me, he mentioned something very different from a need to escape. He explained, "These aren't your typical expatriates who live in

Palm Meadows" (referring to an elite gated community nearby known to replicate American suburbia). He meant that they were *atypical* professional migrants, wanting to immerse themselves in the experiences of everyday Indian urban life rather than shelter themselves from it. The gendering of expatriation in this moment of startup capitalism was a need for flexible bodies to travel the world to shake off the demands of capitalist time and immerse themselves in the dense affective ties and networks of everyday life in Bangalore. These distinctions within the very specific work culture and composition of Captivate's employees are significant because they emblematize the feminization of labor and the production of flexible worker selves that build on existing difference to produce economic value. The valuation of difference and its circulation in a transnational economy is at the heart of this book.

The second group of women at Captivate—those like Jyothi—supported guest travel through the back-end work of building itineraries, updating databases, coordinating logistics, and so on. They all had an undergraduate degree and a few had a master's degree, usually in tourism. These employees were usually the first generation of professionals in their families, and several had migrated from smaller towns and villages.[1] Their spoken and written English took effort, and when I sometimes sent them emails with an invitation to a party or to my house, they would impatiently walk over to my desk and ask me to "just say it in a few words!" While the elite "expat" workers might be searching for escape from their lives in the Global North, these workers sought to make a "home" in the city and to find belonging in the desirable modes of middle-class living that were so tangible to them in other Captivate employees and in the travel itineraries that they so meticulously planned. Their class desires were satisfied by a kind of transference that connected their desires intimately with those of their clients across the world. Company management assessed their value in terms of their relative fixedness—assuming they didn't desire aspirational futures and would stay on in their roles.

These women were the youngest in the office and became my closest interlocutors. My insight into how entrepreneurial workplaces are experienced as experimental by those entering professional work for the first time is shaped by interviews and interactions with them. Typically, their parents had their own businesses or worked for the state government; some had jobs that in India would be considered lower middle class or working class: vegetable pushcart vendor, security guard, building contractor, nurse, and so on. Their castes were more difficult to determine.

Like most industries in India built on the fiction of "meritocracy"— or the idea that skills and talent are objective factors determining success—in the entrepreneurial sector, too, success and mobility are heralded as personal achievements. Yet upper-caste Brahmins made sure to insert references to how particular they were about eating vegetarian food or their fathers' position as "learned men" (professors or priests). Those from middling business castes mentioned the need for their marriages to be arranged with other business families from the same caste. Aside from this, caste status was never explicitly mentioned to me, and I never asked direct questions requiring people to identify themselves with a particular caste or class.

Class was materially evident through an aspiration to an urban middle classness. The six or so migrant women straight out of college, or those who were older but still unmarried, lived on their own in tiny one- or two-room shared apartments or in ladies paying guest facilities. They were able to work late hours, meet strangers at fitness classes, take up weekend hobbies, and engage in leisure activities. In the evenings too, some employees went to a nearby pub with ladies night offers such as free drinks or shopping at a handicrafts sale or street-side (those in their mid-twenties to mid-thirties). The term *ladies* was not just a pointer to gender but also signified the desirable, consuming figure of the upper-caste, middle-class woman, as work like Rupal Oza's (1992) has shown to be crucial to India's transition to a globalizing economy in the 1990s.

In just a few months I came to understand the career growth and desires of Captivate's different kinds of workers. A few of them used Captivate funds for self-improvement to enroll in English-language classes; others took dance lessons for B-boying, salsa, and hip-hop; and others conducted their own romances. Migrants to the city were far from parental eyes and took significant risks with dating—almost always with a man from a different religion, race, class, or caste. They were forced to keep these romances secret, as their parents would insist on their terminating the relationships if they ever found out. Their risk-taking cannot be disengaged from their spatial movements, oriented continually outward toward public classes, weekend hikes, and leisure outings, as compared with the married women, who stayed home, looking after young children, or went out with their husbands.

Although job roles at Captivate were categorized according to the forms of cultural capital that employees could mobilize, there was some (albeit limited) movement between job roles. Those performing back-end work could hope to take on guest interface roles upon mastering certain codes of behavior and speech, although this rarely happened. In my own stay of nine months of fieldwork and then keeping in touch with employees at Captivate, I witnessed only two employees from an emerging middle class take on roles that required guest interactions, both on the phone and in person. Yet individuals experimented with food, drink, leisure, fitness, and travel in ways that may not have resulted in a permanent radical break with their parent's consumption habits and social expectations but offered experience with inhabiting expressive middle-class urban cultures and practices.

LEARNING TO LIVE THE GOOD LIFE

Many of Captivate's employees did not have the forms of capital that could be translated to their advantage in the new middle-class economy that call center workers did (Murphy 2011, 421). While those middle-class service-sector workers had parents who were often part of India's older middle classes, working in stable banking and government jobs, the parents of many Captivate employees were frequently working class, non–upper caste, and most of their mothers had never been employed. They learned how to consume and inhabit Bangalore's new leisure spaces through the comfort and security of group activities provided through work and colleagues.

As an entrepreneurial global travel company, Captivate's work environment cultivated employees as experimental startup founders. They were offered opportunities to act, consume, exercise, and socialize like startup entrepreneurs. I understand this as a means of learning to live "the good life." In the Aristotelian sense, as Hannah Arendt reads it, the good life is an altogether different life for the citizen, one that is "'good' to the extent that by having mastered the necessities of sheer life, by being freed from labor and work, and by overcoming the innate urge of all living creatures for their own survival, it was no longer bound to the biological life process" (1998, 36–37). Captivate offered the ideal space from which to understand how there is more produced at work than the mere functions that earn a wage—the impulse to experiment in and through the office reconfigures our understanding of work and muddles its relations with "life."

Captivate offered opportunities for individual workers to embody entrepreneurial ethics, to build friendship, care, and experimentation into the conditions of everyday work, as I show in more detail in part 2 of this book. The company organized off-site trips to go white-water rafting and adventure sports annually, exhorting employees to move flexibly through the kinds of spaces that their guests enjoy. Several groups of workers were encouraged to innovate with their own labor by suggesting ideas, shortcuts, and changes that would simplify and clarify the workflow. Office lunches were often catered from various neighborhood restaurants so that employees could sample and try new cuisines—as Pushkar said one day, "C'mon guys! We're a global company! Try something new!"

Employees who had completed a few years in the company took "test" trips, on which they stayed at exclusive company hotels and boutiques, making sure the amenities met company standards and making recommendations. These are ways that employees "learned" about the middle-class and elite practices of the guests they served. Often these trips were confusing; employees at Captivate who were young women from a lower middle class struggled to comprehend why a homely bed-and-breakfast ("You had to get your own water!") might be desirable to foreign guests. At meetings that I attended, their team leaders struggled to generate a useful formula that employees could put into play. For example, when discussing why a colorful room with cut-glass windows in a Rajasthani palace might entice guests, team leads noted that "the French like colors a lot," and employees laughed in amusement before continuing to report on how they had milked village cows to "test" an authentic village experience for future guests.

The primary purpose of test trips was a response to what John Urry and Jonas Larsen (2011) call "post-Fordist differentiated consumption," in which consumers react to mass consumption by wanting individualized experiences. Producers respond by tailoring experiences and products to individual consumers' needs (14). "New tourism" is segmented, customized, and flexible—a move away from the standardization practices of mass ("old") tourism (Urry and Larsen 2011, citing Poon 1993). Captivate, as an entrepreneurial travel company, not only wanted to offer guests an experience of the "new tourism"; it also wanted certain forms of habitus to become naturalized among employees: "C'mon guys! We're a global company!" was a call for employees to embody both the entrepreneur's own cosmopolitanism and the desire to try new cuisine, exercise, travel, and sport.

Travel is not a separate sphere from everyday life but part of a series of experiences comprising what Zygmunt Bauman terms the "good life": a continuous holiday for a certain elite (Bauman 2007). Travel marks status; the phrase "I need a holiday" reflects a modern idea that people's physical and mental health will be restored if they can get away and rejuvenate themselves (Urry and Larsen 2011, 5). Both groups of workers—the elite who interacted with clients and the others who implemented these plans through itineraries and logistical planning—were responsible for planning and drawing up elaborate travel arrangements and documents that would materialize the desires and fantasies of their guests. The value they produced through their labor was not use value or *merely* logistical, ensuring people moved from one place to another on their travel. Instead, it was in line with what Kaplan notes as the "hypervaluation of the aesthetic and the celebration of 'experience'" that is so essential to modernity's commodifications (2000, 46) and evidenced by the manifold publications (reports, itineraries, brochures, catalogs) that circulate these promised aestheticized experiences.

For an emerging middle class at Captivate, work in this entrepreneurial travel sector emerged through postcolonial and gendered aspirations; it offered the pedagogical instruction for how to cultivate an appropriate habitus to properly inhabit the new economy of experimental work and life that supposedly reaches its pinnacle in startup capitalism. By participating in the off-site adventures, lunches out, and fitness activities organized by work, and informally by colleagues (see chapter 5), Captivate employees navigated experimental worlds in a group. Being with colleagues who offered different kinds of knowledge about the city allowed newly professional women to learn new forms of embodiment from their colleagues.

From the company's perspective, the investment in employee lifestyles affectively bound workers to the company and created energetic and committed employees. The managing director sent out an email to the entire office one day. It was from a client in London, and it remarked that the nicest thing about booking with Captivate was that all the employees the client interacted with seemed to love their jobs. The company management noted that this was the biggest asset to the company: employees' love of their work. While startup entrepreneurs love what they do because they run their own business, when the company scales up, different management techniques are deployed as modes of governance, to create attachments between salaried employees and the company. The experiences of Captivate employees thus extend and complicate feminist analysis of transnational service-sector jobs. Typically, service-sector workers interact with clients, integrating the labor of brain, heart, and mind for material and immaterial products (Weeks 2011). Yet Captivate's startup roots expected passion, innovation, experimentation, and creativity even from those who did not conduct sales. Each employee was expected to embody the firm.

EXTRACTING FROM THE WORKER

In turn, everyday labor draws from worker subjectivity. Sales team employees at Captivate were required to perform "authenticity work" (Mirchandani 2012) by drawing from their own backgrounds and experiences to enrich client interactions. Unlike the call center model, in which employees are formally instructed in speech patterns and themes, at Captivate employees were expected to draw on their own backgrounds to intuitively "know" how to interact. They were expected to mobilize their habitus to enrich their labor.

As an industry, the more segmented travel becomes, the more it requires tailor-made and intensive attention to cater to customers' needs, demands, and desires (Urry and Larsen 2011). But the model of specialization then not only relies on broad categories of labor advantage—"Third World women" or "special economic zones" as with early waves of flexible accumulation (Molé 2011)—but further parses labor to accrue value from gender, class, and nationality. Feminist theorists have long understood that while work is organized by gender, it is also a site where gender is enforced, performed, and recreated; workers draw upon gendered codes and scripts to perform various aspects of everyday work (Weeks 2011, 209). At Captivate, work was further organized by class, life stage, nationality, migrant status, and an increasingly calibrated and complex set of identity matrices. This is why elite, Western, middle-class, often married and middle-aged women performed direct sales jobs, drawing on their habitus, cultural capital, and individual experiences with travel.

As Chandra Mohanty writes, jobs and tasks are ideologically constructed "in terms of notions of appropriate femininity, domesticity, (hetero)sexuality, and racial and cultural stereotypes" (2003, 2543). She was primarily writing in the context of the flexible restructuring of factory work and offshore informatics processing that rely on the naturalization of gendered traits such as "nimble fingers" (Ong 2010; Freeman 2000; Kondo 1990; Salzinger 2003), or the affective and emotive labor of service work including sex work, sales, call center work, and secretarial work associated with femininity (Brennan 2004; Hochschild 2003; Walkerdine 2003; Pringle 1989). At Captivate, this kind of flexible restructuring and the assigning of jobs to those who "inherently" possessed forms of symbolic capital was a significant strategy through which surplus value was accrued from individuals.

My first inkling of the relevance of such a form of capital emerged when I first talked to Pushkar Subramaniam on the phone, discussing the possibility of doing fieldwork at his company. I reminded him that I had no educational training in travel or tourism, or any work experience in related fields. "That's an advantage," Pushkar said. "We don't look for people with *a formal* training in travel. In fact, we prefer to have people who *fit* the company rather than have the educational degrees. We look for certain *personalities*" (Interview with Pushkar Subramaniam; emphasis added).

Rather than placing value on formal educational training, Subramaniam was suggesting that an assessment of employee potential was key to hiring practices. Success in this work environment also required a mastery over scripts that were unknowable in advance. The office outing might include an off-site white-water adventure or a visit to a neighborhood French café; unlike earlier forms of office work that were confined to the space and time of the office, here employees were expected to be familiar with, or quickly learn, a range of classed embodiments. Class mobility also shaped how workers move up the professional ladder. Some employees were disadvantaged by their migrant status to the city, lower middle-class background, and struggle with speaking English; what was expected from them at work was their presumed immobility. From a management perspective, it was expected that some workers would stay in low-reward and low-paying jobs without demanding raises. It was expected that when they wanted different challenges, they would leave the company, what a company official called "healthy attrition." Thus a study of a service company rooted in an experimental approach to labor and life allows us to understand how these ideals are navigated through a range of prior, unnamed factors that structure how workers enter a world of work without explicit rules and where office life is lived through unexpected adventures.

Studies of women's work show that managers and recruiters reinforce widely held stereotypes about women in low-paying jobs earning "leisure money" to supplement family income (Mies 2012). They seek out women employees, believing them to be inherently better able to perform certain jobs (Freeman 2000). Part of the attraction in hiring women for factory labor has been women's assumed docility and servitude, as Aihwa Ong (2010) and Caitryn Lynch (2007) show about gendered factory labor in Malaysia and Sri Lanka. Not only did flexible economic restructuring produce gendered low-status and routine jobs; these were also shipped out to other countries, mapping race, ethnicity, and nationality onto the figure of the Third World woman worker (Mohanty 2003). At Captivate at the time of my fieldwork, the Bangalore office took on back-end roles for all of Asia and South America. Thus even the company's flexible work practices assess gender, race, class, and life stage to create forms of feminized labor.

Drawing on labor as method allows us to complicate the conversation about global capital and feminized labor. As a method it moves beyond the formative, and polarizing, debates that startup capitalism often provokes. Is global capital manifesting the conditions of its exploitation everywhere, or are workers finding ways to circumvent its totalizing logic? Labor as method offers an approach that sidesteps these questions to examine instead what is produced in the interactions between capital and labor that this book studies. For instance, the allure of participating in the experimentation of startup capitalism often compels young workers to take extra forms of labor and risk to participate fully in the entrepreneurial economy. They do this by creating forms of care and kinship for each other; through these infrastructures of care, they survive and even thrive under startup capitalism. Rather than categorizing these relations within the terms of agency or resistance, labor as method allows us to consider how workers create vital infrastructures of care through which they sustain themselves and produce the basis for experiments in techno-capitalism to unfold. These infrastructures have a productive function: they are key modes of worker regeneration through which new class practices are learned, desires fulfilled, and personal aspirations met. Thus reproductive labor—the work of regenerating labor power—is fundamentally transformed as labor power is regenerated outside the heterosexual household. Following labor to ask what does it do, how does it work, and what is produced through its movements allows us to see new forms and alliances.

Captivate also allowed me to understand how startup capitalism is enacted over a sustained period. Once the crucial two-year period is over, and the startup survives, how does it grow? I found that the emphasis on innovation and disruption transforms into other attributes being valued. The startup sector frames labor in terms of innovation and passion (the immaterial labor of the mind and the heart), but as companies scale up they demand the material labor of everyday work to implement and actualize abstract ideas.

PLACING THE ETHNOGRAPHER

I was to be Captivate's first "intern." This was not a separate job role carved out for me but similar to what Jyothi and Susan on the marketing team did, without remuneration. I would be helping their team with writing content, sifting through tens of Picasa albums, and editing guest posts for the blog. In return I would accompany the office on off-site trips, organized leisure outings, and team lunches, and have my own Captivate email and Skype addresses. I could eat lunch with employees in the tiny snack room and get to know people there. In sum, I would be treated like a Captivate employee. I was sure that this would have its own repercussions; for instance, how would those I was writing about respond to my research?

I found myself in an odd position between the different social classes at Captivate. On the one hand, with a master's degree from the University of London and work experience in national media, I found myself sharing a middle-class outlook, tastes, and leisure life with the first group. And yet as someone who grew up in India, I spoke several of the same languages (Kannada, Tamil, Bengali) as those in the second group. I looked their age, too, and people assumed that I was like them, single, straight out of college, and therefore a willing recipient of excitable text messages on Sundays: "Want to do something funky?" I spent more time with the second group, as I felt more comfortable with them. However, the location of my rented apartment and my "in" with the company through the CEO's brother contested my efforts to easily slip into different groups. Ananth Subramanian and I occasionally went to drink coconut water downstairs; when we came back my outing would be mined for information to know more about the CEO's brother: "How much was lunch?" "What did you eat?" "How was it?" As I explain in a later chapter, there was less interest in the content of the conversation than in the material markers of food, aesthetics, and consumption that offer valuable "knowledge" about consumption practices.

Perhaps the experience of establishing identity and intent is different for foreign ethnographers conducting fieldwork; there is no immediate referent for where they come from or what their status is in their home country. Here in Bangalore, as a "local," making friends meant being hyperaware of our differences. My desire to try to obliterate them and somehow to conduct fieldwork as though I had no history in the city or that my geographies of familiarity in the city could be concealed was in vain. I tried to blur caste and class rules by taking local buses into parts of the city I had never been to before, to eat unfamiliar food at smaller darshinis, and tried to never talk about where I went on my personal time. If I were new to India, perhaps everything about me might seem "strange" and "alien" to my interlocutors at Captivate, yet here as a Bangalorean back "at home," I knew I was being assessed when people visited my fieldwork apartment or, once, at my birthday celebration met my "other" world of friends and family.

Unfortunately, despite my elaborate explanations of what research I was doing, my work seemed confusing to most employees, and eventually people adopted me into their fold as a colleague and perhaps even a friend rather than a researcher. Two years after my fieldwork, when I met everyone again, not a single person asked about my research. In a well-known essay, David Mosse (2006) reflects on his decade of fieldwork at a developmental project. His informants challenged his interpretations of their social work; reported their dissatisfaction and protested to his university management, senior colleagues, and the ethics board; and finally participated in a one-day session at which they raised fifty-six pages of objections to his analysis. Mosse argues that in producing the ethnographic account, he had to refuse the roles allocated to him: "I had to disembed myself, erect boundaries, or put distance between myself and the social worlds I described such that the academic individual was seen to deny the moral person of fieldwork" (2006, 946). His objectors challenged the boundaries raised by his writing, choosing not to textually mediate it but to socially mediate it through the creation of a "moral community" in which Mosse could be re-embedded, reproducing the relations of fieldwork.

Like the development organization where Mosse worked, Captivate too had a coherent representation of itself; by promoting ideals of flexibility and meritocracy, it explicitly located itself as a worker-friendly space. My challenge was to both work at Captivate and to simultaneously understand how its self-representations were created and interpreted by different levels of workers. Working full time lessened my sense of obligation to those through whom I negotiated my entry into Captivate, like the senior management who explained Captivate's work philosophy to me. Anthropologists of labor have long studied labor processes, sometimes joining their interlocutors undercover (Fernandez-Kelly 1984), participating on the assembly line (Lynch 2007; Salzinger 2003), or being on specific teams on Wall Street (Ho 2009). The small scale and flexible workplace of the entrepreneurial economy, with teams of between five and eight people, had no space for observers, making it imperative for my presence to have a tangible beneficial meaning and value for Captivate. In this fast-moving startup economy, I ended up staying longer than many who were recruited at the same time as I was, or even afterward!

As time went by, earlier distinctions between "friends" and "informants" or between ethnography and life did not seem so distinct or irreconcilable anymore. My informants came home for drinks or meals, became friends with Naina, and stayed overnight at my place. I began to spend weekends with them, traveled to meet their families, and attended significant occasions—birthdays, a daughter's first dance performance, and festive celebrations at their houses. My own mobility became intertwined with theirs, tightened and loosened according to shifting contexts of urban space, everyday work, and private life. It is through this tight and entangled set of relations that my ethnography unfolds.

2

GENDERED PUBLICS

Looking Back from the Startup City

ɪ'ᴍ ɪɴ ᴍʏ great-aunt's apartment, overlooking a leafy street in Malleshwaram. Outside a storm is raging, punctuating my audio recording with explosions of thunder. Around us there are framed photographs of the family across the years—tints from black and white to sepia to the faded color of the 1970s and 1980s. The older photographs date from the mid-1900s; in one of them, my great-grandmother is seated in a checkered nine-yard sari, her husband beside her looking preoccupied, in formal shirt and trousers. Her sari and the way she ties it marks her caste as Tamil Brahmin. Below them in a ragged line on the floor some of their seven children sit, squinting uncertainly into the camera.

I visited with my great-aunt—one of my grandmother's younger sisters—during my fieldwork in Bangalore. I had been interviewing women in various small entrepreneurial companies, and my interviews and fieldwork were rich with details of how women negotiated middle-class compulsions to be respectable in public with their own pleasures and experiments in self-making. I was interested to hear how older professional women navigated movements across public and private spaces, and my great aunt, a journalist and teacher, was offering me a sense of her own past.

Historicizing my fieldwork through an unlikely archive of family stories, poems, and scrapbook entries, this chapter examines small and contingent projects of feminist future making from the late 1800s to the present. The women in this chapter were upper-caste and middle-class women, the same demographic that has been mapped in Indian historiography as either burdened by Indian (read Hindu) culture or proudly emblematic of Indian nationalism and able to withstand colonial modernity by embodying the inner spiritual core of the nation (see Chatterjee 1987).[1] This chapter explores how the subject of the middle-class woman might be productively read to anticipate later navigations of neoliberalism and nationalism within the current economy of entrepreneurialism.

I juxtapose oral histories and archival materials from my own family with ethnographic fieldwork in the aspiring startup city to show how middle-class womanhood unfolds the possibilities for feminist future making adjacent to dominant projects of nationalism and neoliberalism. Following labor as method, I move across sites of gendered labor through different historical periods. Rather than imagine such gendered publics of middle-class womanhood as a radical break from the norm and something *new* in the startup city, this chapter helps us contextualize public cultures of the entrepreneurial city as contingent navigations between opposing ideologies to achieve power.[2]

My great-aunt is a family archivist of sorts, writing a biography of her mother—my great grandmother. I arrived in her top-floor apartment just before a rainstorm broke. The audio I listen back to captures the landline ringing insistently with my mother on the other end trying to reach me to ask when I could take her to the doctor. In the foreground is my great aunt's relaxed voice close by the recorder reminding me that she expected us to spend a leisurely evening together. Reading back my fieldnotes as I transcribe the interview, I'm struck by how even simple acts of coming together amidst gendered responsibilities can seem fraught and perhaps even impossible.

My great aunt, whom I call Shanta here, began by telling me how her family came to be in Bangalore in the late 1800s, when her parents got married. Her mother, Ratna, lived in a small town nearby and had studied English in school until she was about nine years old. When she moved to her husband's house in Bangalore, then a small British cantonment town, she was an early teen and the only daughter-in-law in the household. Not surprisingly, she was quickly put in charge of most of the cooking, cleaning, and washing. Ratna was new to this—as an upper-caste daughter, she had been pampered in her natal home and was unprepared to be caretaking an entire household. She found the work overwhelming. She eventually had a sort of mental break and decided she would not—*could not*—work anymore.

How does one protest labor within the household, among those you are expected to love, cherish, and nurture?[3] If the household has been coded as the realm of "women's work," the general category of womanhood is refracted further by histories of difference. For an upper-caste woman in pre-independence India like Ratna, caste lines were firmly maintained to keep her indoors, maintaining the desired sanctity of the home. Isolated and alienated, she registered her protest against incessant labor in the only way she could: she claimed illness and stopped working to lie in bed. She interrupted the time of the heterosexual household that unfolds according to the logic of capital accumulation and caste-class reproduction. Tom Boellstorff (2007, 228) calls "straight time" "an emically salient, socially efficacious, and experientially real cultural construction of temporality across a wide range of political and social positions," and Ratna was protesting her co-option into this linearity.

Ratna's husband was away in the nearby city of Madras (now Chennai) studying, and so her worried parents-in-law began looking around for medical treatment themselves. They lived on the grounds of a hospital (where her father-in-law worked) and called on the resident chief medical officer, a British official. In halting English, Ratna confided to him that she was enormously fatigued. He assured her that he would keep her in hospital for a few months to rest. He informed her parents-in-law that Ratna was severely ill and needed recovery time. When Ratna's husband finally finished his undergraduate degree in Madras and returned to Bangalore, the medical officer asked to see him. He told him of an opportunity in the nearby cantonment town of Kolar Gold Fields, where they were looking for health officers like himself. It would be a wonderful opportunity to move his ailing wife away from the extended family and start a new life.

This is the story Shanta told me, a story that marks Ratna's nascent feminism, her dislocation in a strict Brahmin household, and her restlessness to explore the world outside. Its telling is shaped in distinctive ways by my great-aunt's own outlook: Ratna's desires for freedom were recognizable only by the white British officer, who rescued Ratna from her fate as family laborer. Ratna's feminism, in this telling, was out of sync with her premodern, caste-obsessed household, but she found an ally in the liberal white man, and he cut her free and sent her on to her independent future. In this story, Ratna's desire to find herself was dependent on leaving behind the space-time of her caste-life with her family, so she moved to a small British-run town, Kolar Gold Fields (KGF).

THE INTIMATE PUBLICS OF GENDERED LABOR

In KGF, the British ran gold mines and employed locals as officers and mining labor. It was a mining camp, a predominantly working-class town, established in the 1880s on a model of colonial extractivism designed to serve the British (Nair 1998). Ratna moved and settled down here during a period of KGF's most dramatic growth; between 1891 and 1901 the town's population increased from 24,111 to 70,874 (Nair 1998, 20). She soon gave birth to her first daughter, whom she named Leila after a Tolstoy character she particularly favored. Eight more children followed; two died young. As she raised her children, Ratna also raised beloved cows and buffaloes and cultivated a curiosity about the lives of women around her. She was less interested in well-off women who lived in bungalows in what was called the West End of town, my great-aunt told me. Instead, Ratna ventured to the "row houses" to meet middle-class and non-Brahmin women, whom she convinced of the need to maintain their own income to be independent from their husbands.

Ratna's husband was apparently quite enchanted by British life: he socialized with British officials, wore shirts and trousers, played tennis and football, and attended local soirées. Ratna seemed to have indulged him but did not join this life. For social events, she sent one of her daughters instead. Her own attention was elsewhere. As she ventured out of her own home, she began to interact more with the women in the lower-income row houses in KGF. Ratna worked with the women to start a *samaj*, a community space, and raise a small seed fund to purchase some sewing machines. She lobbied local officials to acquire a small room for her venture: the samaj was filled with women of different castes and classes. The affluent among them were invited to fund the samaj. A sewing teacher was appointed, and women soon undertook small paid tailoring jobs. Soon an English teacher found his way into the group to instruct them in language, and then a music teacher.

Years after the interview, transcribing the audio, I asked my aunt who these women were. What caste were they? In her email reply she told me it was a "casteless, classless congregation of women whose husbands held middle or lower-level positions in the gold fields." They came from various parts of India and were of different religious faiths. Shanta deemphasized caste to imagine her mother as creating a space of gendered freedom within the terms of liberal inclusion. In other words, people disregarded their caste and class differences to create a new community. I heard this language of casteless-ness frequently in my research, usually from upper-caste men who lauded the inclusive entrepreneurial sector they were building. The grammar of the story that I am told is itself a story of a certain feminist history; it begs us to ask for whom these differences of caste and class mattered and for whom they could be surpassed in pursuit of freedom.

But Shanta's story also shows how she sought to create conditions in which her labor would be valued. The samaj offered a concrete and material site at which value was produced: it was a gendered public, respectable for a middle-class and upper-caste married woman to convene.[4] Ratna's freedom from the time and space of her household was crafted in and through the strictures of caste and class life, responsive to her place in a small town run by the British. Her public life intersected little with her husband's. He kept an open house, inviting people to stay for a meal when they visited. Ratna ran the household and raised the children, but she maintained her passion for the samaj as a pursuit separate from her husband. Historians of colonialism remind us that Indian women in this period were expected to acquire European accomplishments but present themselves as emblems of national culture, as traditional yet modern: the figure of the "Enlightened Woman" (Jayawardena 1986, 13).[5] When middle-class women did circulate outside their homes, their movements were purposeful and oriented to the social and—in colonial India—national good.

Nationalist reformers advocated for women's education, freedom of movement, and a turn to monogamy as markers of modernity, development, and civilization. In fact, the historiography of India is filled with analysis of the ways in which middle-class, upper-caste women came to symbolize the Indian nation.[6] Ratna's choice of work and fulfillment was cognizant of these expectations, yet she could not abide by them. Ratna did not circulate in the spaces of colonial modernity as her husband did, acquire European accomplishments, or even consider herself modern. As Sarah Sharma (2014, 13) reminds us, the public sphere is also a time: a free and unfettered time for deliberative thinking. Ratna shows us how citizens are *constituted in* time (Sharma 2014, 13; emphasis in original) through the household, colonialism, and care work.

The lives of individual women like Ratna continually existed in the interstitial spaces between the abstract ideas of the nation and idealized womanhood. Ratna acquired some power and influence and shaped a space for cross-class mingling even within terms that were dominantly acceptable. In this setting, Ratna's experience was not of the large colonial cities but of a young woman from the small town of Hasan, and later, the colonial mining town of KGF. The activities of her samaj were adjacent to and referenced the larger national struggle for freedom but did not strive to join them.

Located as she was, outside colonial cities, Ratna's story offers us a sense of an ordinary life that I know only from family stories and oral histories. Unlike the Enlightened Woman, she was less immersed in her circulation in colonial society than in the creation of a small gendered public oriented to women's development and flourishing and their independence from the demands of the heterosexual household. If nationalist efforts recruited women into projects of modernity (monogamy, English-language education, fashionable clothing), Ratna's efforts formed around gaining skills for financial independence and language proficiency that could ensure class mobility.

As a gendered public, the women were starkly differentiated from the working-class publics for which KGF was known at the time: work in the mining camps that dotted KGF was "strenuous, risky, and relatively low paid," as Janaki Nair (1998, 21) writes. Instead, Ratna's group produced the political through their learning and sewing as part of a public that did not adhere to the demands of nationalist publics, as

Kumari Jayawardena (1986, 17) notes about them—a public sphere of women's writing in the form of books and journals. Ratna's public was also unlike the modern girls of the 1920s, whose pleasurable roaming rendered them as visible figures: women who were "too public."

The public of the samaj was lived in and through the bodily practices of circulating within the town: women moved to the closed space of the samaj and back; at the samaj they cultivated financial independence and self-sufficiency, not unlike the quest of nationalist leaders at the time. Ratna maintained a healthy skepticism of British life in her cantonment town, and her most explicitly political moment might have been when she greeted Mahatma Gandhi when he visited KGF by falling at his feet. Her samaj is an indication of the forms of freedom and labor that gendered publics might assume under British rule in the early twentieth century. Through it, women left their homes with a purpose that was oriented to a local form of life and relation.

The samaj was a modest, even moral endeavor, a public that creates its own political life produced through the embodied labors of women's work and collectivity.[7] Here the samaj enables a form of freedom that enabled Ratna and the other women to come together. I see this form of gendered public life as resonant with the contemporary startup city of Bangalore too. Middle-class women convene in public spaces to practice yoga, run, and linger in the park. These are not necessarily feminist practices, coincide often with dominant forms of neoliberalism and nationalist expectations around gender. I understand them instead as collective gendered publics that enable leisure and pleasure in contingent ways, outside the heterosexual family.

THE PRICE OF FREEDOM

In the late 1940s, a science teacher visited Ratna's home to talk about one of her daughters. Her talent couldn't be wasted by staying in KGF, he said. He presented the family with an admission form that he had procured: it was to a well-known women's college in Bangalore. He suggested they send their daughter along with another sibling to accompany her. Ratna had a matter-of-fact approach to the world. Others in her position might have been anxious about their daughters' loss of respectability by living away from home, but she was not worried. Would they receive a challenging and good education? Would they be safe and cared for? The answers seemed to be yes. She did not need much persuasion, and neither did her husband.

In the first part of the twentieth century, Bangalore was a center of textile production, but by the 1940s and 1950s it began to gain a reputation as a public-sector city. Ratna's daughters were enrolled to study in Bangalore in the 1940s, and a third—the great-aunt who told me this story—joined them in a few years. Women's education during this time was intended to cultivate them into philanthropic activities, as postcolonial historians note. Yet for these sisters, education offered a space of freedom to partake in public life through pleasurable forms of address and recognition.

Shanta, my great-aunt, had had a stolidly bad time at school and was hopeful that college would be the start of a new life:

> I thought "thank god I'm out of that restrictive school!" I heard [that in college] there were fetes and competitions and I had heard that girls could speak on a public stage. I told myself the minute I go to Maharani [college] I'm going to do all of those things! That was the turning point in my life. I had lots of ideas that I wanted to do things in college that I couldn't do in school. . . . I used to watch the notice board and join play reading contests, and joined the magazine! I gave my name to everything and joined all the clubs and it was encouraging. Only a few girls were bold enough to volunteer . . . I wanted to join them all! (Interview with great-aunt Shanta, 2013)

Women's colleges were key sites in a transformation of womanhood, and in Bangalore, Maharani College—where my great-aunts studied— was established as the first college to offer higher education for women.

It was residential, located on an ample campus called Barne Park and formed as the result of a merger between two existing women's colleges, an intermediate-level college in Bangalore and one in Mysore. This would be an arts and sciences college for women, meant to "bring about cultural change rather than prepare them (students) for livelihood" (Shyalaja and Jayagovind 2003). College life held the possibility of participating in a public filled with ideas. Middle-class women were granted legitimacy to circulate in public via these activities, enabling both confidence and skills.[8]

In a city cleaved into an old and a new, the *pete* or old city of Bangalore dates back at least five centuries, and the newer, Cantonment area was developed through the 1800s by British troops stationed in a vacant village near Halasur (now Ulsoor) (Nair 2005, 42). It was in the Cantonment area that streets were developed to facilitate the body in motion (Nair 2005, 47): Anglo-Indian residents and British officials strolled along the main tree-lined avenues, visited theaters and dances, and rode horses and cars down broad streets. Shanta's involvement in college life enabled her participation in this world of motion and mobility associated with the Cantonment. Her movements reinforced the sense of modernity in the Cantonment's leisure pursuits as the middle classes partook of the city's pleasures.

For my young great-aunts, their ability to engage their talents and interests with a wider public world was closely routed and legitimized through college-sanctioned activities: elections, cultural clubs, and campus newspapers (see also Lukose 2009). College activities offered Shanta a chance at cultivating erudition but also the joy of being seen in public, able to craft her own image, circulate among strangers, and hold her own in debates and discussions with classmates. Tarini Bedi's (2007) ethnography of women workers in the Hindu right-wing party, the Shiv Sena, details how the *visual* field of the Shiv Sena is dominated by posters and publicity of male cadres. Women workers desiring to be seen and recognized engage in what she calls a politics of "visibility" through which they bodily insert themselves into urban public spaces to make themselves known. Through this distinction between the visual field and the politics of visibility, space is carved out for gendered bodies who step into public life (Bedi 2007, 1536). The visual field is shaped by dominant men but navigated in enterprising ways through a politics of visibilizing oneself strategically, as Shanta did while she maneuvered space in Bangalore.

As an upper-caste and middle-class woman, Shanta too sought out particular publics through which to imagine and cultivate her self-development; these were arranged around the college newspaper and the debate stage and based on formal learning and discourse. During our conversation, she reminded me how hard it was for young unmarried women to move around in public spaces. Their urban circulation was contained within permissible spheres of development and service to the nation, the community, and their college.[9] She considered her education less a preparation for marriage and service to the nation and more a means to achieve self-understanding. Still, Shanta had to ensure that expectations related to her caste, class, gender, religion, and belonging in what was then a small town cohered with dominant expectations.

She stood for college elections and was elected vice president, a role that required her to participate in evening meetings of the College Council. Soon her two sisters discovered a sketch of her on the college bulletin board with what they considered unsavory text scrawled below it. She had become "too public" a figure.[10] Her sisters pressured her to resign, but she was adamant not to. She replied that her very visible and mobile public presence might tarnish the reputation of her sisters, but she was winning prizes and bringing honor to the college. Shanta's body and its circulation across different publics became quite literally the ground on which battles over appropriate middle-class demeanor were staged. She described to me how young Brahmin women were expected to comport themselves:

In the late 40s I was in Bangalore as a teenage student. If you want to know what life was like for a teenage student . . . you had to walk with your head bent. Maharani's College was a place where respectable middle class Brahmin families sent their daughters, and all the daughters had to get married; the BA [bachelor of arts] was an added attraction because by then they felt girls had to be educated. Many Brahmin families sent their daughters to Maharani's rather than Mount Carmel's College which opened later. . . . In those days Mount Carmel's was a good college but it was run by Christian missionaries; going there was anathema for (Brahmin) girls.

Thus, public life is always already demarcated in and through caste, region, and class. Shanta described how her college attracted women from Brahmin families who were expected to neatly oil their hair and decorate it with flowers, attend school in their neatly pressed saris, and return straight home. Their freedom was established within these norms—intended to bring honor to their colleges and families. Mount Carmel's, a short distance across town, attracted women from other communities (like the Kodava community), who played sports and had a more public life— their bodies were considered too visible, too unruly by Brahmin families, who did not want their daughters participating in such life. As Janaki Nair writes of gender and public space in Bangalore, "a complex matrix of gestures, markings, bodily controls, and language enables the safe passage of the woman through the urban space" (Nair 2001, 302). Shanta too, was guided through public life via the gestures and signs of caste and region. Her inability to create a gendered public that would support her efforts and into which she could safely ensconce herself speaks to the disciplining effects of caste-class and gendered strictures that set the limits for projects of gendered freedom.

Even while Shanta tested the boundaries of freedom for middle-class women by entering public life that disciplined her, another sister, too, chafed under the restrictions of college life. Most young women attended women-only colleges and religious activities, typically accompanied by their siblings and cousins, each of them assigned to keep watch on the others. Shanta's younger sister was one such sibling, dispatched to college with two older sisters watching over her and, she wrote an indignant poem to register her disappointment:

Back in the hostel from Sweet Home,
We sit in our room no more to roam
Back to our books we now come,
Haggard-looking creatures to become (1948, Bangalore)

The pleasures of the public were acquired through specific and intentional circulations, and even these were regulated to maintain women's decorum and demureness. These were fraught publics, recruiting women into pleasurable interactions with college mates and strangers but also regulating them according to caste, class, and gender norms that required them to demonstrate their allegiance to the household and family. For women like Shanta then, self-confidence and self-growth necessitated a highly restrictive movement between dominant expectations around caste, class, and gender behavior. Chela Sandoval comments on feminist navigations between different forms of power: "The differential mode of social movement and consciousness depends on the practitioner's ability to read the current situation of power and self-consciously choosing and adopting the ideological stand best suited to push against its configurations, a survival skill well known to oppressed peoples" (2000, 60). Shanta's recognition of the limits of her circulation reflects how women navigated dominant configurations of power and worked within its contours.

IN PREPARATION FOR GLOBALIZED CONSUMPTION

In the 1990s, India's economy opened to global markets, and consumption became key to national growth. New spaces and practices did not just offer opportunities for the middle-class urban woman to consume and partake in leisure; these publics fashioned the very subject of middle-class consumption through media and national discourses, built environments, and security and surveillance practices.

Following a long, symbolic association of middle-class women's bodies with the Indian nation through colonial and nationalist times (see Mankekar 1999), at liberalization too middle-class women came to visibilize and embody the growth desires of the nation. The responsibility to consume accordingly fell on them. Public leisure and consumption was legitimated for middle-class and upper-caste Hindu women when it was co-opted into the service of the nation. If the Enlightened Woman navigated colonial society, the figure of the consuming "global yet Indian" woman was expressed in the early 1990s via the figure of the New Indian Woman (Oza 1992), who managed the anxieties accompanying the opening of India's markets with Indian respectability.[11] Together, writes Rupal Oza, "these narratives generated a visible public archive in which the new woman entered the popular imagination as an icon of modernity" (1992, 26). The New Indian Woman was a direct product of India's economic liberalization, present and proliferating in a public archive of street hoardings, magazine covers, talk shows, and a leisure culture of bars and discotheques.

She might work in newly privatized workplaces and was expected to galvanize the global economy of consumer and personal goods now available in India. She was consistently framed as independent yet situated within reassuring narratives—"family-oriented," "a loving mother," "a good wife"—and appeared in commercials for domestic appliances (Oza 1992, 31–35). The gendered new middle class was produced through public acts of consumption—a significant reformulation from the association of middle-class women with domestic private spaces or in civic forms of public life oriented to philanthropism or nationalism. Thus, the "new" middle classes born during economic liberalization in India are not "new" in terms of structural or social basis, as Leela Fernandes reminds us, but reference "a process of production of a distinctive social and political identity that represents and lays claim to the benefits of liberalization" (Fernandes 2006, xviii). The new middle classes occupy an ideological position to establish their distinction from other groups in the city through spatial practices including "beautification" schemes; urban "cleansing"; and a politics resonant with liberalization principles of privatization, spatial segregation, and an emphasis on consumption culture.

The public of the 1990s that organized itself around images and discourses of the New Indian Woman also circulated around the material architectures of these discourses. Light-filled spaces of daytime leisure included coffee shops, cyber cafés, fast-food restaurants, malls, pubs, and discotheques. Spatially, new middle-class modes of consumption emerged in and around historical leisure publics, collecting in "town." Bangalore opened its first women-only mall—Eva Mall—just off Brigade Road. Other leisure spots appeared on the city's central boulevards, created by the British as part of the Cantonment area in which they would unwind from their official postings. These spaces were now colonized by India's young new middle classes, experimenting with dating (along with group chaperones) at Macs fast food, accessing the internet through newly acquired Hotmail accounts at Coffee Day, and shopping for glitter spaghetti tops in the underground shops off Commercial Street.

This gendered figure so crucial to India's globalization was produced through matrices of security and surveillance. For instance, the launch of the first pubs in Bangalore was accompanied by publicity touting them as "family friendly," and male bouncers were present to ensure the respectability of consumption within their walls. A man I call Ramesh Melwani, a local entrepreneur, credited himself with launching Bangalore's first pub. I met him at The Underground, one of his pubs in the city's center, to talk about how Bangalore came to enable a public culture around technology work. The pub had barely changed in the twenty years of its existence. It was dimly lit, diffident waiters scuttled around, and large TV screens dominated the space.

Melwani, who called himself the "Father of Pubs" in Bangalore, said he was traveling in the UK with his wife when he was struck by all the pubs he saw. "I thought if they can do it there, then why can't we do it here?" he recounted. When he returned from his travels, he reached out to Bangalore's local "Liquor Baron," Vijay Mallya, who owned Kingfisher Breweries (Karnad 2012). The Pub, Bangalore's first modern pub, was a collaboration between Vijay Mallya and Melwani. Located on a central street in the city's Cantonment area, the pub served beer on tap: the first time in the city's history, Melwani noted. Soon other pubs opened in the area, and the idea of Bangalore as "India's Pub City" was born in the late 1980s. Fried snacks and alcohol attracted scores of young software engineers over the years—"techies" who saw these central city pubs as an extension of their work conversations about software and tech work. Inside smoky interiors, men of all ages, often sporting T-shirts with the names of heavy metal bands emblazoned on them, mouthed the lyrics to hard rock and metal music. A thriving masculine subculture of avid quizzers, rock music aficionados, and techies gathered in the city's modern pubs.[12]

Melwani wanted to maintain what he called the "feel" of his pubs: he wanted them to be family friendly, and he wanted women to visit and feel safe. He imagined his pubs as private spaces—guarded by male bouncers—another first in Bangalore. As middle-class women entered these spaces of consumption, they were guided by the signs of respectability: the pubs claimed a global and modern status, they invited in families and professionals, and bouncers and managers regularly inventoried their clients to ensure class homogeneity. The pubs functioned similarly to what Radhika Govinda (2020) terms "liminal, partially private 'public spaces'" that are produced as "safe" for middle-class women. If surveillance is not just a process through which subjects are watched, but in fact a way to notice how gender is itself produced through regulatory frameworks, Melwani's pubs produce the middle-class respectable consumer; they do not just protect them.[13]

Sometimes consumption ran amok, such as when the wrong bodies entered circuits of public consumption, enjoying a pleasure marked as excessive. Shanta had been disciplined by a public gaze in the 1940s as she became a "too public" figure, reprimanded by the scrawling text on a poster. Middle-class, privileged-caste women were also disciplined for experiencing too much pleasure in globalizing India. In 1999 the Miss World pageant was to be held in Bangalore, and it became the center of a raging controversy between right-wing regional nationalists and left-leaning activists battling over the public, mediatized circulation of gendered bodies in the service of global capital—I read this event as part of the "culture wars fought to define the Indian nation" (Mankekar 1999, 5). Although the pageant was finally staged, it demonstrated how profoundly certain women's bodies become sites upon which national and nationalist discourses are galvanized (Mankekar 1999). The presence of sexualized and feminine middle-class bodies in public threatened to destabilize notions of the proper place and presentation of the nation, here metonymized by the gendered body.

By the early 2000s, such attention on a singular spectacularized event was fragmented into occasional panics surrounding a series of raves and farmhouse parties held on the city's outskirts. These parties were organized by both individuals and event planning companies and, as news about them spread, they were "raided" by zealous members of assorted right-wing groups. These self-appointed vigilante police arrived at the venue with media in tow to "bust" the party, rounding up attendees to shame them by publicizing their names and photographs. Local media then streamed live television footage or printed photographs of young women, their faces hastily bundled in a shawl or cloth covering, ducking out of the party, escorted by police, and held in custody until their parents arrived with bail money.

In a typical instance of how raids on rave parties were reported in mainstream media, a news article from 2009 in the *Hindu*, a staid and left-leaning national newspaper, described such a raid: "29 partying women held; liquor, 40 vehicles seized." As Kareem Khubchandani writes about media "raids" at gay nightclubs that fabricate headline news on local TV channels: "Journalists fold excess, gayness, criminality, Westernness, north Indianness into one another, colluding with police by capturing sensationalist footage that shames partygoers and portrays police as paternalistic heroes" (2020, 35). In the Bangalore raids on dance bars, raves, and local parties, the gendered body represented the excesses of globalization and consumption, needing to be disciplined by the Law of the Father who was represented by media, law, and policing efforts.

In January 2009 I was in Bangalore when the news channels began playing a startling series of visuals one night. At a pub in Amnesia, in nearby Mangalore, young women dressed in jeans and T-shirts were shown being dragged out of the pub by their hair—screaming—by a group of men. The perpetrators later claimed allegiance to a right-wing group called the Sri Rama Sene (Army of Lord Rama). The group's leader appeared on TV to explain the attack: the women were in Western clothes in mixed company, and this defied Indian culture, he said— they needed to be disciplined. Valentine's Day was around the corner, and he promised to forcibly marry any couples who were seen together on that day. Following the attacks on Mangalore, there were similar attacks on middle-class women in Bangalore, all women who were out on the streets on their own. Local activists and concerned members of the public formed the group Fearless Karnataka, Bhayavada Karnataka and staged a series of protests and a Take Back the Night event in response.

Economic liberalization might have constructed female desire as seamlessly extending across the realms of public (consumption) and personal (sexual desire), rendering such distinctions irrelevant (in John and Nair 2001), but how much one could consume, where and how, and which caste, class, and gendered body could access the pleasure of the public, is still calibrated and policed by a nationalist gaze.[14] The movements of liberalization's new subject—the New Indian Woman—were predicated on the proper adherence to heteronormative rules governing the conduct of gendered, classed, and caste-bearing bodies. Sex and sexuality were to be confined to the bedroom and the heterosexual household in service of reproductive futurity that would maintain the virility of a Hindu nation.

LANDSCAPES OF HIGH TECHNOLOGY

In 1999 Karnataka's then chief minister, S. M. Krishna, declared his aspiration to cement Bangalore, the state's capital, into a "world city" modeled on Singapore. This was a material restructuring of space—the building of multilane highways to the airport and large IT parks—but also a firmer integration into a global economy.[15] Bangalore was being fashioned into an "investor friendly" destination, equipped to staff and run twenty-four-hour call centers and manage software for large corporate houses. Through the 1990s, the city geared to perform a host of "outsourcing" functions in which labor is offshored to destinations where cheaper rates and relevant language fluency help maintain margins.[16]

Technology workers are themselves far from being a coherent category of analysis. From its early days, software was an industry that spoke of itself as meritocratic, rewarding—so the story goes—hard work and talent with a good job and the promise of entry into middle-class life (Upadhya 2016). The growth of the software industry in Bangalore was first fueled by an upper-caste base of software engineers. Their caste capital translated into access to an engineering education, and their class capital enabled them to fluently circulate in global IT spaces as they serviced clients abroad on project-based work. This kind of professional technology work was well-suited to upper-caste women. They could avail themselves of taxi rides to and from their homes, were typically sequestered from the city in gated campuses flanked by manicured lawns, and embodied what Smitha Radhakrishnan understands as a "respectable femininity" that privileges class and gender (2007, 198). They enacted middle-class gendered sensibilities to be accepted in their workplaces (Raju 2013).

Such professional work largely adhered to caste and class protocols. Radhakrishnan's research found that middle-class women IT professionals privilege work, but never at the cost of families; practice restraint in their consumption and leisure; and can sense the moral fabric of a certain "South Indian middle-class ethos" (Radhakrishnan 2009, 202, 205, 209)—all findings that must be contextualized within a larger culture of IT defined by its early composition as largely Brahmin and upper caste. Air-conditioned offices, interaction with other upper-caste, middle-class professionals, and international travel for short periods made IT professional work appropriate for middle-class Indian women, who work less out of necessity and more from a need to utilize their education and achieve professional satisfaction (Patel 2010). A recent report by Equality Labs shows that caste is not only still very prevalent in high-technology workplaces but also travels transnationally to manifest as a form of discrimination among Indians in US-based workplaces too.[17]

The publics of IT maintained caste and class arrangements as women largely stayed within the spaces delineated by heteronormative family life, moving between professional office and home in private transport and spending their weekends with families or in consumption oriented to class reproduction. While IT engineers perform software-related work, another sector called ITES (or IT enabled services) created a subsidiary economy of call center workers who work night shifts in India, modifying names, accents, and conversational styles to erase specifically Indian mannerisms and modes of speech (Bhagat 2007; Mirchandani 2012; Patel 2010). This is the transnational service sector that had been expanding globally since at least the early 1980s (Mukhopadhyay 2002), and India joined this boom after its liberalization.[18] Technologically oriented service-sector work emerges around the promises that technology will integrate India into a professional global economy.

Unlike earlier "runaway" manufacturing jobs of the global assembly line (Ng and Mitter 2005, 210), work in professional technology offices (software companies, call centers, startup workplaces) signals the possibility of class mobility. The refrain around feminized work in call centers that Kiran Mirchandani (2012) terms "authenticity work" is based on concerns about skill erosion and the routine nature of "deadend" jobs, with limited possibilities of career advancement (Ng and Mitter 2005, 210). However, these are the jobs that allow young graduates without technical qualifications to enter the world of middle-class professional life and imagine different futures for themselves as professionals. If middle-class women were expected to consolidate the nation through respectable consumption and social reproduction, what space do young workers from outside dominant caste and class backgrounds enjoy?

Given the historical mapping of nation onto gendered bodies, young technology workers who live on their own or with friends are especially susceptible to rumor, gossip, and forms of community and local policing. "I didn't want to work in a call center, you can understand, no . . . ?" a young woman from Captivate explained to me during my fieldwork, a moment I revisit in chapter 6. The dangers to the reputation of young women in call centers are so well known that they do not have to be spelled out.[19] There is an affective and moral charge linked to gendered mobilities. Popular media frequently portray young workers in technology offices as promiscuous and spendthrift; they are rumored to spend their entire incomes on consumer durables and clothes for themselves.[20] Landlords prefer not to rent apartments and rooms to young women employed in call centers. In Anjum Hasan's *Neti Neti*, her young protagonist, Sophie Das, struggled with escaping the continual gaze of her landlord who lived downstairs; he was ever present to notice her male visitors, late hours, and spending habits (Hasan 2009). Even as jobs in the new economy make available professional work and the salaries that enable an independent life, young women navigate the watchful surveillance of neighbors and strangers as they navigate public spaces.

Research shows that call center workers embrace globalization more readily than other youth, own more consumer items, and are conversant in consumption and leisure practices such as visiting malls or eating out. Their middle-class practices and aspirations are enabled by their access to, and ability to learn about and master, aspects of everyday consumption and leisure, including what technology to own, what clothes to wear, mall visits, frequenting restaurants and fast-food joints, and so on. Since most of them are under age thirty and live at home, they have a disposable income with which to engage and develop the crafting of modern selves and their orientation toward global practices (Mirchandani 2012; Murphy 2011). Their ability to enter new middle-class publics of leisure and consumption are enabled by their parents' symbolic capital; it allows them to transform older forms of privilege into assets as they enter spaces of new middle-class life.

Even as the feminized figure of the call center worker is stigmatized, the globally mobile and itinerant figure of the young male software engineer working on software projects accumulates an enhanced value in the arranged marriage "market" (Biao 2011). Gender is produced as a system of meaning through which everyday labor is distributed and valued, through which movements and mobilities of individual workers are determined, and through which aspirations for the future are enabled or limited. Haunting the boundaries of professional worlds of technology, both call centers and IT work, are other, minor histories that index how globalization orders and polices caste, class, and gender even as it makes new spaces. Raves, pubs, parties, and discotheques were raided and surveilled and errant women disciplined; bar dancers were arrested, partygoers were shamed, and Ms. World contestants were banned. Yet by the time of my fieldwork in 2012, middle-class bodies were being invited

Figure 8. Day's schedule at the Startup Festival, 2013. Photo by author.

into public spaces and to experiment and innovate with how they made space and fashioned themselves. What changed?

LIFE IN THE STARTUP CITY

In 2014, back in Bangalore for fieldwork, I found myself fielding various invitations to public events, including Yoga in the Park and running clubs. I attended an activist intervention inviting us to occupy public spaces as gendered bodies. At this, entrepreneurs with whom I was doing interviews very early in my fieldwork invited me to an event at which we had all been told to wear our most risqué clothing and to take public transport to get to the venue (Gupta 2016). How were gendered publics now so resolutely forming in public spaces, intending to be visible?

Lata Mani (2014) writes powerfully about "sex and the signal free corridor," showing how neoliberalism functions as ideology, structuring an imagination of personal freedom. Freedom, she writes, "comes to be represented by the young, desiring, unfettered subject able to choose his or her path, partner and forms of consumption, constrained neither by tradition nor any other material factor. Unrestrained choice and obstacle-free mobility comes to be woven into the very ideal of freedom" (Mani 2014, 2). Cities are crucial sites for the symbolic economy of neoliberalism, offering a material and affective site from which to imagine a liberation from the economic inequalities and injustices of the past (Mani 2014). This is a compelling vision for both feminist activism and startup capitalism: both imagining liberation as mobility, unfettered access to public spaces, and the dream of a future in which the shiny new city affords personal freedoms.

In startup Bangalore, entrepreneurs—and entrepreneurial citizens more broadly—are expected to shed the burdens of being a postcolonial subject in order to cultivate the risk-taking and adventurous spirit of startup capitalism. This postcolonial desire for freedom in startup worlds is akin to what Lily Nguyen describes in Vietnamese entrepreneurial circuits: "The moral affect of freedom stood in contrast to a long cultural history that viewed transnational relations through the sobering gravitas of colonialism, sovereignty, and independence" (2018, 3). Worlds of open source design and hacking are experienced by some Vietnamese designers as providing the opportunity to cultivate a cosmopolitan identity, traversing the nowhere of their immediate world, a sensation and feeling, the frisson of transnational encounter not overdetermined by colonial subjugation (Nguyen 2018). At the Startup Festival, an entrepreneur enthusiastically explained to me the excitement of new encounters and possibilities here:

The first thing they [aspiring entrepreneurs] might drop is their full-armed shirts and chinos and . . . find themselves walking around in shorts and T-shirts. . . . [P]eople [earlier] bet on a stereotypical character who they thought would make money, [but] did not make money. The way the eco-system is changing now, people don't hesitate to be who they are. VCs are beginning to look beyond that to say, "he might be an alcoholic, but he's looking to create something cool." (Interview with Startup Festival organizer, March 2013)

In his references to shedding stigma and focusing on creating some-thing compelling and new, this entrepreneur (an organizer of the festival) was also suggesting that age-old expectations of caste behavior and class status needed to be put away in the startup economy. Another festival organizer, the US-based Vlad Dubovskiy, said in a media interview, "The idea is to convey that entrepreneurship is a lifestyle rather than a career." This lifestyle is cobbled together through different spaces and activities, piecing together the distinctive identity of the startup entrepreneur by curating the self. There is no single site at which the startup entrepreneur can be produced; instead it is by moving through different spaces that the startup entrepreneur is performatively enacted. Moreover, new spaces are produced through these circulations in the space of the startup city aligned with global entrepreneurial ecosystems.

Public-private partnerships in the city have shaped its public parks so that paved walkways run through them, bushes and plants are neatly trimmed, and uniformed security guards police whether entrants carry food or not, often checking bags and wielding a *lathi* at couples who get too close on park benches. City government increasingly seeks out private investment and partnership in running the city as a sanitized, modern technology hub (see Mukherjee 2008; Nair 2002). The city is "beautified," populated by the fit and energetic middle classes, a symbol of global modernity in which runners frequent the early morning streets and yoga sessions take place in public parks (Gupta 2020). This neoliberal middle-class city, spruced up and ready for private investment, is cultivated in the imagination of Bangalore as a startup hub and enacted through postcolonial publics seeking visibility and personal freedom. An entrepreneur organizing the Startup Festival explained the transformation of a professional into an *entrepreneur*, well-versed in the arts of cosmopolitan city life and its varied startup publics:

> [T]hat's why you see 6 o'clock in the morning [as the start time for each festival day] because it also tells you, "Dude, you have to be physically, mentally fit to be able to take on this decision, it's not easy. You have to party till two in the morning and you gotta make it to your breakfast meeting because there's an investor waiting to talk to you. So you gotta be able to balance both." (Interview with Startup Festival organizer, March 2013)

From the festival's itinerary I saw that each of its four days was broken down into activities, events, and sessions. Zumba, yoga, running in the city events; networking, *pecha kucha*–style pitching sessions; and dozens of drop-in visits to startups in the neighborhoods hosting this event. Evenings were reserved for plenary sessions, followed by drinks and networking. Heart signs were everywhere; this was Do What You Love through the day. The festival indicated a need to master experimental time, fitting even rejuvenating activities into the strict calendrics of an energetic and productive startup day through what Sarah Sharma (2014, 89) might call "speed therapy" in her discussion of lunchtime rapid yoga sessions offered to corporate workers.

Participation in the Startup Festival required attendees to be mobile urban subjects. With sessions on the itinerary beginning at 6:00 a.m. and ending long past 10:00 p.m., festival participants were expected to be active and energetic. By lunchtime on every day of the festival, designated areas were opened for networking. Aspiring startup entrepreneurs were meant to work lunchrooms and festival venues, handing out business cards; circulating; and engaging one another in talk of technology, funding, and collaboration. In the evening, the action shifted to massive plenary sessions, and then finally the day ended at a neighborhood pub or bar for socializing over drinks and snacks. Public spaces across designated neighborhoods—bars, pubs, parks, and side-walks—were transformed into potential sites for the performance and production of startup founders.

Not only does the startup economy imagine business as an "open playing field" focused on possibility and futures rather than class, gender, or caste histories. It also imagines entrepreneurship as centrally defined by practices of mobility and freedom, visibilized by the new middle classes in an "open city" to be conquered by entrepreneurial energy. These are gendered publics too, but they are in service of nationalist and private capital's vision of entrepreneurial futures of profit and value, thus reimagining space according to future-oriented time. These futures are also mapped in caste-time, as the sociologist Ramesh Bairy reminds us of how modernity becomes coeval with Brahmanism such that "for brahmins themselves, their early entry into the spaces of the modern was made possible not by their structural location—not by the sheer fact of being (and recognizable as) 'Brahmin.' Rather it was because of apparently non-caste factors like their keenness to invest in education, to migrate to cities, to take up modern occupations and so on" (2016, 114).

Thus, participation in technological worlds of IT and startup en-trepreneurship is itself structured by educational backgrounds, rural-urban migration, and fluency with inhabiting the *urban* caste-class landscapes and networks of professional life.[21] This chapter has shown how gendered publics find forms of influence and self-expression that emerge adjacent to dominant norms of nationalism and neoliberalism.

Shanta's samaj, which reconfigured heterosexual and straight time and space to carve out small collectives of gendered learning, and Ratna's college activities, which limited her movements through the strictures of class and caste respectability, are reminders of how gendered publics are shaped through overarching norms, sediment-ing movements in time and place. And yet their incremental bids for freedom and collective belonging in a gendered public achieved confidence, freedom, and influence for them. These contingent gendered publics might not be Feminism writ large or with a capital F, yet they brought them into contact with class and caste others and in pleasurable connection with strangers. These are everyday challenges to the norms of gendered public space, enacted by individual actors through their practices of running, convening a group, participating in a debate club, and performing yoga in the park—akin to what Asef Bayat (2013) calls a feminism of everyday life.

In the neoliberal startup city whose public spaces are cultivated within the grammar of urban beautification, women running on city streets or practicing yoga in the park are also shaping gendered publics. These publics shift between the demands of entrepreneurial life and productivity and the participants' own desires for moments of quiet reprieve from families and their communion with both city spaces and others chasing similar pursuits. Rather than consider these radical feminist acts, this book pursues these gendered publics to understand how they are shaped through the space-time politics of techno-capitalism.

3

PRODUCING THE ENTREPRENEUR

Embodying and Gendering Value

DAY ONE of the Startup Festival, Bangalore, India. At an open field, I was handed a free T-shirt, white with a big red heart on it, and a small, glossy foldout brochure for the festival. I struggled into the T-shirt, putting it on over my clothes, and joined others around me who were peering at maps trying to decide their day's plan. Over four days, those of us registered for the Startup Festival would participate in learning how to be an entrepreneur, visiting startup offices, and preparing to network but also to exercise as constitutive parts of this new embodied regime of labor. In this chapter I detail the recursive process of producing the entrepreneur as someone who is recognized as a successful figure *because* of [his] entrepreneurial actions and demeanor, rather than prior to it.

Through my fieldwork at this festival, I locate how startup capitalism translates forms of caste, gender, and class status into desirable value that is rewarded through funding.

Notions of risk are key to how entrepreneurial ideas are valued, and I adopt an understanding of risk that locates it socially and culturally not only as a function of business but also through forms of sociopolitical difference. Startup capitalism produces a social world of risk that, I show, carves out a certain figure as the desirable entrepreneur. Risk is expressed and celebrated not only through this figure but through [his] mastery of experimental space and time. If labor as method helps us trace the new forms and alliances of hitherto discrete activities that we can now link together as part of a system of labor, this chapter follows labor as method into the home, office, and networking venue to understand how the risk-taking entrepreneur is produced under startup capitalism.

As I crossed the busy main street of Indiranagar, one of Bangalore's "startup neighborhoods," I entered a residential stretch of street and peered at the brochure map, trying to find my location. Low-slung bungalows posted scrawled signs for math tutorials and English-language classes—signs of another local entrepreneurship. I wondered which of these buildings discreetly doubled as a startup office for the hotel business I had elected to hear about at 10:00 a.m. After a few harried phone calls to the helpline number on my brochure, I discovered that a small bungalow with a winding staircase right in front of me was in fact the travel startup I was looking for. Bangalore's new economy of small startups is densely embedded within residential neighborhoods. Unlike the spectacular sprawl of IT campuses on the city's outskirts, the new entrepreneurial economy is based in rented bungalows and within home offices fronted by discreet signage.

A group of us crowded into what would have been the former living room in a house. It was now an open office, a startup for travel. Attendees of the Startup Festival were here to discover what it takes to launch a successful startup. The startup founder casually leaned back in his chair and crossed his hands atop his head. He began: "We [the two founders] were seated at a bar on New Year's Eve and got talking about this crazy idea for a travel business. We scribbled our notes on the soggy napkin on which our beer was placed, and that was the start of the company."

The audience was still. We listened in silence. The man next to me wore a black T-shirt that read "Superman"—the S was a dollar sign: $uperman. The entrepreneur continued. Those hasty notes made on a damp napkin spurred the two former "techies"—male, middle-class software engineers—laughing over a beer late one night, to spontaneously turn into tech entrepreneurs. My field notes continue with excerpts of the conversation: "interrogate your own assumptions"; "back your gut feeling"; "you have to interest the VC (venture capitalist) in the first 5–10 minutes to impress him"; "you have to diminish the distances between you and him; for Americans you need to be straight. With Brazilians you need to be chatty and friendly"; "you cannot be sentimentally foolish."

Launch stories I heard in Bangalore resonate with those from elsewhere—the maverick entrepreneur, the inspirational idea hatched through collaboration at an unlikely venue, the risky jump away from a corporate job into the world of entrepreneurial innovation. These stories circulate as evidence of Bangalore's new belonging in a global ecosystem in which eccentric entrepreneurs take great risks with their garage-based startups.

Books and films like the biography of Steve Jobs (Isaacson 2011) or the film about Facebook founder Mark Zuckerberg (Fincher 2010) crystallize classic entrepreneurial narratives of risk and create the figure of the startup founder as a maverick man who refuses stability and rejects middling success to pursue a wild and fantastical dream. As Deborah Piscione writes in a popular book about Silicon Valley and startup entrepreneurship, risk is "the most vital apparatus of our time" (2014, 10);

without risk, there can be no reward. Within neoliberalism, it is individuals who bear the burden of risk.[1] Writing about the risk-taking of the dot-com era, Gina Neff notes a general cultural and political landscape that celebrated and naturalized economic risks "by urging a casual, even positive, attitude toward losing one's job" (2015, 3).

In this chapter I offer a different reading. I suggest that risk is not self-evident and situated in the individual but is produced specifically as a relative *distancing* from caste-based and gender-coded work.[2] An analysis of risk in Bangalore reveals how forms of difference (religion, class, caste, and gender) shape the possibilities for people to enter startup capitalism. Entrepreneurs are not just people who innovate; their innovations need to be hailed as adequately risky for them to be recognized as entrepreneurs at all. Risk itself is not value-neutral terrain but produced in relation to the fabricated figure of the ideal entrepreneur.

The historian Ritu Birla (2008, 2) notes that, according to early twentieth-century modernizers in India, indigenous merchant capitalists who operated through ties of kinship, clan, and caste required a radical makeover. Their supposed entanglement in customary webs regulating partnerships and the division of parental property posed a challenge for India's progress. Thus, a defining feature of Indian modernity was the staging of the difference between the public world of the modern market and the private world of the indigenous capitalist. I show that today's entrepreneur continues to publicly maintain this separation, but [his] success capitalizes on directing (the private worlds of) caste, class, religion, and gender into the recognizable figure of a startup entrepreneur. Even as the entrepreneur refuses the affiliations of caste and gender in the service of a supposedly meritocratic field, these negations serve to naturalize an upper-caste, middle-class male as the startup entrepreneur worthy of funding and success.

Startup capitalism thus tries to make itself by undoing caste, a process that involves narrating first how the entrepreneur needs to learn how to take risks and affirming that it is new for the entrepreneur. But for which caste communities is risk-taking and business a new venture that has to be learned? As entrepreneurial networkers explained to me at the Startup Festival how risk had to be learned, I was offered a sense of who is imagined as the figure of the entrepreneur. The discussion in the first section of the chapter explores the emphasis on risk-taking as a new trait that must be taught and that sets up the middle-class, upper-caste brahmin as the sine qua non figure of entrepreneurship, to whom—and through whom—entrepreneurial discourse is addressed.

To understand how such an idealized figure is hailed as the entrepreneur, in the second part of this chapter I take seriously the narrative device of the "pitch" to show how it is read across embodied performances of gender and caste. In the third part, I ask how we might understand the production of the figure of the entrepreneur from the fringes of startup worlds. Traveling quite literally to the city's outer neighborhoods to meet women entrepreneurs at home and with their families, I detail the material temporal and spatial itineraries that are essential to produce the mobile, risk-taking entrepreneur, able to conquer time and space as he works across time zones and networking spaces. The final section takes up sites of entrepreneurship in which women are explicitly addressed: business school programs, corporate schemes, and informal networking sessions. I show that gender is framed as a "problem" to be solved and ask what this tells us about how labor is valued. Deploying labor as method, I travel across the spaces and temporalities of startup capitalism to understand the production of the entrepreneur.

REJECTING BRAHMINISM, TAKING RISKS

It was barely light when the first event of the Startup Festival began. The streets were dark and deserted; dogs occasionally wandered around sniffing for food scraps. Still at home, barely awake, I dressed in a rush and ran out to the nearest large intersection, hoping to find an auto to take me to any of the morning events. By the time I saw the first few autos—around 7:00 a.m.—I had already missed the early morning fitness sessions. They were listed under the energetic title "Pump," and offered a choice of yoga, power cycling, studio workouts, or open area runs. Somehow, while trying to find transport I had even missed the 8:00 a.m. "Reload" sessions, at which I could have met a mentor or a venture capitalist. (Not surprisingly) I was in time for a set of events called "Crawl," at which I could select a neighborhood startup and hear about its journey.

The itinerary of the festival was intended to produce middle-class publics of startup entrepreneurship. The overarching message was to show entrepreneurship as a valorized form of risk-taking: by indicating the early mornings of fitness, days of workshops, and late evenings of networking, we were to understand the temporality of startup life. It was never ending, a physical test of fitness that also required the participants to engage in *zumba* class or be casual with strangers at a bar. The itinerary was itself a test to ascertain who could produce themselves as ever available to join a startup public and thrive under mobile configurations of time and space. I felt I had already failed the first test by my inability to find transport and move across town in the early morning.

By the time my auto finally arrived halfway across town at Indiranagar, I found several others milling around a small outdoor space where we could register for the festival inside several open tents. I picked up my free T-shirt and a map and itinerary. It was a white T-shirt with a red heart and hot air balloons on it, signifying a passion for work and the buoyancy of new ideas. The T shirts doled out for free at so many startup events were mobile signifiers of belonging in the risky and adventurous new world of startups. Unlike corporate T-shirts worn by the many IT workers in Bangalore, which were usually collared and buttoned, all-black, and with their logo clearly visible, the Startup Festival T-shirt was casual and collarless, in reds and oranges, available to everyone who registered, as an invitation to join this world and announce one's belonging in startup life.

The T-shirt signaled the other—less explicit—form of risk that was expected as essential to the production of the startup entrepreneur. This was the transformation of the skilled and highly educated techie into the casual startup entrepreneur. New forms of startup entrepreneurship encourage upper-caste and middle-class men to invest their talents and labor into their own enterprise and away from the back-end labor of Bangalore's software world.

After Bangalore's Startup Festival, I sat down with one of its organizers to understand its attempts at building a social infrastructure that would produce risk-taking. He explained:

> Entrepreneurs don't land a date! On Valentine's Day they are sitting alone in a pub having a beer! Entrepreneurs in general as individuals are looked at as unemployed and unemployable. There's a little bit of social stigma that people carry that business is not good, and from an old school thought process then you're not doing the right thing . . . "Be a good son, do your engineering, take up a job, and get married." That's what people look at as a path of career growth. We said . . . how can it change? It can only change if you build an identity around what you do. (Fieldwork interview with festival cofounder)

In this narrative, the desolate entrepreneur challenged the normative life of middle-class, upper-caste heterosexuality: he resisted his parent's pressure to pursue a respectable career path, find a stable job, and get married. This seems like the incitement to embrace an individualism that situates self above kin. But although it is not mentioned explicitly, the telos of this life—an engineering degree, duty to care for your parents, and a professional job, probably in computing—signals a form of specifically Brahmin masculinity. It includes the familiarity with urban life that comes from generations of urban living for young Brahmin men who are sent out to integrate into urban milieux, the caste networks that they then mobilize to acquire jobs, and the familiarity with cultural and class codes through which one can integrate into modern environments, as Ramesh Bairy (2010) writes about the naturalization of Brahmanism into institutional life.

This narrative gestures to what Smitha Radhakrishnan (2011) calls a specific "South Indian ethos" when discussing IT workers—it is the cumulative benefit that accrues to South Indian Brahmins whose families have benefited from generations of technical and elite education and who translate their caste capital into the class capital and educational credentials required to succeed in the contemporary work worlds of IT.[3]

The language of risk is part of a global startup culture, but it is refracted through material and place-based infrastructures in Bangalore. At an event held at INK Talks, a young entrepreneur asked the audience to remember what it was like "wooing a college crush." For a few moments, the audience was lost in a reflective silence. He broke us out of our stupor to urge us on to action: "You should be similarly obsessed with chasing a business idea!" Developing a college crush is a noninnocent act in India: romantic love outside one's caste and religion often necessitates eloping and invoking the wrath of the natal family. Yet the rhetoric was mobilized here to spur the production of a modern self, freed from caste and gender norms, ready to find its passion.

The production of risk through caste and gender logics became further evident when I attended a dating event with Naina, whom I introduced in chapter 1, and a friend of hers. The event was conceptualized specifically for entrepreneurs, intended to normalize—even popularize—the practice of dating entrepreneurs. At an open-to-the-sky venue, we heard from entrepreneurs about their startup journeys, then broke into two groups. One set was divided into opposite-sex pairs to learn ballroom dancing from an instructor. The other group sat around shared tables and learned about whiskey tasting from a representative from Jameson, the Irish whiskey company.

The rationale of the event itself neatly encapsulated the logics of reproductive time; dating an entrepreneur was risky because dating was assumed as foreplay to marriage and marriage was assumed as a heterosexual economic arrangement of financial codependence. The dating event intended to produce the maverick, risk-taking entrepreneur, ready to challenge the norms of brahminism. Yet it maintained the logics of startup capitalism, centering risk-taking, passion, and a class-coherent group who would learn ballroom dancing and whiskey tasting, thus signaling their ability to move in global circuits of leisure and consumption necessary to acquire venture funding.

These three examples—the pedagogical thrust of the Startup Festival, wooing romantic love at INK Talks, and the dating event—signal how the dominant figure and imagination of the entrepreneur is produced through casted, gendered, and classed logics. While much of the focus of entrepreneurship has been on what people innovate, my fieldwork shows that reigning techno-scientific imaginaries shape who can be hailed as an entrepreneur. At the Startup Festival, organizers were in search of a figure who was risk-taking and adventurous, shaking off the "burdens" of caste affiliation and gender norms to circulate with ease in middle-class publics.

Startup entrepreneurs in Bangalore court the badge of willful eccentricity. Yet while seeming to refuse caste-based alliances and the respectable professionalism of Brahmin upper-caste telos, they still maintain the conventions of middle-class consumption and desire for heterosexual family life, and map their value as economic profit generated for the community and nation. This refashioning of time within capitalist logics to produce forms of experimental life reworks caste and gender and maintains class coherence in deference to capitalist value and risk.[4] Thus, even as risk is produced as a resistance to the specification of caste, gender, class, and region, it continually traffics in them, in effect naturalizing them (Thomas 2020).

Startup capitalism seeks to rework these practices by removing individuals from these expectations and dense networks of caste and kin to situate them *within other such ecosystems*.[5] Risk is thus not the production of individuals who bear its costs but the combination of caste, class, and gendered privilege to produce new forms of entrepreneurial heroism and risk-taking. The entrepreneurial ecosystem, with its own rituals and networks, its own expectations of mobility and cosmopolitan networking, is reworking class, caste, and gender capital into the production of experimental life embodied by the new startup entrepreneur.[6]

THE PITCH: SPECTACLE AND SPECULATION

At the Startup Festival, sessions with founders of entrepreneurial companies opened to questions from the gathered audience. We asked the entrepreneur how to brand startups. How do products differ from services in the startup world? What was Bangalore's readiness for growing a startup? We left with his parting words: "If you feel for what you do, you feel your ownership, you can generalize that into entrepreneurship." When other participants in the session asked the founder for advice about how to become a startup entrepreneur, he explained that his own journey was unpredictable and marked by forms of risk-taking that he could not anticipate. "There are no rules to become a startup entrepreneur," I noted down diligently as my ethnographic note. "But risk-taking appetite is a pre-condition."

The origin story is thus a retrospective account of enterprise, drawing on the past to hypothesize about the future. Arbitrarily selecting a past moment of brainstorming, the startup entrepreneur produces himself as existing outside of the dominant capitalist logics of time and space—here he is, unencumbered by family at a late night bar, ideating the impossible. Or then again, here we see him at 2:00 a.m. on a Skype call with collaborators around the world.[7] Thus the openness to experimentation and to trading in speculative futures is key to startup capitalism.

At the Startup Festival, afternoons opened into larger interactive sessions. Swarms of startup aspirants jostled each other to be noticed by panels of venture capitalists. To do this, they had to publicly demonstrate the value and worth of their product—and thus of themselves. One afternoon, I sat in a large foyer space that had become a venue for a planned pitching session. In front of us, participants took turns energetically pitching their entrepreneurial ideas to skeptical venture capitalists. This required specific storytelling scripts; pitches typically followed the Japanese *pecha kucha* style, in which presenters are given twenty seconds each for twenty slides, for a total time of six minutes and forty seconds to impress diverse audiences.

Participants distinguished themselves by their creativity and uniqueness, producing, in Arendtian terms, storytelling as the performative dimension of human action and speech in which dimensions of the self are revealed (Meehan 1995). This is an embodied performance; class, caste, and gender are read through the body as the vital, embodied, and entangled scripts accompanying the visuals and narrative of planning and innovation. We listened to a young man pitching an idea for a nutrition startup, and as we listened we also assessed his class position: Did he know and truly understand the elite clientele who might sign up for such a service in India? Did he have the capital to access the expert dieticians who could offer cosmopolitan meal plans for an urban audience? Was his an urbane masculinity that could appeal to a gendered middle class?

The pitch events were part of the pedagogical training of the Startup Festival. Attendees watched for pleasure, but they did so to learn what worked in a pitch and how to adapt their own pitches to be compelling. As audience, the spectator anticipates another spectacle in which they will finally be actor (see Meehan 1995). The interactions between the public and the performer unfolded not through the rational terms of universal discourse that marks a pitch as good or bad but rather through assessments of caste and class, performances of gender that signal risk-taking behavior, and the pleasures of anticipating one's own performance. The fiction of these events maintains that these are unique performances of individuality. Yet individuals are not entirely in control of their stories—the stories emerge from how bodies are read and how they adhere to relevant scripts.

A startup entrepreneur explained to me that he did not initially have an idea for a startup. He and a group of friends knew they wanted to launch one, and they spent months brainstorming ideas. When they finally came up with the idea of a cooking robot, they retrofitted an origin story so that the idea appeared to have emerged organically. He laughed as he explained to me that this was a strategy for investors, creating a compelling narrative in which the team "always knew" they wanted to do this. Yet the idea itself emerged through the possibilities of structural location.

As upper-caste, middle-class young men with no family obligations or debts to bear, they could fashion themselves as risk-taking entrepreneurs who were jumping headlong into entrepreneurship. Their familiarity with the busy worlds of working parents and urban living came from their own lived experiences. In their pitch, they talked about how they hated to cook and wanted an invention that would automate meal making. The innovation first (de)valued the labor and skills of cooking, reading it as a mundane activity that should be automated. The gendered labor of cooking, its intergenerational knowledge transfer, and the science of balancing spices were written over by the promise that technological innovation could free us from this work. Cooking itself cannot be read and valued as "innovative"—it has to be abstracted from local context, scale, and appeal to vastly different markets in order to acquire value. The cooking robot could not have come from a working-class woman; it required a class confidence, monetary backing, and risk-taking masculinity to produce the idea as a startup.[8] This is part of the visibility and hype integral to the startup economy.[9]

Aspiring entrepreneurs embody and narrate traits of risk and innovation and convey these to the assembled audience. I sat with Malathi, a middle-aged entrepreneur whom I had met at a previous session and whom I had ridden to this venue with in her large Toyota Innova. She was traveling between sessions in the car with her driver. As we watched, a young man took center stage to explain his idea for a food startup to the audience: it was the app I mentioned earlier that assesses nutrition and hydration and makes recommendations. Malathi was visibly moved by his presentation; she nodded vigorously through it and clapped loudly when he finished. After his pitch, the young man returned to the audience and sat down in front of us. Malathi immediately leaned toward him: "I loved it!" she said. He looked relieved, then vaguely hopeful. "Are you an angel investor?" he asked her doubtfully. "No, I'm an entrepreneur," she said, and he quickly turned away, disappointed.

Malathi and other audience members were thus not removed from the space of the pitch but an extension of it; watching the other entrepreneurs pitch onstage, they speculated about their own participation and "even the deferred pleasure of one's own anticipated enjoyment" (Landes 1988, 100, quoting Marie-Hélène Huet's work). The affective economy of the pitch thus circulated through a reverberation between the embodied performances enacted on center stage and the hopefulness and anticipation of audience members. This nebulous and permeable space between audience and actor generates the figure of the entrepreneur as a speculative figure—both performing what one could be and the hope the audience has for their own future. Yet the language of affect does not adequately convey the structural imbrications of caste, class, and gender that render some bodies only capable of producing "failed" enterprise.

Later, at another venue, Malathi finally raised her hand to share her startup idea. The small hotel conference room we were at was packed with festival participants. Women rarely put up their hands or took center stage at the festival unless they were organizers or on a panel. The masculine figure of the techie entrepreneur was the central referent for startup entrepreneurship—the silences around gender "paradoxically highlight[ing] the masculinity that implicitly defines them" (Rofel 2002, 185). One woman even explained to me her background in software engineering, beginning: "At first I was a tech guy."

Like several women at the festival, Malathi was dressed in trousers and a shirt. She wore cutaway trousers ending mid-shin with white sports socks pulled up to meet them, and an oversize black jacket hanging loose. This was a conscious choice away from the *salwar-kameez* she usually wore, and I read her clothes as her performance of an urban masculinity. Indeed, women attendees at the festival often chose masculine clothing of loose pants, oversize shirts, and no makeup, rather than the more feminine salwar kameez or blouses and pants. Forms of dress, like Malathi's clothes, challenge gendered hierarchies of power by navigating clothing and bodily comportment: a bodily resistance to gendered disciplinary procedures (McDowell 1994; Ong 2010; Fisher 2012; Freeman 2000).

Along with a friend, Malathi had devised a product for children's education based on her experience with her own son. It would fill a gap she had personally experienced as a parent, she said. She was nervous but earnest as she spoke up from her seat next to mine at an investor pitching session. The whole audience fell quiet when she finished, waiting to hear the feedback from the panel of venture capitalists listening to her idea. She explained the need that children have for this, and the gap in the market. She was working with a cofounder, also a mother.

The panel included four funders, one of them a woman in a sari. The only women in saris were powerful ones—venture capitalists or senior entrepreneurs. The panel looked bored at her description and became visibly restless as she spoke; finally one of them quickly cut her off. Rather than directly address her product, he repeated the classic mantra in circulation for entrepreneurial success in Bangalore: "A lot of times people don't know what they want until you show it to them," he said. "We should drive the market, not vice versa." In other words, entrepreneurs should not merely fill a market gap as Malathi proposed; they needed to create a desire for their commodity, make people want it, and somehow encourage consumers to feel that they cannot live without it. It seemed from his tone and his suggestion (which did not address her product directly) that he was dismissing Malathi. Why did her product seem unimportant when he barely knew anything about it? On what basis did he assess and dismiss her proposal as not adequately risk-taking?

Malathi's body was being read as a middle-class, upper-caste woman's body. Her product—one for children, emerging from her own experience as a mother—gestured to her role within the domestic household. The combination of upper-caste, middle-class womanhood worked contrary to the configurations of caste, class, and gender capital that were being valorized at the Startup Festival. The ideal and feted startup entrepreneur was a highly mobile figure, able to rid himself of caste expectations, mobilize middle-class masculinity, and move with ease across startup spaces and temporalities in the city. His pitch—clothed in the language of passion and innovation—obscures the forms of capital that enable his production as a fundable entrepreneur.

Even as the startup entrepreneur signals his value as an investment, a *worthy* speculative investment, his future is determined by his past. Histories and lineages of caste, class, and gender produce the startup entrepreneur as a good future investment. As entrepreneurs stage a refusal of caste, they still benefit from its relationship with modernity and accrue its advantages. Further, they maintain the gender norms that seek to develop entrepreneurship as a form of masculinity. The emphasis on refusal, on risk, and on circulation produces startup entrepreneurship as a form of masculinity. It is fabricated from the material histories that produced the IT worker, although it is now trying to abandon its association with back-end work toward a nationalist masculinity of innovation and risk.

RISK AND MOBILITY

The startup entrepreneur is thus produced as a fetishized figure; his value cannot exactly be pinpointed or articulated. You "just know" when you have a good idea, many entrepreneurs repeated to those looking for advice. Similarly, assessing the pitches made by aspiring entrepreneurs, venture capitalists appear to be searching for a certain kind of investable figure. They have already mobilized their internal image of what a successful innovator looks and sounds like. Lisa Nakamura writes of the "digital fetish"—an example is Apple's iPhone—that it acts as both a commodity and a noncommodity that can be used by makers to create films and music (Nakamura 2011) in an entrepreneurial economy that fetishizes self-sufficiency and creativity.

I extend the idea of the fetish further to consider the startup entrepreneur as a fetishized figure—his body itself needs to signify a special and exalted status. This fetish is created through an invisibilization of the social and material reproduction of caste as an animating feature of an economy that refuses to acknowledge its presence. Additionally, the fetish conceals the reproductive labor that offers certain bodies as available for self-making and circulation in cosmopolitan publics.[10]

Malathi heard the advice offered to her and nodded eagerly; she would return to the drawing board to reformulate her approach. Her product needed to be located within a different subjectivity—not linked to her reproductive labor as a woman, innovating for her child and other children like him. Instead, she would need to produce and later leverage herself as a quixotic, unpredictable, "fun" entrepreneurial self that can shape such a product and thrive in a financial climate where "the early entry to the market is through who you know," as a venture capitalist at the session told us. This process of generating risk-taking and producing oneself as a fetishized figure is built from gendered bodies, caste capital, and class mobility. Despite her masculine clothes, Malathi's body was read as feminine, and too close to the domestic realm of local entrepreneurship to attract a venture capitalist's attention. She later told me that her idea emerged from her experience with the education of her young son. By fulfilling an existing need, she was not seen as taking enough of a risk—she was not mobile enough to circulate in Bangalore's spaces of venture capital funding and networking.

Startup entrepreneurs shape and frequent urban publics that congeal around tech-talk and trends and brainstorming at bars and pubs. Technologists hanging out with others who "get it" form a "public constituted through a shared sense of concern for the technical and legal conditions of possibility of their own association" as Christopher Kelty (2005, 192) explains about geeks in Bangalore. In Lilly Irani's fieldwork of design practitioners, like-minded professionals coming together in experimental art and design scenes gravitate toward others who share their tastes for self-actualization, developmental good, and nation building (Irani 2019, 113). Scenes here are cultural infrastructures useful for offering an outside to work among others who could also be helpful *for* work (Irani 2019, 113; emphasis in original).

These kinds of immersions are vital for startup entrepreneurs to constitute themselves as such. Networking interactions typically take place in the late evenings or, as the bleary eyes of startup entrepreneurs made evident, on international networking Skype calls all night. In a sprawling city of eleven million with a metro perpetually under construction, a bus system that affluent middle classes almost never take during leisure time, and three-wheelers that stay stuck in interminable traffic snarls, commuting takes time, money and energy. Staying up all night and commuting for networking or to meet casually to brainstorm is not an option for everyone; those who can enter this world of disruptive startup capitalism tend to be mobile, cosmopolitan enough to circulate in the social spaces that support and produce startup capital, and unattached to the "straight time" (Boellstorrf 2007) that would-dilute their participation.

Watching the fabrication of risk through performances of hype and masculinity signals startup capitalism as a relationship between men (investors and capitalists) that is passed down to other men (startup founders)—a phallic exchange (see also Rubin 2011; Wiegman 2002) codified in the beer bars, networking meetings, and investor pitches that maintain the symbolic order irrespective of the occasional presence of women in these spaces. These exchanges codify the figure of the idealized startup entrepreneur as masculine through forms of risk-taking and mobility.[11]

In Bangalore, the celebration of unfettered movement through space and time is formative of startup capitalism. An emphasis on movement is further refracted through India's postcolonial condition, in which entrepreneurs circulate metaphors of travel to signal their cosmopolitanism and ease in unmarked contexts of global startup entrepreneurship. In Lilly Nguyen's ethnographic work on startup entrepreneurs in Vietnam, she describes this desire for travel and to learn from white European hackers within the terms of a feeling of freedom that comes through the frisson of encounter (Nguyen 2018, 4). Encounters with traveling entrepreneurs offer the possibility of relocating oneself outside the subject position of the laborer to whom work is handed. Indeed as *entrepreneurs*, here in Bangalore, festival participants imagined themselves as free to mingle in a marketplace of globally circulating ideas and capital.[12]

The Start Up Festival's own everyday itinerary of pitching, dense networking, and financial and logistical scaling also reflects a neoliberal urge to move unfettered across diverse forms of space and to scale an idea exponentially.[13] It is the scaling across space and time that differentiates a startup from other kinds of entrepreneurial ventures, lending it value and making it fundable.[14] If entrepreneurs want to open a small entrepreneurial business, they are expected to take out a loan; venture capitalists justify their investments in a startup when there is evidence of risk-taking. The risk-taking is predicated on expansive scaling, attached to bodies that can circulate.

Alongside movement across space, there is also a value placed on circulating across time zones. I was invited to an accelerator lab where entrepreneurs were living on-site, developing their products with collaborators. On the day I attended, a venture capitalist had been invited to hear some pitches and offer feedback. A few minutes before the scheduled start of the event, I entered a small boardroom. A screen hung from one wall, and the aspiring entrepreneurs were seated around a long wooden table. Some hovered around the table, tweaking their PowerPoint presentations and whispering fiercely to each other until the last minute. Finally, the head of the lab cleared his throat to introduce the event.

Throughout, the venture capitalist sat upright and alert in his chair, listening carefully and making suggestions. He often asked the presenting team if they knew what competition existed for their proposed product and why that product had failed—or how it was doing—and queried them on anticipated timelines. One of the innovations was a product that would use text messages to send directions to those without a smartphone and GPS.

"What if someone texts a request at 3:00 a.m.?" the venture capitalist, Anant Subramaniam, asked. "Will you be able to respond?"

The team replied that they have a third member in the United States who took on a shift while the India-based partners were asleep.

"I have a one-year-old, so I am usually up at 2:00 a.m.," the venture capitalist replied. "I'll text you then to check if I get a reply."

This "mock" pitching session demonstrated that even within the testing space of the accelerator lab, there is no "soft launch" and no trial run. Products and services are expected to be market ready when entrepreneurs approach investors, and this means an immersive twenty-four-hour commitment or an outright rejection. The venture capitalist asked for growth timelines and then advised the team to project for a period of three months; anything longer than that is impossible to predict, he said. This is an intense and concerted period of growth, crucial to the evolution of a startup. Not being able to commit time in the ways required eliminates some entrepreneurs from the race for funding.

This assumes a young middle- to upper-class demographic who have no family or financial commitments. Religious and social norms and gendered expectations disadvantage and preclude others from participating in Bangalore's startup economy. Although entrepreneurs in Bangalore speak of startups as meant for "anyone"—that is, not just the young, not only men, and not only the middle classes—women's ability and willingness to adopt risk and embrace passion are mediated not only by their obligations toward reproductive labor but also by the labor politics of class and caste.

Startup entrepreneurs also extend themselves in time and space, reaching out to aggressively acquire advantages and accumulate valuable resources. After the pitching session, one aspiring entrepreneur at the lab hopefully hovered around the visiting venture capitalist after the official session. The entrepreneur was imploring and deferential; he wanted more feedback, more ideas, and more contacts. His body reached out in space—a phenomenological challenge for feminized bodies, as Iris Marion Young (2005) shows. Young terms this ambiguous transcendence or a subjectivity located not in consciousness but in an embodied sense of who we are. This prevents women-identified bodies from moving outward in space and results in them thinking of their own bodies as objects that are passive rather than as having the ability to achieve transcendence.

In Bangalore, as in other capitalist contexts, some bodies could not enter these distributions of time and space under startup capitalism.[15] I asked Malathi if she would stay on for the plenary session at the Startup Festival that evening. She peered worriedly out of her car window as her driver navigated us around neighborhoods. We were trying to find the startup venue for the next event we planned to attend. "I'm on the schedule," she said. Malathi wakes up before her husband and son—at

5:00 a.m. every day—to talk to her collaborator. She then prepares their meals for work and school respectively and makes everyone breakfast. Being "on the schedule" leaves little time for networking events or to attend social events at the Startup Festival.

LIFE ON THE FRINGES OF THE STARTUP CITY

My experience visiting Malathi at her home was like my experience visiting the homes of many women entrepreneurs. It took me two hours in a bus to get to her address, and as we inched along the streets, crowded even at 1:00 p.m., I tracked the changing city landscapes as though a diorama stretched before me. Many of these streets were along the bus route of my high school bus, and in the late 1990s they had been densely knitted with tree cover and spotted with low bungalows and small gardens. The trees have been razed, streets strangled on either side by the debris and construction material for new overpasses and the planned extension of the Bangalore Metro. Gradually we arrived at an extension of an older neighborhood, known just as "Phase Seven," signaling its growth away from the original neighborhood.

Approaching the destination, we turned into a narrow street, and suddenly massive buildings arose on the horizon. The road widened at the entry to Malathi's apartment building, one of several, tightly packed in a landscaped web of gated community life. I filled out my personal details at a register at a little security booth outside one of the buildings before I was allowed in through the pedestrian gate. On my left a glass-walled gym revealed young people working out on exercise machines a few floors above street level. On my right elderly people chatted, watching screaming children bicycle past them. Children's playgrounds, a clubhouse, and smooth tarred streets wound around the complex; this was a typical middle-class residential gated community in Bangalore.

I found Malathi on the seventh floor of her building, in a small and carefully decorated apartment. There were plastic flowers in tiny vases and stuffed plush toys in the display cabinet. TV maintenance men crowded the tiny living room area, working at straightening out a cable connection, while her four-year-old son shouted above their confabulations, insisting that his TV viewing schedule not be disrupted.

Malathi employed a maid who did some cleaning every morning, but she cooked for her household; packed their lunches; and took care of her son's tuition, sports, and play schedules on her own. Hers was an arranged marriage to her husband, now in his forties, a senior manager with a bank in Bangalore. Her parents lived in Mumbai, a major metropolis, and Malathi had been a professional before she was married. She had a self-assured air but seemed dubious about her ability to be a "good" respondent to my questions, repeatedly insisting that she was not representative of women entrepreneurs. She and I sat at her dining table, talking in between the interruptions of the maintenance men and her son.

Malathi told me she did not have the time to engage in Bangalore's startup world. She balanced her business with parenting, waking up at 4:00 a.m. to work on the new product before the rest of the household demanded her attention as the day broke. Malathi's schedule challenged the familiar complaint about women entrepreneurs: that they only devote the tail end of their days to their business, after family commitments have been taken care of. Instead, she began her day by thinking about her business—4:00 a.m. to 6:00 a.m.—a time when many startup entrepreneurs are finally going to bed. Other startup entrepreneurs peak and network in the evenings, but Malathi was at home with her family at that time. For those in the startup sector who live on their own, small and shared apartments in the center of town are affordable. Younger entrepreneurs who live with their parents similarly are often well-located in central neighborhoods. Attending networking meetings, collaborating face to face, and immersing themselves in Bangalore's startup culture requires hopping on a scooter or motorbike and arriving at a central destination without too much planning.

Middle-aged and middle-class entrepreneurs like Malathi are spatially segregated by their need to have apartments large enough for their families. Married women's middle-class life and living patterns prevent them from traveling in and around sites of the startup economy. Malathi's reproductive labor for her husband and son tied her into ideals of domesticity and segregated gated community life. If her entry into startup worlds was shaped by her reproductive labor, this labor also shaped the product she devised. She explained to me that when she organized groups for mothers to meet, she made it a point to tell them that she had created an educational resource for children. The resource itself was a form of reproductive labor, solidifying the caste and class capital she made available to her son.

Some months later, I spent some hours on a bus to reach the home of another entrepreneur, whom I call Ruhanna. She lived in a small two-bedroom apartment in a massive gated complex but without the amenities of a pool or clubhouse. A heap of slippers marked her doorway. Inside, her one-year-old baby was wailing in a crib in the center of the tiny living room, and a young man sat attentively on her faux leather sofa as she advised him on his new project: celebrity management. Finally, the young man left and Ruhanna turned her attention to me.

I pulled out my recorder and began talking to her about my project in between the baby's gurgling and occasional high-pitched wails. Just as I asked my first question, the doorbell rang, and this interaction followed:

INTERVIEWER (HG): Oh! Shall I get it?
RUHANNA: Oh no, I'll get it. That's my older one, Rohit.
[She opens the door and a young boy of around ten enters.]
RUHANNA: Hello! This is Hemangini. That's Rohit.
HG: Hi! How was school?
ROHIT: [Grunts] (inaudible).
HG: Good?
[Ruhanna laughs.]

ROHIT [in a whining and accusatory tone, to his mother]: You're
   going out?
RUHANNA: No, no, no. I'm not going out. She's here to see me. I'm not
   going out.
HG [enthusiastically, attempting to forge an informal bond]: And you!
   I'm here to see you! And your brother!
RUHANNA [to Rohit]: Come. Will you wash your face and all? And
   change your dress . . . get ready? I'll talk to . . .
[Baby interrupts by gurgling loudly.]

It was only 4:00 p.m., but Ruhanna's attention was forcibly splintered
between a cranky (and exhausted) ten-year-old, a year-old baby, her
need to contribute to charity causes by consulting and sharing her networks, and her willingness to talk to me. I could see the immense resistance from her son just at the sight of me; I imagined the tantrum he
would throw if she stepped out right now. I wondered how many hours
she had for her business. She told me how challenging it was to attend
networking meetings with no possibilities for child care. Middle-class
mothers with young babies in India typically have the assistance of
their own mothers or extended families in cities like Bangalore, where
hiring a full-time nanny is relatively unusual except for the elite.[16]

Startup entrepreneurship misleadingly foregrounds flexibility as its
key advantage. For some entrepreneurs it means the ability to work
erratic time schedules as they make themselves always available for
collaboration. For others, like Ruhanna, this fiction of flexible time assumed she would be able to both care for her child and work simultaneously; her labor doubled and evaded accountability under the guise
of flexible work.[17] Ruhanna had no family on hand, and her husband
had not taken time off from his corporate job to care for the child during the day. As I talked with her that afternoon, she persuaded Rohit to
care for his younger brother while she talked to me.

After we finished, I accompanied Rohit downstairs to play with
his friends while she minded the baby. As his friends ran out of their

apartments and rushed screaming down the stairs, they asked him who I was. "My mother's friend!" he told them. The other boys wanted to know what his mother did. "She has her own business!" he yelled to them as they all turned in the stairwell at breakneck speed. "She has her own company!" Rohit was clearly proud of his working mother and used her status to his advantage among his ten-year-old friends.

They clutched my hands as I chaperoned them across a wide street busy with hurtling buses and swerving motorbikes. They quickly unclenched my grasp on the other side, running into a comic store library opposite, where they borrowed some books. We then made our way back to the apartment building, where they played downstairs. Ruhanna, the entrepreneur, was stretched between her children, taking care of her home, cooking, volunteering, supporting her husband, and networking, but she also tried to grow her business. Spread thin laterally, across many responsibilities and commitments, she was also spatially isolated in her apartment building and tied down to being with the children. Similarly, it took Malathi two hours each way to reach events and meetings, battling Bangalore's notorious traffic.

Another entrepreneur I met told me that after her child was born, she took two months of maternity leave before her office moved far away. It took her four hours in travel to commute back and forth. That time added to eight hours of a working day made it impossible for her to work at the office anymore, so she turned to entrepreneurship. Many busy women entrepreneurs, isolated from the nodes of business and networking that make startup capitalism possible, provincialize the ideas and strategies of startup capitalism by incorporating them into everyday life. When I asked Malathi how she met neighbors in this massive, anonymous-seeming community, for instance, she told me: "I network downstairs" in a matter-of-fact manner. "While [my son] plays on his bicycle."

When she expanded on this, I realized that she used *networking* to mean "meeting people" rather than more specifically to connote exchanging information with those in professional settings who could benefit her business and increase her connections. At first glance, since Malathi was not active in Bangalore's entrepreneurial networking circuits, I classified her use of the term networking to mean the imaginative labor of locating herself within entrepreneurship's rituals and practices. But in fact what Malathi shows us is that if startup entrepreneurship cultivates networking as a set of informal meetings over drinks and leisure, then her labor of meeting and mingling too had the possibility of meeting useful strangers. She *did* network downstairs in a way that helped her advance her product: with other children playing and parents supervising, she could meet new customers and acquire new collaborations. If startup entrepreneurship develops forms of experimental life in which people forge speculative futures for themselves, it also requires us to imagine new spaces and activities as possible sites of potential value.

Women like Malathi and Ruhanna challenge the self-representation of the startup industry as one solely driven by risk-taking and passion. What supports the semblance of risk-taking is a social world that defines who and what constitutes investable risk. Participating in and creating risk as desirable requires forms of mobility and immersion. But as these vignettes show, such risk-taking in the dominant mode of startup capitalism is shaped by forms of urban growth that structure spatial segregation, reproductive labor, middle-class heterosexual family life, and the ability to circulate away from home to build dense connections across social settings.

Malathi's and Ruhanna's experiences reflect both power geometry (Massey 1994) and power chronography (Sharma 2014). Doreen Massey's (1994) work on gender and place challenges the assumptions of time-space compression (Harvey 1991) and of fluid movements and communication across space. For Massey (2018, 151), this perspective misses attention to power geometry: "For different social groups and different individuals are placed in very distinct ways in relation to these flows and interconnections. This point concerns not merely the issue of who moves and who doesn't, although that is an important element of it; it is also about power in relation to the flows and the movement." Anna Tsing's (2004) conceptualization of friction too as a zone of awkward engagement between the global and local is helpful—here, it is a collision between the promises of startup capitalism and its reality. And if space is relational and differentially experienced, Sarah Sharma reminds us that temporalities are too. Power chronographies are based on a conception of time as "lived experience, always political, produced at the intersection of a range of social differences and institutions" (Sharma 2014, 15).

Summoning the confidence, vocabulary, and vision for a startup idea that adequately traffics risk is a performative production of entrepreneurship learned and mastered by participating in incubation labs, attending startup networking events, and circulating around the city for leisure and consumption. When Ruhanna and Malathi networked in their apartment buildings and conducted meetings at home over the wails of a newborn, their mingling of public and private reflected both power chronographies and power geometries.

BODIES OUT OF PLACE: "A FISH OUT OF WATER"

Even within the space of an incubation lab, where innovations are grown and nurtured through exposure to different kinds of expert knowledge and advice, women encounter forms of risk by negotiating respectability politics. Entering such labs is prestigious and valuable because of the access to collaborations, funding, and visibility to others in the startup ecosphere. Startup founders apply to participate in these spaces and often spend days, weeks, or even months at such labs, working around the clock to develop their ideas. I was invited to a new incubation lab in Bangalore and saw this as an opportunity to understand how value (and more tangibly, *financial* value) is assigned to ideas.

The lab was a short walk away from a stop on Bangalore's then fledgling metro system, so I took the metro there on the afternoon of the event. I wandered around a bit before realizing that—yet again— the unnamed and unmarked spacious bungalow on my left was in fact the accelerator lab. It was a repurposed bungalow, redone with wooden floors and shining white tiles. Two security guards zealously manned the entrance, and inside I found tight knots of entrepreneurs hunched over laptops on raised tables, polishing their pitches. This current batch had ten entrepreneurs, competitively selected to join, and they now lived in this house, honing their ideas. This premise of immersion and collective living already ruled out this opportunity for those who could not take time away from families and salaried jobs to participate.

One of the company's directors had invited me there; she was a young woman who moved actively and energetically around the lab and an aspiring startup entrepreneur herself. She described some of her ideas to me. One of her early ideas received money from an angel investor, yet she could not pursue it, as she explained to me. She identified as Muslim, as did her family, but she described her religious background to me as "community."

DIRECTOR (MEHNAZ): "I could not take it [my startup idea] to the next level although I had received funding for Rs 50 lakhs because . . . ummm . . . things got really bad at home. So . . . I come from a really conservative family where even working as a corporate is not acceptable.

INTERVIEWER (HG): Because?

DIRECTOR: So the basic expectation is . . . the community expects you to just finish your education and get married and that's it. That is the regular routine and that is how you are expected to be. But I happen to be the most adventurous person and I happen to always be the talk of the town [laughs]. I am like a fish out of water in my community right? [laughs] So, anyway, now things are so much better, because I have this habit of "starting up" even from my college.

HG: So how did that happen? When did you decide that you wanted to start something?

DIRECTOR: It was always on, right, because my dad is an entrepreneur. (Interview with Mehnaz)

The director, Mehnaz, explained that she did not—could not—pursue her plans with the startup because of her family's resistance. Through her awkward laughs and her strategic choice of words ("like a fish out of water," "talk of the town") she distanced herself—an aspiring startup founder—from the rest of her community. Her first innovation, however, was related to a meal service for Muslims during Ramzan, the holy month of fasting, worship, and gathering.

Like many other women I met in Bangalore's startup world, Mehnaz described everyday life and herself in a startup lexicon. She had "validated a pinpoint" (meaning she achieved an anticipated outcome) on one idea, wanted to use technology to "scale" her father's old-school silver business, and was inspired by the popular stories of young entrepreneurs who defy the odds to establish their own international companies.

Yet despite her growing fluency and familiarity with startups, her family was reluctant to allow Mehnaz to work on her own. As a young Muslim woman, she said that in her "community" it is unthinkable for an unmarried woman to branch out on her own to take a risk on a startup. Additionally, as a member of a middle-class but not rich household, she had to contribute to home expenses, so she navigated these expectations and norms by taking a corporate job to fund her startup with her salary. She took up a senior position at the incubation lab where she worked now; her own startup plans were on hold, and she hoped to return to them soon.

Mehnaz possessed all the innovation and passion expected of startup entrepreneurs: she was a serial innovator, her businesses were "disruptive" as startups are expected to be (they challenge existing ways of doing business in a particular industry, as with her idea for providing a meal service for Ramzan), and she routinely worked through the night. These practices offer cues that Mehnaz was well-versed in the practices and traits through which startup founders recognize each other. She found the risks pleasurable and became excited as she spoke to me. Yet despite her mastery of the ways of being a startup founder, she encountered specific material, social, and religious constraints on actualizing her dreams of building a business.

Armed with a business degree, inspired by her father's entrepreneurship with a silver business, full of startup ideas and great drive, Mehnaz was still not a participant in the lab but its curator: unable to become a startup entrepreneur herself. Her attempts to devote concentrated amounts of time into launching a company or to scale her father's business were constrained by social and familial expectations that she keep regular work hours, work at a respectable salaried job, and stay close to home (rather than running a startup requiring late hours and interactions with strangers and mobile practices around the city).

In other words, for Mehnaz's family, their daughter's passion threatened to derail her from the expected temporalities of gendered life for a middle-class Muslim woman: education, marriage, staying at home. Religion, class, and gender converged to frame Mehnaz's passion for work as illicit and dangerous; the "fish out of water" was tamed by her family's expectations that she reign in her passion to work a salaried job. Even as she emphasized the particular constraints of her own "community"—meaning her middle-class Muslim family—I was reminded that Hindu women faced similarly unsurmountable blocks to their entrepreneurial aspirations. Religion intersects with middle-class propriety and respectability, foregrounding startup entrepreneurship as desirable for young upper-caste men while precluding it for many young women. Gender is thus distilled through matrices of caste, class, and religion as a site for possibility within the so-called meritocratic world of startup entrepreneurship.

WOMEN'S NETWORKING MEETUPS: THE LABOR OF PRODUCING GENDER

Through my fieldwork I encountered efforts to encourage and support women entrepreneurs through dedicated training and mentorship. For instance, the reputable Indian Institute of Management (a business school in India) has targeted training programs for women entrepreneurs. Goldman Sachs (the investment fund) has a global program, run as an online course, to equip women with "practical tools and knowledge to help you successfully manage the demands of growing your business." Here, entrepreneurs are afforded the ultimate flexible options of skilling and reskilling themselves, a key part of neoliberal economies that require us to prepare ourselves for ever-changing market conditions.

I signed up for the Goldman Sachs course, and once I had chosen what business skills I wanted to develop, I was offered options to bring their learning to bear on specific situations and ideas. For example, in a "Grow Your Business" module, those who signed up (it was free) could learn how to identify a good opportunity, select a growth opportunity, and note who was geographically proximate to them on a map. Each module allowed the user to learn new concepts and apply them to one's own burgeoning ideas. Women participating in these formal and informal programs were expected to already have the wherewithal to enter a wider world of entrepreneurship that requires dedicated time, energy, and the ability to scale. Individuals were empowered, and they empowered each other. Michelle Murphy (2013) writes about entrepreneurialism within neoliberal economies as a cultivation of human capital: each of us is believed to have a latent potential that can be developed to produce economic value.

If the competitive, male-dominated world of startup capitalism does not recognize women as entrepreneurs, the targeted efforts of women-only groups focus on individual empowerment and skills with a similar discounting of the larger structures within which women are supported in their efforts to be recognized as entrepreneurs or to be funded. Programs seek to connect women with each other and to create avenues for them to teach other aspiring women. Early during fieldwork, I met women from an informal women's networking group who conducted similar training sessions for each other. In one session, one woman taught a group how to make a spreadsheet during a breakfast meeting. In another, local women-run businesses organized a day of pop-up events in a specific neighborhood to spur consumption. These events work within larger structures of gender and caste, seeking to move into existing entrepreneurial spaces rather than to challenge the broader social constraints that shape gender.

At another networking event for women entrepreneurs that Naina took me to, I watched how the sessions became spaces to perform and reinforce gendered norms. For example, at one networking meeting, held at the same time as the Startup Festival, fourteen women sat around a long table at a small conference room in a startup founded by a woman, receiving advice from a well-known venture capitalist. We went around the table sharing our "origin stories"—how our companies began, and why. I took notes detailing these businesses: a phone-based app for women's safety, a service that brings tailors to your doorstep, a human resources consultancy for recruitment, a party service for inflatable trampolines for children's birthdays, a sports public relations company, a cosmetic dermatology company, and an innovator of children's products.

When asked to elaborate on their business, women spoke of a need to "give back to community," provide a "service to the nation," "act as a role model," and so on. Each narrative was shaped by a discourse of value addition, affirming that the entrepreneur was creating more than economic value—it was the gendered labor of community and nation building that the women emphasized.[18] For example, a technology entrepreneur introduced herself with this narrative:

Money doesn't inspire me. To run the operations that would [be necessary] but after knowing that the purpose is all about touching lives and giving the best of others, I don't get motivated with money. If I'm able to see a genuine smile on others' face, then it's really rewarding. Everyday I start with, "I'll touch one life." I don't know whose it is, maybe even a dog but without that I don't go to bed. That gives me a lot of happiness at the end of the day. (Prakriti, technology entrepreneur)

Women performed and iterated gender continually by emphasizing how their gendered subjectivity inspired their business or how they were prevented from accomplishing a key goal owing to gendered expectations. The session was advertised as showing women how to succeed in entrepreneurship; in practice it unfolded as a session at which women created incremental space for themselves in the masculine world of startup entrepreneurship by affirming their gendered presence.

Naina, seated next to me and bristling with impatience, did not want to talk about how gender shaped her business. "What's with all the sob stories, dude," she texted me impatiently in the middle of the session. Across from me, another friend, a gender-nonconforming aspiring entrepreneur, similarly expressed to me that she felt alienated from the session. As a coder, she was enchanted by the possibilities of technology work, and this session made her feel distinctly out of place.

These attempts at incorporating "women" into entrepreneurial worlds that I encountered in my research reveal two approaches to navigating gender in startup capitalism. Institutional mechanisms to address the "problem" of women's entrepreneurship assume that women have inherent entrepreneurial potential that is untapped. These programs attempt to incorporate women into already existing entrepreneurial worlds by teaching them the logistics, know-how, and grammars of expected entrepreneurial behavior.

The second approach unfolds at the informal level, where women encounter each other as a marked "Other" category within the normative world of entrepreneurship. Acutely aware of their difference, they make space for themselves within the masculine codes of startup capitalism through iterative and repeated performances of their gender. Through their origin stories, embodied behavior, and the events they curated—ladies nights and Sunday brunches were some that I attended—women performed a gendered femininity to insist on its place in startup capitalism.

The institutional approach of disregarding gendered constraints to insist on women's inherent potential to be entrepreneurial and the informal approach of performing gender roles both isolate gender as a problematic. In the first, the "problem" of gender is that women are not entrepreneurial enough: they have to overcome their gendered inhibitions and lack of networks to join the world of entrepreneurship. The other problem of gender is that it surfaces in informal networking through an almost obsessive focus on detailing itself. Gender is discussed, performed, lamented, and celebrated, thus overdetermining its singularity and erasing its instabilities and the ways it manifests in relation to caste, region, and class.

PRODUCING THE ENTREPRENEUR THROUGH RISK AND VALUE

Risk is relative: it emerges through its interactions with forms of sociopolitical difference such as caste, gender, and class. As entrepreneurship unfolds in experimental time, claiming a distance from caste-based and gender-coded work, it naturalizes the effects and interactions of forms of difference and specificity that are constitutive of the figure of the entrepreneurial man. Origin stories that valorize certain forms of risk-taking and masculine caste advantage fetishize the startup entrepreneur as a highly mobile figure, traveling easily through time and space. The time-space continuum of startup entrepreneurship galvanizes national time—meaning the postcolonial thrill of global mobility—as well as the mobilities required to participate in networking time and collaboration time that extend across time zones and across urban neighborhoods that are unequally accessed by entrepreneurs.

In thinking about risk as related to the creation of economic value, I follow labor as method, asking how the material spaces of the city—its blockages, distances, and enclaves—isolate some entrepreneurs, committing them to arrangements of heterosexual reproductive labor in ways that are unreadable to dominant circuits of startup funding and valuation. By immersing myself in the household calendrics of women entrepreneurs, I suggest that upper-caste, middle-class domestic arrangements allow for their own forms of entrepreneurship—provincial iterations of networking, mentoring, and innovation. Yet these struggle against the valorized forms of masculinized risk-taking and urban/national mobilities that are required to acquire startup success and value.

By the end of my fieldwork, Malathi had still not found a funder for her product or taken it to market—and nine months is a long time for such incubation in the startup world. Women entrepreneurs like Malathi are subjectively shaped in the space and temporal frames of the middle-class household. Malathi was uncertain that she would be a good interview subject for me: "I don't think I am representative," she said, repeatedly. "I don't mind meeting you, but I'm very new to all this." Malathi's product (based on children's need), her firm situation within the temporal and spatial rhythms of her household, and her only occasional and somewhat awkward circulations in Bangalore's larger startup world shaped her love for her invention as the *wrong* kind of love—nurturing familial and domestic love—rather than the supposedly unfettered passion for innovation and risk that startups demand.

Startup founders are expected to show passion and initiative—but they are also serial entrepreneurs, meaning that they are expected to continually innovate. Being overly attached to one idea is detrimental to them; their love is fleeting, contingent on the product's success. Malathi also loved her product, but it was her only one; she developed it over years, and all her energy and time outside work was spent building this product. This kind of single-minded devotion and care differentiated her from startup entrepreneurs who take multiple risks on a range of innovations and celebrate failure as integral to their innovation.

When women pitch ideas that have emerged from their gendered life experiences, these are read as examples of reproductive labor—ideas that enhance domestic life or child-rearing or are oriented toward care work.[19] The work of maintaining middle-class and upper-caste social reproduction (in the form of birthday parties, educational enhancement tools, and dog spas) is not valued in economic terms, and when women seek to innovate around these labors, those are unfunded too. Startups are defined by their scalability and reach, so these innovations are entrepreneurial, but not "startups," as they are not valued as ideas that can be technologized into an app and scaled.

The business ideas of the women I met during fieldwork shape a detailed registry and record of uncompensated gendered labor. They mark attempts at subsidizing this labor, outsourcing it, and putting a price on it. Women's insistence on their ideas as valuable and their businesses as innovative are their demands to have gendered labor recognized. Their "failures" are a record of the ways in which women's work is both naturalized and relegated to the uncompensated realm of the household.

As long as women's work in the home (the work of social reproduction) is not recognized and compensated as labor, women are considered a latent labor force who need to be cultivated to produce value for the economy. This is the "problem" of women's entrepreneurship for global corporations and business school curricula. Yet the real problem of women's entrepreneurship is the differential value accorded to gendered labor. This chapter has shown the multiple ways in which religion, caste status, and gendered labor uphold and make possible the ability for some entrepreneurs to become valued innovators while others' dreams are deemed too local, too small, and too specific.

PART TWO

THE ENTREPRENEURIAL EVERYDAY

Figure 9. Graffiti on a wall at the Startup Festival, 2013. Photo by author.

4

THE OFFICE

From Entrepreneurial Exuberance to Embodied Exhaustion

〰〰〰〰〰〰〰〰〰〰〰〰〰〰〰〰〰〰〰〰〰〰〰〰〰〰〰〰〰

AT THE ORIENTATION for newcomers in my first month of work at Captivate, I joined others stiffly sitting around a long table in a glass-fronted conference room in the center of the office. Pushkar Subramaniam, the company's managing director and co-founder, had just returned from an extended business trip to the South American office, and we new recruits had been waiting for our first meeting with him. Pushkar is a former international tennis player. Tall and lean, he moved lithely around the office, often stopping to chat with employees at the various open bays that structured space and separated teams. He was dressed semiformally in a tucked-in shirt and trousers and energetically conducted this meeting alone.

The anxiety in the room was palpable. We sat awkwardly, getting restless and fidgeting with the small spiral notebooks we had been given. Occasionally someone bent over their notebook to furiously jot down something. Pushkar had told us we would not be learning anything today, just getting to know each other. He was casual and conversational, trying to put people at ease. "Relax!" he said, firmly. Despite this instruction, when we went around the table doing introductions, I could sense that his casual demeanor and invitations to converse heightened the anxiety among those not fluent in English. They worried about this informal environment, in which they were unsure about what they might be called on to say. As part of the first round of introductions, we were asked why we chose to work there and what our dream holidays were. "South America," I said when it was my turn, and we continued through a string of "Switzerland's" before an unexpected "Paris," and then another "South America" from a young woman I had barely spoken to, who now exchanged a conspiratorial smile with me.[1]

Pushkar's comments to us emphasized a flat work structure, rather than a hierarchy.[2] He wanted to be called by his first name. Yet for many of Captivate's new recruits, predictable hierarchies were reassuring. Formal codes can be learned and mastered, whereas the informal "conversational" style of a startup or entrepreneurial office requires an ease with language and socializing that is unfamiliar and seems unknowable. Many employees insisted on calling him "sir" despite his pleas to be more casual.[3]

Pushkar explained that at Captivate good ideas were implemented, whoever they came from. Rather than hours clocked, Captivate named flexibility and meritocracy as key modalities to ensure work. The company centered flexible work policies and job roles as a sign of its difference from IT jobs. This chapter examines "flexibility" as a kind of boundary object (Star 2010) that allows us to study work arrangements even as they are interpreted differently by groups of workers. For entrepreneurs and elite workers within the company, like Pushkar, freedom was enabled in negative terms: it was the absence of bureaucracy that allowed individual creative labor. New startups promise to increase women's workforce participation by increasing flexible work choices, but research among platform economies finds that workers are coerced into working longer hours under the guide of flexibility.[4]

I first introduce managerial fantasies of flexibility, locating them as a celebration of postsocialist and neoliberal modes of work. I then consider how discourses of flexibility were interpreted differently to allow workers to assert themselves as self-confident postcolonial subjects and as entrepreneurial agents in the office. The chapter ends by asking what bodies were offered the pleasures of flexibility and the visceral limits of such a workplace approach as felt through exhaustion, illness, and pain. In these pages, we journey along a brief arc of entrepreneurial work cultures: from exuberance to exhaustion.

FLEXIBILITY AS FREEDOM

Pushkar escaped from his meetings one afternoon to finally sit down with me for an interview. This doubled as lunch, and we sat at an Italian café outside Captivate. I scrambled to balance slices of thin pizza with asking him questions and taking notes. Pushkar told me how he imagined work at Captivate to be inspired by meritocracy and flexibility, which entrepreneurs often reinforced to me in my fieldwork as the two central tenets of startup capitalism. He explained that he was interested in "work done" rather than hours clocked. He outlined a vision of flexibility that would allow him to be productive: flexibility *as* freedom. Pushkar said:

> I don't like a very monotonous structured typical way of doing things; for me a job where you have to do everyday the same thing and be bound by a certain rigidity everyday.... I'd feel trapped! ... If I feel like that, it wouldn't be fair for other people to feel like [it]. It's important to equip people with skills and responsibilities and ownership but let them figure out how to do it and give them that amount of flexibility so that they actually enjoy it rather than saying "Oh my god I have to" ... clock in the hours and face time and all the things I hated. We didn't want to build a

company that had that. . . . But, for me, flexibility is genuinely trusting someone to figure out how they're going to do their jobs and succeed in their jobs with their own balance. (Interview, Pushkar Subramaniam, October 2013)

Pushkar described a method of management in which individuals would be entrusted with the freedom and responsibility to create their own conditions for optimal productivity. Melissa Gregg describes this condition of work as a mapping of masculinity, a "vision of mastery and control that entails freedom from obligation but not from work" (2018, 91). This is the freedom *to* work, not from it; such freedom is a gendered prerogative—the mapping of masculine power, "[the] power to command, to walk out the door, to deny the work of nurturing and the material fact of interdependence" (Gregg 2018, 93). While expecting the individual to exhibit control over time here is a masculine performance, another form of flexibility in vogue is expressed through a preference for feminized labor that emphasizes "autonomy, spontaneity, rhizomorphous capacity, multitasking (in contrast to the narrow specialization of the old division of labor), conviviality, openness to others and novelty, availability, creativity, visionary intuition, sensitivity to differences, listening to lived experience and receptiveness to a whole range of experiences, being attracted to informality and the search for interpersonal contacts" (Martin 1995, 97).[5]

Entrepreneurial economies bring together these two forms of flexible work in a binarized structure of gender disciplining such that managers seek to empower individuals to take charge of their time (masculinized flexibility) and to generate value through enabling flexible (feminized) labor that is spontaneous, sensitive to difference, cooperative, and ever responsive to market demands. Under earlier Taylorist models, workers were expected to perform their tasks with machine-like efficiency and precision. There was a clear distinction between the worker and their work, as Leslie Salzinger (2003) explains well in her ethnography of maquiladora workers. The new spirit of capitalism invites, and demands, a flexibility that draws from personal assets to enhance work. There is emphasis on authentic human relations, interactions, life skills, adaptability, and in general a more "human" face to work (Boltanski and Chiapello 2007, 98). Working at Captivate before and during a period of immense change offered me a vantage point from where to witness the construction of flexibility as a boundary object that combined a desire for a startup masculine mastery over time with the feminized flexibilization of labor.

In a later interview with Krishna Iyengar, who devised Captivate's automation efforts (more in the next chapter) and subsequently became the company's chief technology officer, he elaborated on how technology enables flexibility as freedom. The technological imaginary of work freedom was understood as the ability to do creative work so employees could reach their full potential. Krishna outlined the questions he asked himself when he developed technology for the company:

> Are we effectively using the human capital available to us or misusing their [employees'] time? We need to deploy capital in a way that's beneficial: are employees [really] doing sales or something else that's nonproductive? Being conscious of what work is being done helps them to be efficient—there are two metrics:
>
> 1. Time taken to get the job done and
> 2. The number of people needed to get the job done
>
> (Interview with Krishna Iyengar, September 5, 2018)

For Krishna and Pushkar, flexibility was thus the combination of both masculine control over time and feminized labor. Technologically, it was the ability to clear one's task list of mundane and routine activities that could be done by someone else. But it was simultaneously the effort to direct technology toward enabling more sensitive and custom-made interactions with clients. This duality is key to several interventions in artificial intelligence, for example; Abhishek Sekharan and Ambika Tandon (2021) provide a brief overview, noting that some analysts project the loss of jobs with AI, while others predict AI technologies will enhance human technologies.

When I interviewed Krishna in 2018, many Captivate employees had already been laid off. He was working on machine learning that would further introduce technology into the office, but this time it was intended for the more senior jobs. It would anticipate appropriate affect by excavating key details from past emails as a reminder to travel consultants. This way emails would seem intuitive and personalized. The focus of this automation also reveals which employees brought most value to the company. Krishna explained that he understood "human capital" as a valuable resource that needs to be protected:

> [N]ow every job has a high salary, with high intellectual needs. Each job needs to have these. The pool of qualified candidates is getting smaller, it's hard to find these people so getting this talent and making them do boring jobs is demotivating for an employee. How do we ensure that our capacity is put to best use so what we have not underutilized or overutilized people? Tech plays a big role in this. (Interview with Krishna Iyengar, September 5, 2018)

Pushkar and Krishna were describing ideal workers as those who transcend the realm of what Hannah Arendt might frame as the "social" (the reproductive labor of the home and its associated affects), removing themselves from its demands.[6] Work itself is defined by entrepreneurs and technologists as having high intellectual needs, without boring labor. Clocking in at stipulated times, having to coordinate one's labors with others' schedules, and committing to time-consuming bureaucratic processes are all described as fundamentally inefficient and wasteful. In managerial terms, a lean startup workplace and the right technology could free the neoliberal sovereign worker to achieve their highest human potential. Ideal jobs in startup capitalism take their place at the top of Abraham Maslow's (2022) hierarchy of needs, as a startup networker explained to me; he described his job as connecting people: "creativity and self actualization," both of which, he said, keep him happy.

This techno-utopia is summarized in Aaron Bastani's (2020) vision of a future of abundance: a fully automated luxury communism would supposedly innovate and automate, recasting contemporary crisis into potential for a new future of luxury and plenty. Yet my fieldwork specifies how these visions of automation need to consider the frictions through which they are materialized. Relations of debt and obligation, of classed desire, of relational freedom: these are the essential modes through which such futures are inhabited and unmade.

Flexibility might be routed to Captivate's leadership as part of a global managerial compass, taught at business school. But an insistence on time and work control and utopic futures of meaningful existence among entrepreneurs also takes on a special resonance in India. These promises of flexible work emerge as the aftermath of software jobs in which Indians labored for overseas clients and worked relentless hours on project time.[7] Flexibility is thus imagined by startup entrepreneurs as more than a managerial practice—it is a postcolonial dream of the idealized conditions of work. It is an aspiration for freedom, a discovery of one's highest potential and productivity. Yet this is an elaboration of freedom that assumes as its project the freeing of the liberal self from social encumbrances: no more back-end work that is the repetitive and reproductive labor maintaining global IT.[8]

Flexible approaches to work hold out the promise to free employees from numbing work to reimagine worlds and innovate toward new horizons. The promise that anyone can create a technological innovation is widespread in entrepreneurial India. In Lilly Irani's *Chasing Innovation*, children are reminded to be their authentic selves, moving away from a "BPO worldview" of low-paid repetitive data entry work; instead they say, "I CAN"! (2019, 61, 64). In Carol Upadhya's *Reengineering India*, at an orientation session the CEO tells new recruits, "One of you could do something amazing—everything is possible" (2016, 181). These contours of freedom resonate with Arendtian understandings of freedom, as outside the frame of the social. For Arendt, the realm of the private is an encumbrance on the political; it is a domain of repetitive, monotonous work related to nature and housework (see also Beauvoir 2007). Selves come into being through action and speech in the public sphere. While the public self is courageous, multiple, and heroic, giving birth to selves through action, the private self is subjected to the demands made on it by nature and its body.[9] In the entrepreneurial workplace of Captivate, too, flexibility is articulated as a freedom that is liberated from the social.

However, with this promise of leaving behind an encumbering social is also a neglect of the "social" of identity—histories of caste, the deprivations of class, the discriminations of gender—to enter a new world in which anything is possible. This imagination also works with and through forms of gendering, as I showed with how startup masculinity maps time and power and expects and invites feminized work. This invisibilization of how the liberal empowered and entrepreneurial self is produced actively negates how upper-caste worlds of entrepreneurialism normalize caste habitus as modern, scientific, and in line with technological progress.[10] How does flexibility articulate within the worlds of caste, class, gender, and region that cohere the social lives of workers at Captivate and perhaps elsewhere? Flexibility, I will show, is also an invitation to bend and move with obligations of duty, responsibility, and diligence.

FLEXIBILITY AS A PERFORMANCE OF CLASS

I spent an afternoon with Purnima, a travel consultant at Captivate, leaving work with her around 4:00 p.m. for the day, as she planned to carry on working from home. She had client phone calls to make, and these were best conducted in the privacy of her home; she needed this isolation since the office only offers a few quiet conference spaces. We went to a new café near the office. Small groups of women were scattered around us in the open back area sitting at wrought iron tables, sipping lattes and eating the red velvet cupcakes that were very popular in Bangalore at the time. Purnima was relaxed and friendly and, although still in the middle of her working day, dressed casually in a sleeveless top and fitted jeans.

She had been at Captivate for several years and always looked completely at home in the office. She often shouted out to other team members across cubicles, chatted with colleagues about her—and their—personal lives, and showed an avid interest in office goings-on. Her work required a phone, a calling card, a data card, and a laptop with Skype to reach clients. On the way out of our meeting she told me, laughing, that she would do some work on her phone in the car, as her driver steered her through traffic. Her driver formed part of the human infrastructure through which Purnima both signaled her class status and was able to maintain it, moving easily between café, office, and home, and—as I show—later to evening socializing.

The role of a travel consultant at Captivate was an elite one, involving feminized labor. Travel consultants listened carefully and attentively to clients before making suggestions for itineraries. They maintained a veneer of hospitality, care, and concern: hallmarks of the "Captivate Travels experience." Purnima told me that she had left a previous job in banking because of the stressful work life and the pressure of having to lead a team. Here at Captivate she found the work pleasurable, and she sought it out. "The first thing I do when I wake up," she said, "is roll over and check my phone for new email. I don't have to, but I want to because there might be someone replying or asking more questions, and I'm curious."

The initial conversations that Purnima and her team had with prospective guests were informal. They relied on the employee's ability to strike a rapport with the guest and establish some familiarity early on. While they casually conversed with their elite Western guests, Purnima and her team understood their travel needs; translated guest desires and dreams into choices for concrete itineraries, activities, and hotels; and maintained a level of confidence that assured the guests they were in good hands. Employees in this role could not commit lapses in English or grammar in the emails that they wrote guests or appear uncertain and flustered in phone calls. This expectation of labor was concealed; I was never clear who might or might not become a travel consultant. While I worked at Captivate, some employees who framed itineraries wanted to eventually work in a role where they directly sold to guests, but there was no direct path from back-end work to client-facing roles (and the distinction between "work" and "roles" itself insinuates the class component of this labor). Purnima's work in sales was masked by the title "travel consultant," which suggested billable hours rather than the salaried work that it was. This was how Purnima explained to me what she did:

Even though you're . . . getting in revenue for the company, it's not direct sales. You don't do cold calling . . . or harassing someone to [buy]. For me it was more like an extension of my personality since I love talking, I love traveling and I like India.

What I like about this job is that you're allowed to do it (work) in your own individual space and your own individual style. If you give us one guest, we'll all have different views on it, in terms of the itinerary, or what we would plan for the guest and how we would approach the guest as well. We are never asked to curb that, which is very important. Like our email writing styles . . . everyone is different. (Fieldwork interview, Purnima, September 2013)

Although making sales calls was a primary part of her job, Purnima explained it to me as "an extension of [my] personality." Purnima's individual flexibility and her classed access to private resources granted her the mobility that was important to her; her workspaces included her car, her bed, and her home. She also valued the freedom of taking each call differently, outside of a sales script. Purnima personally disliked long emails; she preferred to just pick up the phone and "chat" with someone. The discomfort with long email played out in different ways at Captivate: to nonelite workers, the energy required to read through several paragraphs felt exhausting. For middle-class workers like Purnima, email detracted from her ability to deploy her feminized labor in ways she was comfortable with.

Purnima was not the only consultant who referred to work as a "chat," reinterpreting labor as a personal set of actions that then assumed a different affective dimension. Rather than being a stressful "sales call," it became a "friendly chat" with a stranger. Her freedom was also enabled by the flexibility to move easily in and out of the office outside of stipulated hours, dressing informally, as she preferred. Unlike the larger IT companies and banks where many employees had previously worked, Captivate did not stipulate a strict dress code or a separate leisurely Friday "dress down" option.

Purnima's use of various forms of flexibility (ability to choose her clothing, adopt erratic office hours, and deviate from a script in her calls with clients) enabled her sense of freedom. She offers us a route to read freedom differently: not as the self severed from the chaos of the office but as the self produced as desirable by being able to coordinate work according to both social and professional itineraries. Purnima's flexibility at work, class status, and access to money allowed her to try out the new coffee shops, participate in yoga sessions with other travel consultants, and attend the new karaoke night at a nearby bar. Thus, the flexibility at work was alluring for Purnima not because it freed her to work without constraint but because it enabled her to craft a gendered and classed self *in keeping* with work protocols.[11]

Flexible work offers the possibility of a social, class-based life for professional women as they circulate in elite spaces and maintain the practices that designate their social position as middle class. Unlike other professional middle-class people, they are not employed in bank jobs and software work that require strict clock-in hours and rigid work protocols. Thus for Purnima's family and those of other elite colleagues, her job was desirable because it enabled her to be present for her familial obligations when necessary. It was still seen as work, but it was recognized as *flexible* work.

For employees themselves, flexibility offered more complex meanings. Employment in an entrepreneurial company like Captivate allows work to be interpreted as "not work"—its very concealment offering the key to class belonging (Weeks 2017). Thus, unmoored from a practice of labor, work can be misrecognized as a middle-class leisure pursuit, unfolding at home or in the car, flexibly moving in between spaces and resisting its categorization as salaried employment.

As middle-class travel consultants came in late to work after making international phone calls at erratic hours, the calibration of their day between "home" and "work" became blurred.[12] Unlike others who visited fitness classes at 7:00 p.m. after a working day, consultants scheduled classes earlier, at 5:00 p.m. When I requested interviews, they met me at 4:00 p.m. or for lunch at a neighboring café. As their activities spilled out of the neat order of contained workdays, they could be mistaken for middle-class women of leisure, their days peppered with yoga classes, visits to cafés, and nights out. Their labor was performed at home, in private, since they needed silence and private space, yet this retreat of labor into private space and the performance of leisure in public frames their work primarily in terms of an enjoyable pastime.

Maria Mies's ([1982] 2012) historic study of women lace-makers in Narsapur, India, traces how women's labor comes to be seen as "leisure" or "part-time" work as it is performed in home spaces, while middlemen who sell their work and engage in the public world of commerce come to be seen as engaging in labor. This older, material Marxist analysis is an important reminder that travel consultants still had work to do at home and calls to make. Flexibility can also transfer the burden of work onto individual workers—an important facet of platform economies when workers have to compensate for longer travel times by extending their hours (Tandon and Sekharan 2021). For elite travel consultants, too, flexibility enabled them to rearrange their labor and leisure and to convene groups around their activities. However, work extended into the spaces of their homes, as they worked later into the night and according to the availability of their clients. Thus their classed ability to manage work across spaces enabled them to do *more* work.

FLEXIBILITY AS A GIFT AND MORAL OBLIGATION

If Purnima's case shows us how flexible work enables circulation in middle-class life and pleasures derived from its pursuits, Radhika's case shows us how the flexibility at Captivate drew workers into meaningful moral relations. Radhika was an employee of Captivate who left a high-pressure job at a global bank to join this smaller workplace. She had disliked the work environment in her previous job, uncomfortable with the idea of Indian employees constantly deferring to white British bosses. "It was like colonialism all over again," she said to me. She had come on board at Captivate as part of the initial team and was a travel consultant, on the same team as Purnima. The purportedly "informal" nature of her friendly chats with clients shaped her experience of work as one that was warm and desirable; she did not view her relationships with clients as one of servility. Instead, she represented herself as an equal with the elite white foreigners whom she typically talked to everyday, sharing her expert knowledge of Asian destinations. She did not regard herself as employed by potential guests, and instead spoke about her work within the terms of a gift economy, as a "return" of what she owed the company for the flexibility and freedom it afforded her:

> Over here there is more ownership [of work]. It's not forced upon you; you do it on your own. . . . [T]he moment you get flexibility, you want to

return it back again, right? When we joined, our working hours were 9.30–6.30. That was the office hours . . . but because of our UK, US and Australian guests, we can make calls from home. The moment you get that flexibility, you get interested. I've always said that the flexibility you get over here is amazing. Literally amazing. This is mainly for travel consultants. (Fieldwork interview, Radhika, October 2013)

Although she worked around the clock, as a travel consultant she was free to choose her hours and place of work, and this appealed to Radhika. This freedom framed her work as convenient, desirable, and pleasurable. Radhika was not the only employee who described her work in the personal and social terms of "gift-giving," which anthropologists interpret, following Mauss (2000), not as a duty-bound offering but as the "cultivation of personal relationships and networks of mutual dependence; and the manufacturing of obligation and indebtedness" (Patico 2008; Yang 1994, 6, see also Patico 2008). Mauss (2000, 3) suggests that the reciprocity in gift-giving was in theory voluntary, but in fact obligatory: to give something is to give a part of oneself, and it is dangerous to keep this moral and spiritual liability (which is a part of someone else). The flexibility offered to Radhika adheres to the logics of global management. It might not seem to the observer a significant personal gift—flexibility is a part of the work process after all, not a selectively distributed incentive—yet she interpreted it as a form of generosity and felt compelled to give back through her labor. Radhika thus dislodged flexibility from its value as a managerial ideal to enhance productivity; instead she located it within the realm of the social. Radhika met the managerial terms of flexibility—enabling efficiency, maximizing human capital—with the language of personal obligation, the affect of mutuality and dependence. She celebrated it as an anti-colonial stance: an Indian company that did not defer to white clients.

It was not only travel consultants who imagined flexibility-as-freedom through work. Ahana was in her early twenties, with a bachelor's degree from a local college and a job at Captivate updating databases. She was part of a small group of women who spoke in Tamil and knew each other from college; they had introduced each other to Captivate. When Ahana told me she enjoyed her job, I wanted to know what she enjoyed about it.

INTERVIEWER (HG): What do you enjoy about working here?
AHANA (A): Flexibility.
HG: In what sense?
A: You don't have too many restrictions here: "You cannot do this, you cannot do that." You have a lot of opportunities to try new things and learn new things. We had this thing with [CEO] one day [when he said to us]: "You have to give me ideas that you think if you do will improve someone else's work." I gave this idea: there are too many templates. . . . [W]e can simplify them and use just one.

He liked the idea, not everyone encourages such ideas but he said you can go ahead. So that became my project. . . . I came up with new designs and they liked it. . . . [W]e have five templates now in place of twenty-five.

There's a lot of opportunity for you here to explore. If I had joined KPMG or Ernst and Young, my work would not have got recognized.
(Fieldwork interview with Ahana, Aug 2013)

What Ahana called "flexibility" was an articulation of the freedom to join an experiment. Ahana regarded Captivate as a young company that was bold and ambitious and, like her colleagues, she was eager to be recognized by management and to claim ownership for work processes. Unlike in the corporatized work environments of KPMG or Ernst and Young (as Ahana imagines them), Captivate employees were given flexibility and freedom to innovate. Ahana shows us how the discursive effects of imagining work as freedom end up reinscribing techniques of governance. "Free" to innovate, she generated an idea for a standardization of templates that she then became committed to implementing: it was her idea, after all, not a demand made on her by management. Proud of her own idea, she was now committed to the extra labor of implementing it.

When used by the managing director, *flexibility* meant something very different from when travel consultants who moved in and out of the office at all times of day talking to guests used it to describe their working day. It referenced yet another set of meanings when used by junior employees seeking to align themselves with the company's core stated values—although they did not really avail themselves of any of flexibility's intended benefits (work from home, flexi-timings, subjective modulations). Flexibility, as a strategically deployed shifter, can only be interpreted "in terms of the speaker's position, in a specific place, time, social context, or some combination thereof" (Urciuoli 2008, 214).

My interviewees did not resist work; they welcomed it into intimate spaces and sought out more. While we might read this as an instantiation of capital's power to obscure the conditions of labor by positing it as lovable, I offer here a reparative reading of conditions of work to suggest that these ethnographic moments reveal a remaking of the significance and material value of work.[13] For many at Captivate, this job was preferable to a specific other. For Radhika and Purnima, it was an alternative to jobs in banking that had rigid hours and yoked workers to what they described as colonialism all over again. Workers like Ahana who performed data entry and back-office work had first competed for jobs in accounting and also in call centers, which offered wide opportunities for professional jobs in Bangalore and the industry that self-represents as creating a large new Indian middle class.

Yet for most of Captivate's nonelite workers and first-generation professionals, their undergraduate nonspecialized degrees from local colleges and their class background as children of drivers, security guards, nurses, and low-level government officials prevented their entry into the upwardly mobile ranks of IT engineers, who were expected to already have the cultural capital to move across global projects (see Upadhya 2007). Hiring consultants and recruitment websites sent them to smaller workplaces such as Captivate. Captivate only paid about Rs. 20,000 (or $200) a month for a "fresher" or recruit straight from an undergraduate course in a local college, but for working women it was preferable to a job in a call center, where night shifts were routine and that threatened their public reputations.

Although employees at Captivate did not own company stock or benefit from its profits, they participated in creative labor practices as they built the future of the company. Ahana understood flexibility as enabling her construction of herself as an enterprising and creative worker who could offer value to the company. Unlike Pushkar and Krishna, who understood freedom as the need for the agentive subject to develop its full human capital and achieve creative potential, Ahana instead aligned herself with a larger project of meaningful work that she helped to shape.[14] My interactions with Captivate's workers reinterpret flexibility and freedom from their claims of maximizing human capital to instead locate them within practices and beliefs that articulate the realm of the social as shaped by class, colonial pasts, and desires for mutuality.

COMMAS, PERIODS, AND EMAIL ETIQUETTE

At Captivate, Pushkar Subramaniam imagined his workers as inspired individuals, in tune with the overall goals and values of the company, rather than as Taylorist subjects waiting to be instructed and guided.[15] The flat hierarchy was reflected in his approach of extrapolating his own work experiences to his employees; the expectation was that what worked for him would apply to his staff, too. Subramaniam wanted to give employees the agency and training to make decisions that allowed them to work at this or another time, at home or at the office. Once they were empowered to exercise this kind of flexibility, the management rationale went, employees maximized the use of their own time. This empowerment could be achieved by equipping employees with skills training, responsibilities, and ownership.

At Captivate, teams met monthly to assess their own performances and to update others on their plans for skills enhancement. The company offered money to employees to update and upgrade their skills. I attended some meetings of the marketing team at which the assistant manager, Jyothi, sat us down in a conference room and asked us to list what we had learned that month and what our goals were, looking ahead. She herself had shifted roles over the years, from being a product executive (laying out itineraries and coordinating bookings) to travel consulting, to doing translations, and finally to website work. Everybody contributed their "future goals" via a Google document that was accessible to all of us. We read each other's lists before the meeting. One employee said he would learn more HTML coding skills, another said she would step up her SEO (search engine optimization) abilities. Each outlined specific steps they would take to achieve these goals.

Skills discourses, found on the internet and in specialized classes (such as the ones Captivate employees visited) are based on a neoliberal imaginary that workers are responsible for mastering skills, and that skills are quantifiable even when they are "soft skills" such as leadership and communication. Bonnie Urciuoli (2008, 211–12) terms this the notion of "worker-self-as-skills-bundle"—not only is labor power a commodity, but the worker's very person comprises commodifiable bits. Yet the money offered to employees at Captivate to enroll in courses to gain skill sets was rarely used. Pushkar Subramaniam was especially puzzled by this fact and asked me if my research could explain it; he wanted to understand why employees did not avail themselves of such funds.

My fieldwork suggests the reason is that management at Captivate and workers themselves shared very different understandings of the meaning of work. When Pushkar Subramaniam explained his rationale for how the office should function, naming skills empowerment and flexibility, he was proposing a master plan in which employees would take charge of their own lives, upgrade their skills, and ensure their own freedom to chart their careers. His imagination of employees was of free, entrepreneurial actors. They would conduct themselves through a rational and maximizing use of the liberty accorded to them.

Yet as I have shown, flexibility works as a "boundary object," as it refracts the social onto the formal world of work. For many workers, flexibility was interpreted and galvanized toward enjoying the pleasures of being middle class, channeling a spirit of debt and obligation and offering participation in creative work projects. Workers rejected the compulsory skill development available to them through additional office schemes and programs, instead inserting themselves into a different ethos of work. Work was not an investment to become better selves—investments in their own and the company's future—but rather offered the opportunity for present satisfaction and escape from the unjust labor relations of the past.

Some workers at Captivate did not associate the work there with flexibility at all, an example of how flexibility converges with the gendered and classed logics of masculine projects of mastering time and feminized labor of continual and cooperative work. Men from regional towns who could not seek recourse in class habitus were not offered magical promises of flexibility, and they did not seek them out. Sanjay, an employee who joined Captivate from another smaller, regional travel company, encountered Captivate work processes instead as templates for learning and acquiring professionalism. He wished to cultivate himself according to the disciplining logics of corporate behavior.

Sanjay had moved to Bangalore with his wife, leaving behind both his hometown of nearby coastal Mangalore and the expectation that he would become a Brahmin priest like his father. At thirty, Sanjay loved to travel and had even enrolled in a local college to learn tourism management. He spontaneously planned trips for his friends and developed an interest in photography—learning the "tourist gaze" (Urry and Larsen 2011) through which to view his environments with the lens of the novel or unfamiliar. He got a job with a local travel company planning trips to nearby destinations. Then a senior from college told him that Captivate Travels in Bangalore had an opening. At Captivate, he could learn how to plan global tours and be on a team that drafts itineraries for South America:

INTERVIEWER (HG): What kind of a place was Captivate [when you joined], was it different from Maquilab [his old local tour company]?

SANJAY: Definitely. Vast difference actually [*sic*]. So Maquilab, it was a small company, and we used to talk in local language many of the time—that is Tulu actually—because all local people . . . local faces. And after coming here it was so professional here. In our old office whatever you do, it is all your own work.

However it is, it is your own work, you can do however you want to do. But here it is not like that, it is so professional here. You have things to do, you have things to follow . . . very professional manner, so . . .

HG: When you say "professional," what exactly do you mean?[16]

[Long pause]

SANJAY: I can say "style," "working style." So there people used to come to our office and ask, "any tours?" and I used to talk to them, I used to get the booking, I used to get the hotels and nobody was asking me, "What you are doing?" Finally, they used to pay me . . . they used to pay the company, that's all done. Nobody will ask me, "What you are doing?" "What did you talk with them?" "How much you are quoting?" "What hotel you are giving?" Nothing! It is all my plan.

HG: Oh. So they just train you and you do whatever you want.

SANJAY: Whatever you want, you can do. Something like that. But here it's not like that. We have system, we have some software where all things are updated and we have to follow, we have to do the trip according to the rules and regulation. We have margins set up and . . . it is not like "I feel this guy [client] is very poor and I can . . . add just 5–10 percent margin or something like that." So it was not actually professional (referring to old job) but it was good experience because it was all my own; whatever I can do, freely I could do. Here it is not like that. Very professional in all the way. (Fieldwork interview, Sanjay, November 12, 2013)

What Sanjay described to me about his old company was what was offered to elite Captivate employees on the sales and marketing teams: the discretionary freedom to chat with customers and decide what to offer them without following a set script. The middle-class women travel consultants at Captivate valued this about their jobs; in a "chat" they could be "themselves" and share their personal experiences with guests. The freedom that Purnima and Radhika described to me built on their classed cultural capital, drawing on their experiences, forms of speech, and ease in interacting with Western guests. Additionally, they interpreted work within the terms of friendship—so that it seemed like a "choice" to work, rather than a necessity—and utilized their flexible job timings and protocols to cultivate classed pursuits of fitness and leisure.

Yet Sanjay, doing the back-end work of creating itineraries, did not experience this flexibility. Further, for a class-aspirational young man, the guidance to be informal, conversational, and off script would probably not be attractive. It would impede his learning of professional style and interaction. Sanjay considered the flexibility to draw from subjective experience and personal discretion a sign of *disorganization* rather than the rationalized efficiency expected of a global company. To him this "personal discretion" that employees like Purnima and Radhika employed was a reminder of the "local" practices of his old company. Purnima appreciated being able to wake up and roll over in bed to check her email; Sanjay, a migrant to Bangalore whose mother was a homemaker and father a priest, would consider this a disgraceful lack of professionalism.

Sanjay's need for standardization, protocol, and procedure demonstrate what empowering and liberating work meant to him. He appreciated that his managers at Captivate used commas and periods consistently in their emails. Nobody cared in his old job about email composition, he said. If you were sending out a quotation for a tour, you sent an email anyhow. Here at Captivate everything had to be perfect. If grammar lapses occurred or a period was absent, managers sent back emails requiring they attain perfection. Sanjay did not find this tiresome or needless. He valued the attention to detail; he praised the fact that emails could be sent back if they were below standard. His devotion to practice, script, and discipline resonate with Saba Mahmood's (2005) understanding of agency not as the liberation from disciplining procedures but in fact as a mastery of them. Sanjay's experience helps us understand the lasting significance of colonial formations of technoscience that emphasize categories and classificatory regimes as a hallmark of contemporary technology work.[17]

For Sanjay, the practices of flexibility- as freedom that his colleagues cherished were a form of improvisation, a vernacular "making do" or *jugaad*: business on the fly. "Any tours?" a customer asked, and Sanjay whipped something up for them, deciding margins, hotels, and travel on his own. At Captivate the flexibility to "let people figure out how to do it," in the CEO's words, was a disadvantage for those from an emerging middle class, a man like Sanjay for whom standardization and protocol offered key learning and class mobility and confidence. The way that flexibility is interpreted and valued is through social histories of class, gender, and regional mobility.

UNFREEDOMS: EMBODIED EXHAUSTION IN THE OFFICE

Despite the enthusiastic energy around me at Captivate, my own experiences at work sometimes felt oddly out of sync with entrepreneurial exuberance. My already weak eyes reddened and watered after hours at the computer, sifting and sorting through photographs to weed out the unattractive ones that did not match Captivate's travel style. The seemingly endless flexibility promised at work was directed to flexibility for travelers, who were offered a range of choices. There were magical *havelis* converted into boutique hotels, infinity pools overlooking rainforests, an isolated adobe hotel-house in the middle of a rocky desert. I spent hours parsing the magical hotels from the standardized hotel chains that Captivate distanced itself from. As the affluent white tourists in the photographs traveled the world, warmly greeted with red powder *tikas*, marigolds, and *aratis* in India, or sipped cocktails after a safari in the Kenyan outback, I was immobile, rooted to my chair, racing against time to clean up the photo albums.

Every now and again Susan, my manager at work, would come up to me, looking over my shoulder at the screen, asking "How's it going?," and I had to have more to show her than the fact that I had been chatting for the last hour with my teammates. I could intensely feel my body collapsing as I peered continually at the computer screen, editing and compiling streams of text and photographs. By evening the sky would darken outside, and the white tube lights flickered on: a sign for many women that it was time to leave work. They left in twos and threes, sharing rides or waiting at the same bus stop. Each group that left reminded the rest of us that we needed to hurry up our work, even as cubicles around us emptied.

By 7:00 p.m., the office became quiet. The sounds that carried were phone conversations from the logistics team, calling hotels, drivers, and travel agencies to coordinate last-minute deals and details. Sometimes the young men on the logistics team waited in the office until midnight, when they slipped into Captivate T-shirts and left to pick up a guest at the airport. The invisible infrastructure of drivers powering the new economy was suddenly visibilized as a feature of Captivate Travel—a feature that guests were paying for.

Senior employees often worked late, confiding that they could not bring themselves to refuse tasks. As team managers granted the same "flexibility" to innovate with work that Ahana had, they stayed long hours finishing extra projects and tasks. Our collective experiences marked how freedom is embodied and experienced through forms of vulnerability. During my fieldwork two employees became weak with neurological ailments and muscle impairments, but they themselves never explicitly connected their physical fragility to work-related stress and strain. Colleagues pointed out that they worked so hard that their injuries did not have time to heal, possibly prolonging their recovery. During an interview with me, one of them, Jyothi, offered the familiar explanation that the freedom and flexibility to learn and develop herself was one of the central reasons to work at Captivate, allowing her to learn different kinds of work and even engage in more than one job. She was recovering from a stress-related illness:

> I'm 100 percent sure it was stress and the way I was sitting like this [demonstrates by showing me her wrists placed awkwardly] and doing my laptop work or whatever.... Two months complete bed rest. What am I doing? I'm working for Captivate lying down and when it was worse then I'm calling up a friend.... [S]he was in constant touch with me and I'm saying, "I'm doing this [work] but I can't type." So she says, "You just speak it to me." I'm speaking to her on Skype and I'm just speaking to her and she's typing it out.... [laughs]... I like to work.... I like to be busy, I like to do different things and if I didn't do that I wouldn't enjoy life so much. Perhaps. (Fieldwork interview, Jyothi, July 27, 2013)

The flexibility as freedom approach of Captivate immobilized Jyothi's body. Captivate's flexible schedule expanded the extent of work she could—and did!—do, filling in the minutes of her day even when she was at home, and on the weekends. The "freedom" of flexibility engineered a physical breakdown as work seeped into her everyday life and well-being. Yet she considered this desirable; the satisfaction of doing "different things" helped her to "enjoy life so much." It is telling that this excerpt ends with her saying "perhaps": both trustful and skeptical that the abundance of work was what made her life worthwhile.

After several years of working on different skills, training and retraining herself for this flexible neoliberal market, Jyothi ultimately left her job. For years she directed her body to align with the resonances of entrepreneurial work—treat the company as her own, work late hours, become completely immersed in the job—but finally there was a disaggregation of love and work as her body collapsed. The cost of aligning work and affect was corporeal, borne by her spinal cord. Embodying freedom by directing it toward more work breaks down the eager and pliant body of the worker, causes illness and impairment, and ultimately forces a departure from the company itself (Gupta 2019b).

Susan, my own manager, severely damaged her wrist by continuously (re)building company websites, yet she soldiered on. Her juniors whispered to me that she was headed for a breakdown of some sort. Her wrist was in a cast, and she turned to robotics to compensate for her handicap—becoming a cyborg worker (Haraway 1996), one for whom neoliberalism was "lived on the skin" (Molé 2011). My research found high attrition rates across levels in the startup work environments where I conducted fieldwork. As flexibility circulated as a promise and a practice of everyday work, its corporeal costs detailed which bodies it rendered most vulnerable. At Captivate, those who spoke of the company as "family" and interpreted flexibility as a form of duty, obligation, and world building were the most susceptible entrants into the promissory freedoms of entrepreneurial work. Detailing the "vital energies" (Vora 2015) that keep alive the promise of flexibility-as-freedom unfolds a biopolitics of corporeal costing: the body as truth-telling device (Molé 2011), revealing the material costs of labor.

Not everyone at Captivate spoke of enjoying freedom and flexibility. Natasha was an employee who worked in a technology role for the company and lived far from the office. She often termed her commute a "risk" because she had to cross miles of potholed streets and traveled to work on a small scooter that did not shield her from the frenzied traffic and uneven conditions of the street. She told me that she had been dissuaded from working from home by her managers. Although she had a laptop and an internet connection, she was expected to clock the facetime that Pushkar hates. Natasha found it increasingly difficult to commute and to reconcile herself to office timings. Soon it became an office joke that she was "working from home," almost as though everyone acknowledged that this was a ruse to conceal her slacking off.

After my fieldwork ended, Natasha lost her job at Captivate. She wanted to use the flexibility of timings offered to the elite travel consultants. Her job, working with internet statistics, did not require her to be present in the office. Yet the notional flexibility offered did not apply to her. When Natasha lost her job, an equivalent job was offered to a part-time consultant based in the US: he performed some of the same work functions for much higher pay. Natasha's case suggests that flexibility and freedom are only conjoined to feel empowering when they enhance the ability to be available for clients. While discourses of flexibility as freedom travel as a liberatory ideology of contemporary entrepreneurial work, in everyday life they are negotiated through classed desires and the norms of gendered labor, and felt by vulnerable bodies.

THE MULTIPLE VALENCES OF FLEXIBILITY

Flexibility is imagined by entrepreneurs and elite technologists as a distancing from the social to achieve one's true potential in a realm of action and creativity. For them, flexibility is the freedom to do more work. The central subject of work is the capable individual who exhibits a startup masculine mastery over time and a feminized flexible approach to labor. But workers practice flexibility otherwise. For them flexibility at work might be the ability to align life and work more closely, to enter moral obligations and responsibilities that are meaningful and anti-colonial. Flexibility might also be an invitation to build worlds in which workers produce themselves as creators building a new company. These practices of flexibility suggest that it is a boundary object, emerging through life histories and desires for futures of mutuality, pleasure, and self-confidence.

Flexibility as freedom was thus articulated with different life trajectories and material resources in radically diverse ways. Ahana, Purnima, and Radhika welcomed it; with flexibility they had creative ideas for work, shaped desirable selves, and imagined themselves as global workers. This discourse met its limits in Sanjay. For him, flexibility did not signal the possibilities of play and creative work.

Tracking the arc of the laboring body, what we might call labor as method once again, also shows the limits of flexibility. Vulnerability and dependence among ill or injured workers rethink the sovereign subject of entrepreneurial work. Flexibility not only names a project of individual selfhood but situates bodies and worlds within webs of dependence, care, and concern. Aspirations to flexibility as freedom as they unfold in the Western liberal tradition are unable to attend to the cadences and registers within which freedom was lived at Captivate. Through my fieldwork, I encountered interpretations of flexibility that reflected workers' acute awareness of their limited opportunities and circumscribed possibilities. Flexibility was the opportunity to enfold oneself within networks of obligation and care and as a relational practice. Work in the new economy offers both the entrepreneurial dream of agentive, creative maximizing of human capital and its response in everyday reinterpretations of this vision.

5

LOVE IN THE OFFICE FAMILY

Infrastructures of Care

ON ONE STORMY monsoon night at the office, some of us were working late when a downpour began. Very quickly, the streets were flooded, and we stood helplessly at the entrance to the office downstairs, stuck inside, water swirling below us.[1] The bus stop was just across the street, but in this rain and with backed-up traffic, the service was erratic. Buses were so full there was no space for new commuters. Two young workers beside me—Apu and Asha—began receiving text messages from worried parents wanting to know where they were. Stuck there, Apu defiantly asked for the cell phone number of Captivate's managing director, Pushkar Subramaniam. "I'll call him!" she declared. "We need company transport! How are we supposed to get home?" Employees bent to look at their insistently buzzing phones, scrolling through the contacts.

Even as they searched, Apu seemed to have a change of heart. She pursed her lips. "Poor fellow," she said. "He's already so stressed out this month. Let's not add to that!" Finally, with a few others who had come down to the entrance, the group split into smaller ones, and they ended up sharing autos to a larger bus stop and taking buses home in the pouring rain.

"Do What You Love" (DWYL) has become an unofficial manifesto of startup capitalism, exhorting workers to pursue the promise of fulfilling and creative work. But how do you pursue that vision when you are not an elite entrepreneur? This chapter shows how the impetus to do what you love at work refracts into other forms of affective life that resonate with workers. They translated the impulse to DWYL as a mantra for profit into desirable forms of experimentation and consumption that were personally pleasurable and sociable. They reframed entrepreneurial discourses of passion into unconventional ideas of family and care. And they accepted office invitations to celebrate religious festivals as performative expressions of their own idealized womanhood.

These affective infrastructures of work—and *at* work—are so much more than the incitement by late Apple cofounder Steve Jobs to "Do What You Love." It is hard work to build, maintain, and repair these relations among workers that I understand as infrastructures of care. But such work is not merely an extractive process that depletes workers. Infrastructural work is also regenerative and creates interdependencies among workers that shape unexpected friendships, kin relations, and desires.

I build on the idea of infrastructures here in the sense that Abdou Maliq Simone (2004) uses "people as infrastructure," emphasizing not just physical infrastructures but the capacity of individual actors to engage in collaborative practices that are inscribed with multiple identities. Julia Elyachar (2010) also points to social and noninstitutional networks to theorize as an "infrastructure of communicative channels" the semiotic commons through which people in Cairo create a resource that can be put to use by the poor. Kai Bosworth explains two directions in which theories of "affective infrastructure" have flowed, and here I take his work in the direction by which the indignation resulting from a scant infrastructure might be channeled back into "an affirmative politics that would grow the capacity to organize the infrastructures of everyday life such that they produce more enduring flourishing rather than alienation" (Bosworth 2023, 65). Fieldwork at Captivate showed me how nonelite workers create the infrastructural conditions possible for their own thriving. Yet these infrastructures of care are not available to everyone; they are differentially distributed and accessed.

If the contemporary economy is thought to "guzzle care" and sap social reproduction (Fraser 2022), I show how forms of care outside the heterosexual household might in fact regenerate social relations and produce new imaginations of family and kin. These are not always world building and life affirming; often they serve to reinforce hierarchies and striate workers. The contribution of this chapter is to show the affective life mobilized to create infrastructures of care that are vital for the social reproduction of workers. It invites us to think of entrepreneurial passion beyond the highly visible entrepreneur into the lifeworlds of workers as they desire, care for, and befriend each other to sustain experimental life. I first consider what it means to DWYL at work from the entrepreneur's perspective. I then follow this affective urge to see how it becomes dispersed into everyday life, exceeding and disrupting the kind of happiness that is meant to generate company profit.

DO WHAT YOU LOVE AT WORK

Pushkar Subramaniam, Captivate's managing director, was back in Bangalore from his recent trip to London, and he was very excited. Captivate had just conducted an event for its former clients over a catered meal at the Taj hotel in Buckingham Gate, and the managers all agreed it was a great success. Captivate consultants had showcased new destinations from their Asia, Africa, and South America teams, and employees had met returning guests over dinner and exchanged travel notes. Upon his return, Pushkar updated the Bangalore office of Captivate via an email:

> One guest even asked me about how we instilled the passion and created a nonhierarchical culture where people genuinely seemed to be excited about our cause rather than just doing a job. This of course made me feel very proud and I believe that it is our people and strong sense of purpose to really enchant guests and derive happiness from that activity is what separates us from the rest. (Email sent to All Captivate email address)

Pushkar's emphasis on happiness reflected one of the company's greatest desires: to create a workplace of happiness and DWYL at work. Further, this love and happiness would increase customer satisfaction and, ultimately, company profit. Pushkar's description of happiness worked productively: happy employees conveyed their sense of work satisfaction to guests, who were motivated to travel with the company. As a disciplinary technique, happiness has a promissory nature to it. Sara Ahmed writes (2017, 48), happiness "is often assumed to be an end point: as what we want to reach, as the point of life, the aim of life."[2] At Captivate, happy employees made happy guests who traveled with the company, becoming ever more happy. Happiness is promissory because it breeds more happiness—but it is not benign: instead it is the crucial route to capitalist profit.

Pushkar's own biography illustrates how he embraced what I call—following Miya Tokumitsu (2015)—"Do What You Love" forms of work that fuse the self with work and foreground the importance of love in choosing work. Among the promises of "lovable work," Tokumitsu (2015, 8) writes, are public visibility, social mobility, and worker autonomy. Pushkar's own route to entrepreneurship exemplifies this trajectory. After working in corporate finance in the United States, Pushkar went to business school in France. He realized while on a trip with friends in India that travel would be a good sector to launch a new business. He envisioned the company with a business school classmate and received initial funding from one of his professors. Upon graduating, the two founders of Captivate Travels and their wives (truly fusing love and work) traveled all over India to understand the sector they were diving into. As they traveled, they got a sense of what other, cosmopolitan, travelers like themselves might be seeking. They situated their own experiences as a kind of template from which to build the company and grow it through a workforce that would share their values.

Gradually, over the next few years they expanded their company from Captivate India to include Captivate South America and Captivate Africa. These other branches also center a love for travel and familiarity with destinations as the core focus of the business. As Pushkar told me, "We don't look for people with a formal training in travel. In fact, we prefer to have people who 'fit' the company rather than have the educational degrees. We look for certain personalities." When Captivate hired guides and consultants, it looked for people who were well-traveled and able to communicate their own experiences to guests and to convert that mutual love of travel into sales. These are key attributes of affectively laden work that Williams and Connell (2010) describe as drawing on workers' social and cultural capital to produce value in sales and to recast work as a kind of leisure activity.[3]

The emphasis on "love" and "fit" in the interview process at Captivate privileged certain subjects—middle class, cosmopolitan, fluent in English—as being able to love this job in elite travel. The language of "fit" with the company's values concealed the forms of professionalization and class capital required to be hailed as a suitable candidate. As women who worked at Captivate told me, they were asked about their favorite travel destinations during their initial interview for the job. Thus, rather than emphasize their degree or seek out tangible skills, a familiarity with classed language and an affective relation to work was always at the core of the business. Despite these being the screening procedures, employees also told me that they had referenced travel destinations they had never been to. The disciplinary techniques employed to screen employees could also be subverted as employees claimed suitability and simulated class practices at Captivate.

When I began fieldwork there, Captivate Travels had scaled up to being a company with over one hundred employees in Africa, Asia, Europe, and North and South America. It was not a startup but a midsize company. However, it still valued and celebrated its entrepreneurial roots. Employees who had been with the company since its inception spoke to me proudly of the long hours that they put in and the ways they had learned how to nurture the company when it was a fledgling entity. Indeed, the tropes of loving work (as Pushkar mentioned in his email) but also an accompanying narrative of "work-as-family" arose repeatedly among employees. Over drinks at a rooftop bar one night during my fieldwork, a former employee proudly recounted how many hours he had worked when the company was launched. He narrated his labor as a sign of intimacy and commitment to his colleagues and to the company itself—he had worked *as though* this were his own company.

These stories were told not as examples of labor exploitation or hours worked without overtime pay, but in the spirit of entrepreneurial business as examples of how the company was shaped as "family"— the "we" of the company that Kathi Weeks (2017) notes conceals the precarious labor hierarchies at work. Why do people work long hours and say they love work? Scholars suggest that people are spurred by a continual hope that labor conditions will improve or that they will find more work (Tokumitsu 2015, 88). This is key to how Lauren Berlant theorized cruel optimism: "a relation of attachment to compromised conditions of possibility whose realization is discovered either to be impossible, sheer fantasy, or too possible, and toxic" (2011, 24). But if we shift our question from asking why people say they love work to ask instead how they articulate these attachments and what those mean to them, we discover what *else* is produced under the sign of lovable work. This chapter shows how "loving work" is diffracted across bodies and spaces such that it produces *more* than managerial injunctions to be happy at work and entrepreneurial incitements to love work.

During my fieldwork, the Captivate office had about thirty employees based in Bangalore. They claimed different backgrounds by way of class, caste, gender, and nationality. Most senior employees (about seven of them) had customer-facing roles, including in marketing and as travel consultants selling itemized packages (for more about these labor hierarchies, see chapter 1). These employees included several foreign nationals who were Indians and had left jobs in banking and other professions to join Captivate. They had upper-caste and middle-class origins and wanted professional work that enabled them to live middle-class lives—work from home that allowed them to do yoga, have evening drinks with colleagues, and "chat" with customers. Their understanding and location as middle class reflects my understanding of class not only as structural but as performative, signaling a familiarity with modes of comportment, fitness, and leisure that distinguish them as middle class (see Freeman 2015; Liechty 2003).

In addition to these customer-facing employees were the nonelite workers on the teams that animated the back-end sections of Captivate's work. I described this team in chapter 1 as those from middling castes or, when upper caste, from smaller towns and villages in India outside the major metropolitan areas. It is tempting to classify Captivate's workers along the lines of class and caste, but in fact the value of their work was additionally striated by the region they were from, their nationality, and their racialization. For example, someone who was not upper caste but British Asian (as a UK national) had far more mobility to travel and flexibility at work than an upper-caste and middle-class Indian.

In general, I call "nonelite" those workers on back-end teams, often migrants from smaller towns who had moved to Bangalore to study and work for a few years, deferring to a family expectation that their marriages would be arranged by their parents when they were in their mid-twenties. The larger group of back-end employees included both men and women, although in general the office was staffed by women (there were a handful of men across teams). These forms of labor are feminized even when not performed by women: "To be femininized means to be made extremely vulnerable; able to be disassembled, re-assembled, exploited as a reserve labor force, seen less as workers than as servers" (Adkins and Jokinen in Mirchandani 2012, 104). If the new spirit of capitalism is about the communicative, empathetic, affectively laden self, this feminized labor and subjectivity was key to Captivate's business model.

Company management understood that there was nothing intuitive about summoning appropriate and profit-oriented forms of happiness. Before we hit tourist peak season, a sales trainer in Canada Skyped to Captivate offices around the world to teach the sales team how to increase guest confirmations. He emphasized that listening was key to sales. Guests needed to feel understood, as though they were talking to a friend. Once a guest's needs were understood, the consultant would guide the guest away from expressing "needs" toward placing greater value on their "wants." This enabled a simultaneous shift away from rational calculations and price-sensitive decisions into a realm that was "emotional," or feeling and perception based. By listening carefully, understanding the guest, and becoming a person the guest can relate to, the consultant engineered a shift from the column of "needs" to the opposite column of "wants" as shown in the following graph.

Initial phone calls began with the Captivate executive on the phone with a guest. At this point the guest was hypothetically at the bottom left of the graph: someone just needing help with travel who had made an initial inquiry. Through the phone call the Captivate consultant would gradually move the guest along the continuum to end at the top

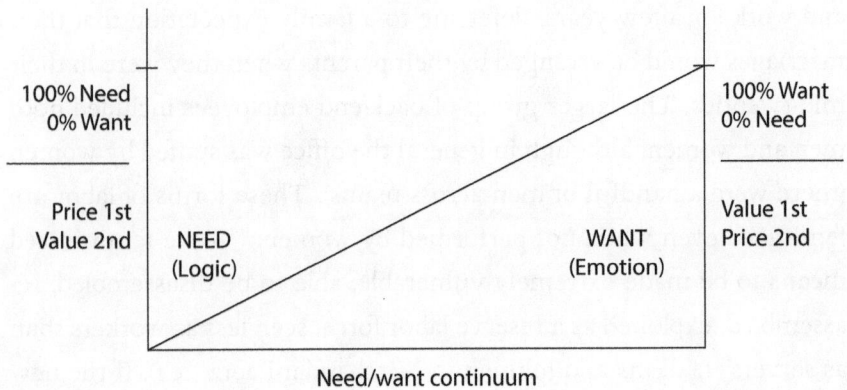

Figure 10. Sales training graph used at Captivate Travels, 2013.

right, a realm saturated by want. This point on the graph was somebody who greatly desired the experiences, photographs, and feelings possible with a specific Captivate holiday. Happiness for profit was produced through this directed movement from left to right. This was one of the main takeaways from the sales training. It resonated with the capitalist diktat to create needs and desires where there were none, fabricating a fetish out of a commodity or service.[4]

If I have shown how happiness and love are expected at work even as they are taught and consistently naturalized, what happened in everyday work at Captivate was more than a mute or extractive rendition of appropriate affect. Workers deviated from the pathways of happiness expected of them. Adjacent to the dominant sign of happiness, I found more fragmented affects of everyday life and work. The everyday graph of workplace happiness deviates from the neat and orderly line moving guests and workers to cultivate desire and joy. Instead, the generative affective life of the office includes forms of relational care and sentimental labor that not only are oriented toward capitalist productivity but also strive to secure one's own pleasure and desire as they articulate with idealized scenes and settings of work.[5] I understand these forms of care and desire as an essential part of the social reproduction through which Captivate's workers replenished and rejuvenated themselves through their friendships at work.

What I am showing here is the disjunctive journey of happiness as it travels through entrepreneurial economies of DWYL. Management expectations for happiness draw on the labor and care of workers through a process that also produces new experimental socialities and affective immersions into current conditions of labor. This same fragmentation of affect—into desire, contentment, pleasure, and thrill—mutes the possibilities for explicit workplace organizing in the tech sector that we might see elsewhere.[6] Our sodden tryst with the downpour at the beginning of this chapter marks the disjuncture between work that is intended to be undertaken in the spirit of happiness and love and the material feelings of abandonment and underresourcing that unfold in the everyday workday. There is a tension between the persistent invocation of the "company family" and "employees as partners" who all DWYL and the material conditions of precarity and underresourcing in the office.

In the next few sections, I develop labor as method as an approach to the ethnography. I follow affect to first understand how happiness is produced through concrete forms of work. I then show how workers process and circulate versions of DWYL that build on their own pleasures and desires. Durable but unequal forms of care and concern shape everyday work and frame the essential infrastructures necessary for startup capitalism to survive and even thrive.

ELITE WORKERS: HAPPINESS AS LIVING THE GOOD LIFE

Work at Captivate began with an inquiry from somebody wanting to travel but not knowing how to begin their research. One of the first things I was taught as an "intern" on the marketing team was how to write content that would attract search engine optimization (SEO). I had to insert keywords into my text, alluring guests to the company's site and ensuring Captivate Travels showed up as a top hit for queries such as "vacation + Patagonia" or "luxury travel + safari." This was an exercise in trafficking through various images of imperial nostalgia and the excitements of empire: quaint colonial bungalows vied for space with lavish tents set up on the outskirts of Kenyan grassland, where guests could watch the Great Migration over a cocktail.

Once the guest landed on Captivate's website, they filled out a query form. As soon as someone in Captivate's office received this, they phoned the guest for a personal chat. This "chat" was key to Captivate's approach. The informal interaction that unfolded outside of a set script distinguished Captivate's team from a call center for a major travel agency. The guest was speaking to a "real" person, someone who had most likely traveled to the destination they wanted to go to and would rely on their own experience to advise the guest. There was labor involved in consolidating the sense that the person the guest spoke to was "real," and this is what Kiran Mirchandani (2012, 2), in her study of call center workers, terms "authenticity work" involved in transacting with consumers around the world through a product that is itself the "responsive, caring, connected self." In the experience economy of the service sector, creating an authentic experience requires employees not to come across as fake or scripted: "By being themselves, workers can convince customers that they know and care about their real needs" (Mirchandani 2012, 5). Yet the production of this real self happens not only through labor but also, crucially, through the leisure of the worker.

While the literature on call center work marks how labor value is extracted from workers to produce an alien persona that can meet customer demand, companies like Captivate imagine their work differently.[7] As I explain in chapter 4, employees didn't get a script to base their interactions on, and they were expected to draw on their own life experiences to inform their calls. Thus the imbrication of life and work was not only a neoliberal strategy to extract more work; it produced experiences and affects that could enhance customer interactions. Travel consultants described specific locations to guests with great familiarity. They offered suggestions of where to go or what to do that sounded like "insider tips" by virtue of being shared by someone based in India. They might align themselves with the guests by describing their own vacation travel to the destination. But then they also distinguished themselves from the guest by demonstrating their knowledge of local food or road conditions.

Sameness and difference were negotiated in order to simultaneously project oneself as both like the guest and sufficiently different from them as to be able to claim expertise. This continual modulation by the elite travel consultants of their subject position was derived from a reserve of social and cultural capital. It was consolidated through the recruitment of middle-class workers who sought to further enhance their leisure and fitness such that consumption was a key productive activity that displayed cultural competence and accentuated one's labor value and sense of belonging in the experimental workplace.

The small team of travel consultants who made these phone calls to guests offered the primary personal contact with Captivate's clients: they were the "face" (or the voice) of the company. Travel consultants were well-traveled and presented themselves as warm, outgoing, and sociable—they became "friends" with the guest over phone calls.[8] Along with actively mediating sameness and difference to generate happiness for their guests, they also cultivated themselves as creative professionals by embracing the ethos of DWYL.

When I passed by the desks of the travel consultants at Captivate one afternoon, I saw a Post-it note stuck on a cubicle wall. It outlined a plan for the next few months. I was confused about whether this was a work plan or a personal plan—it involved significant time to be spent in Goa, a nearby beach town, and other plans to travel to Kerala, a neighboring state represented in the travel industry through placid backwaters and tropical forests. This ambiguity between work and leisure was productive for the company; it allowed personal pleasure and happiness to be routed into expertise, and for happiness to be derived at work without extra cost for the company. Since travel consultants could travel and work at the same time, for many the job at Captivate was a lifestyle choice, remunerating them to live a good life. The good life was not one separated from capitalism's alienation but carved out within it.[9]

Elite workers performing sales work at Captivate took a significant pay cut from their earlier jobs to work as travel consultants there and explained that they did not consider their sales calls to be "work." This decommodification of work is reflective of aesthetic labor (Williams and Connell 2010) that blurs lines between labor and leisure. Making sales calls did not feel like "work" for elite Captivate workers because they channeled class pleasure, travel experience, and social skills into performing sales calls. Their labor was invisibilized because it drew on classed backgrounds and experiences: their cultural capital in other words, to use Bourdieu's (1986) term to describe value that is not merely economic. Referred to as "consultants," they were called on to amplify their own knowledge and familiarity with the classed experiences of elite travel.

By living the good life and instilling the desire for such a life in their guests, work processes were always quickly folded back in to leisure to approximate the experience of good living, surrounded by happiness. For instance, Purnima, another travel consultant at Captivate, invited me to have coffee with her near our office, and her driver took us there. I watched as she took calls on her cell phone, as we were often stuck for long periods in traffic snarls. Mobile technologies such as the cell phone and the laptop hosting Skype calls with clients continually facilitated these exchanges between work and private life, allowing each to channel the other, as Melissa Gregg's (2011) work on intimate technologies shows. Yet in Bangalore, these technologies are also forms of advantage that can be used by the elite to compensate for the slowness of public and urban infrastructures.

Purnima employed middle-class infrastructures—her driver and private car—to enable a good life in which she could chat with clients while on the move. While this is a form of productivity (in which the worker will work everywhere), Purnima and others were also able to draw on personal capital to intersect labor and leisure. For instance, she invited other travel consultants to her gated community, where she had organized a yoga teacher to give private classes in the club house. Occasionally the travel consultants explored new bars and pubs together; sometimes they went out to sing karaoke.

Contemporary analyses of labor, including Kathi Weeks's (2011) writing, show how worker subjectivities are rendered in the service of capitalist profit: integrating the labor of brain, heart, and mind for material and immaterial products. Kalindi Vora (2009) describes as "vital energy" the transmission of value from individuals and communities to clients overseas through affective and biological labor.[10] In corporate contexts, each employee is expected to embody the firm: affective labor produces certain kinds of laboring subjects. Purnima Mankekar and Akhil Gupta (2016, 25) describe the spaces of call centers in India as a traffic of affects, with workers continually anticipating the needs of their clients to satisfy them. Thus bodies and customer demands, labor cycles, and leisure pursuits are continually infecting each other.

These theories of affect in the service sector partially build on Arlie Hochschild's (1997) insights on emotional labor, in which she shows how the gendered labor of service work is an uncompensated and unrecognized but vital element of most service sector work. They also take inspiration from the materialist feminist analysis of the family that demonstrated how romantic love conceals the labor of reproducing and maintaining the heterosexual family.[11] My fieldwork at Captivate showed me how these affects do not just circulate in the office but draw on urban environments and classed longing in equal measure. Through these extensions, labor and leisure enrich each other in a continual feedback loop that translates into profit for the company through producing creative, cosmopolitan worker-consumers. If the dominant model of work situates the employee as an elite entrepreneurial figure directed toward company profit, how does happiness circulate for other non-elite workers?

PLEASURABLE BREAKS FROM REPRODUCTIVE LABOR

Only a handful of employees at Captivate, like Purnima, interacted face to face with guests. Like others at a more junior level at Captivate, I had the same work rhythm every day, although with a commute time of half an hour compared with their average commutes of an hour or more. I left home a little after 9:00 a.m., walked to the nearby metro stop, and took a ten-minute ride on it. On the other end, I walked for ten minutes, to arrive at the office around 9.30 a.m. Mimicking those around me, I would drop off my lunch box in the small tiffin room before settling at my desk. Work always seemed slow in the mornings; the office was quiet as people logged into email, work tasks, and Skype. We spent the day mostly fixed at our desks.

Most of us at Captivate were engaged in everyday work that involved the reproductive labor of maintaining websites, logistics, and accounts. I understand reproductive labor as the work of social reproduction that is crucial, value generating, and feminized work that—although vital for capitalism—is taken for granted and either wageless or undercompensated. Early social reproduction theories focused on the wageless "housewife" as the figure on whom capitalism depended for generation and regeneration, and as Alessandra Mezzadri writes, "Capitalism was first and foremost dependent on processes of generation and regeneration—biological as well as social—of the worker and of commodity labor power, which mostly took place outside what were considered the classic domains of production and value-generation" (Mezzadri 2019, 34).

In contemporary contexts, the figure of the housewife is dispersed through the global economy and laboring outside the home; cleaning, caretaking, and recreation are all activities that are life–generating but increasingly unfolding in public and semiprivate spaces. Thus the importance of the home as the "backbone of reproductive services is waning" (Federici 2020, 45). As Kalindi Vora (2019, 44–45) explains of outsourced service work, it is a form of labor that has inherited the low status attributed to feminized labor, supplying low-wage work to free others to do higher-valued work. I felt this devalued reproductive element viscerally in my own work at Captivate as I spent hours cleaning out online photo albums by deleting and tidying hundreds of photographs of Captivate hotels and destinations that were not suitable for the website, to present a face of the company that would generate value and profit and be desirable in the global tourist economy. Next to me, Albert worked on the accounts team, repeatedly reaching for his phone and switching between social media screens and work interfaces to enliven his day. Now and then we coordinated our breaks, swiveling our office chairs to chat or persuade someone to leave the office for a short walk in the neighborhood.

For most of us, work was not exciting or unpredictable even if it might have been essential for the company. We did not love it or hope for it to become better. My own tasks at Captivate were determined by Susan, of Scottish origin, who worked on the marketing team. She had trained me to distinguish valuable and unique photographs of Captivate destinations from more routine ones, and I had to sift through thousands of photographs with this cultivated eye. I knew every day that I would have to repeat the task of cleaning out photo albums for hours, sometimes taking a break to write website text for the Captivate blog. My manager often came by my desk to check my progress and to assign me more tasks. Affective immersion into lovable and pleasurable pursuits was thus not attached to work as it might have been for Purnima and other more elite workers, but occurred as a punctuation of the workday and a break *from* it. Unpredictable breaks were the ways in which we too could generate happiness and pleasure *at* work, although not *from* it.

The circulation of affect occurred within and between work processes, similar to what Mankekar and Gupta (2016) describe as affect animating the social. They describe call centers becoming erotically charged spaces as workers labor alongside each other, cut off from other social relations by the demands of night work (31–33). In my fieldwork, breaks from work were also opportunities for employees from different work teams to socialize; nonelite workers sometimes joined the more elite workers at Captivate for drinks out. Leisure spaces thus became performative spaces of claiming class belonging and knowing, creating new class identities rather than merely reinforcing office role-based groupings.

Occasionally, the office would give a team money for lunch out or an expedition to the bowling alley. Affective life generated in and out of work kept us charged as we visited nearby bars, went dancing, and explored the city together.

One evening some of us planned to go dancing after work. By 7:00 p.m., even as the office emptied out, we walked over to a pub that was having its Ladies Night a few streets away from the office. These nights were popular in Bangalore at the time of my fieldwork and allowed women to get two free drinks and enter a pub without paying a cover charge.

I joined a group of six other women from different teams, and we laughed our way across a somewhat dimly lit and broken sidewalk to arrive at our destination, a small pub on a second story a few blocks from the office. We wound our way up a narrow stairway and entered a still vacant space at 7:30 pm. An indigo blue circle was stamped on our inner wrists upon entry, and we were ushered to a low table surrounded by stools. There were few choices for complementary drinks,

Figure 11. Captivate Travels employees enjoying a beer after work, 2013. Photo by author.

and we made our selections almost immediately, then proceeded to pick the cheapest snacks to share. All the while we tried to generate excitement through banter and teasing to ease the discomfort of being out with colleagues from different teams whom we barely interacted with at work. This was a contingent community, formed in its perusal of the pleasures of the city at night, yet we needed each other to explore the unfamiliar city at night.

Shonali started us off with a suitably scandalous story to set the mood for the evening. She was a quick-witted twenty-two-year-old, always dressed in fitted jeans and sleeveless blouses, joking with others around her. She and her best friend from college, Supraja, had both joined Captivate together and shared a small, rented apartment nearby, as their parents lived in another part of the country. On some weekends they contacted me to ask what I was up to; they were always looking to pass time pleasurably. (One Sunday, for example, they entertained themselves by hooting at passing men from their upper-floor apartment window and then ducking to avoid being seen.)

On this day she recounted the last time she had been to this bar. She had come with her college friends, a group of young women, and she said, "I was wearing short shorts, they came till here" (she gestured to high up on her thigh). They had danced until early in the morning. When it was time to leave as the bar closed, she reached into her handbag and discovered she had not brought her wallet and had no way of getting home. She was forced to call her boyfriend at the time. "He was so mad!" she exclaimed, clearly enjoying the memory. "He had to bring his bike early in the morning, he was cursing me the whole time!"

As I have noted elsewhere (Gupta 2017), when Shonali and Supraja moved to Bangalore, their parents expected that they would work a few years after completing their tourism courses at college and then return home to have arranged marriages. For Shonali this was to be when she turned twenty-three, a year later. Shonali continually navigated and challenged these terms: she had an interfaith relationship (a Christian boyfriend) and joked that her parents would be scandalized if they ever found out about this premarital relationship (she was a Hindu). She had at some point moved in with her partner, becoming close to his mother. Despite her parent's wishes for her to practice endogamy and continue the reproduction of their caste and community, Shonali's affective disposition transfigured her world.

At the bar, she completed her story to loud laughter and then insisted we all down our drinks, hoping that the quick intake would compensate for the diluted alcohol in the cocktails. Soon we were on the dance floor, a tiny open space, arbitrarily demarcated by the arrangement of the bodies that were now pouring into the bar and heading straight to dance.

At work, Shonali updated logistics for Captivate hotels, a series of daily tasks that could not contain her affect. On her team women laughed loudly and joked almost continually with each other. We often heard their laughter across cubicles; it was uncontrolled and sudden, resisting the expectations of professional work etiquette. If happiness was the expected outlook to bring to work, it was also meant to be appropriately contained. Happiness at work is the motivational poster on someone's cubicle wall, a dedication to their work; it is not to manifest as these uncontrolled explosions of affect. Their manager frequently reprimanded them—too much laughter, she told them; they were too loud, others were watching.

After an offsite trip that I describe in chapter 6, Shonali developed an ambiguous but flirtatious friendship with a man from another team. As her laughter rose across cubicles, they often exchanged glances, occasionally stopped to chat with each other (ostensibly about work), and performed vivacious extroverted selves on full display for the office. Shonali also took lessons in belly dancing and salsa and was enrolled in a professional dance troupe, with which she performed for corporate events, often earning the equivalent of her full monthly salary at Captivate from a single show. One evening at my apartment, a few of us sat together as I attempted to eke out some "interview time" in between the everyday rhythms of work. I scanned my questions and began addressing them to Shonali. She seemed to have already decided this was somewhat of a joke, an alibi for a fun and informal evening. She explained to me that her parents were arranging her wedding. She was twenty-three, articulate, and energetic. I asked about her plans over the next few years. She looked around at the others in mock disbelief at the question. "Obviously what my mother-in-law tells me to do of course! What kind of question is this?!"

Supraja, Shonali's friend, was a little older, at twenty-six. When we both began working at Captivate, she had just changed her phone number in order to intentionally forget and delete older contacts. "I don't want to be able to contact my ex," she explained. "I want to forget his number" (see Gupta 2017). She had met her ex-boyfriend when they lived opposite each other and had been dating for nine months, until one day with little warning, he told her his marriage had been arranged to someone from his caste and abruptly moved out of his apartment. Supraja told me this story when we were out one night, and it agitated her enough for us to need to leave the bar and wander the neighborhood looking for a streetside stall that would supply her with a few loose cigarettes. Standing on the edge of 100 Feet Road, busy even at 10:00 p.m. on a weekday night, she took furious puffs of the cigarette. Later, back at the bar, she explained that she wasn't craving a long-term relationship, but she missed the physical intimacy.

Supraja's parents had begun to hunt for a suitable groom, but unlike Shonali, who was full of excitement about a married future, Supraja was not interested. "Do you think they'll find someone for me who likes rave parties?" she asked me once, hopefully. She had attended weekend-long rave parties on the outskirts of Bangalore several times a year with her ex-boyfriend, and this was an important aspect of mutual companionship for her. For Supraja and Shonali, their lives as a first generation of single women professionals in a city known for its nightlife and leisure distributed happiness so that it was not experienced in and through the primary site of professional work but rather in moments of intimacy, dancing, and revelry across varied sites that were adjacent to—but not contained within—their work worlds. When I knew her, Supraja left Captivate as she came close to turning thirty—she was already much older than most of her colleagues. Her parents were concerned that she was unmarried and living on her own. She moved home for a few years and then back again to Bangalore. When the pandemic laid off workers, she lost her job and turned to working as a full-time artist, spending her weekends on short travel trips with friends and her days sketching commissioned pieces.

The happiness that the management at Captivate expected may have been the kind that is oriented to profit, but there was a surplus of affect produced in the everyday: erotic intimacy, embodied pleasure, and the revelry of collective after-work life. These exceeded the ordered line of the need-want graph that directs happiness toward profit. While some of the more elite employees at Captivate suitably channeled affect as a productive form of labor, for most others, affect erupted out of the norms and etiquette of the workplace to guide desiring bodies and pleasure-filled evenings. I consider this too as the work of social reproduction: replenishing workers, rejuvenating their lives through dance, music, sex, and the pleasurable evenings of a night out at the local sports bar.

Prior studies of technology workers in India have found that upper-class and caste modes of speech, dress, and behavior reproduce the middle-class family in India. Smitha Radhakrishnan, for example, uses the idea of symbolic capital to explain how the "respectable femininity" of Indian IT workers is central to a "symbolically authorized middle-classness" (2011, 51). Yet among the non-upper-caste workers of Captivate—and under startup capitalism more broadly—there were deviations from respectable femininity, and from the normative compulsions of upper-caste life unfolding under the patriarchal gaze of the family. Young women who lived on their own and outside the arrangements of caste-based kinship reproduced their lives and desires away from the unit of the household and the patriarchal gaze. In the next section I shift focus from the capricious intertwining of affects, bodies, and spaces to examine how relations of affect produce formations of care at work that queer the idea of "family."

REIMAGINING THE FAMILY AS A SITE OF CARE

Most women at Captivate could have secured comparable jobs in call centers but did not want to risk the public stigma that accompanies call center work. Sushma, a Captivate employee, explained to me, "I did not want a call center job . . . you know why, no?" She paused briefly but definitively in the middle of her explanation, and I nodded, knowing what she meant. Her pause gestures to the dominant circulation in middle-class discourse of call center work as stigmatized for young women. Respectability is named as a central contradiction for South Asian women, who navigate expectations that they will behave with the docility and restraint expected of middle-class and upper-caste women along with being successful professionals.[12] As Michiel Baas writes, "In Bangalore, working at night is both a burden and a sign of success, of making it happen, of working successfully hard" (2007, 66). Captivate's workers who were unmarried and living on their own could refuse the disciplining of their bodies and desires into middle-class and upper-caste respectability, but for those who had been divorced or lived with their families, their status was already precarious, and maintaining it was partly achieved through their choice of work.[13]

IT companies in Bangalore are frequently located in large, gated communities with facilities for leisure, rest, and fitness (see Baas 2007) that mark them as middle class and thus a suitable and desirable place for upper-caste women's work outside the home. Architectural markers such as glass and chrome exteriors are accompanied by the mobile signifiers of middle-class work: the chartered buses with corporate office names taped to the windscreen ferrying in employees, or white cabs hurtling across nighttime streets to transport women employees working late shifts (see Patel 2010). Sprawling lawns and campus eateries ensure workers can remain within these gated communities for meals, fitness, and leisure. These multinational office campuses ensure the preservation and reproduction of caste, class, and gender as women are transported between the homogeneous spaces of home and the typically upper-caste spaces of technology work. During my research on the contemporary neoliberal startup economy, workplaces were not supported by such large-scale infrastructure. Instead, in small offices of rented floors and low-slung bungalows, professional women assumed responsibility for their own well-being, leisure, and safety. They did this through building and maintaining what I understand as infrastructures of care. Care and social reproduction are not synonymous;

instead, care is *one site* of social reproduction, one mode through which life and capitalist relations are reproduced at once (Mezzadri 2019, 37).

At Captivate, Sushma, who lived alone with her mother after her father passed away, felt the burden of establishing herself as a respectable woman. She declined jobs at call centers, knowing that office cabs would move in and out of her neighborhood for her drops and pickups at odd hours of the night and early morning. She found Captivate an attractive alternative. As a global entrepreneurial firm, it offered her the respectability of an office job without needing a technical or specialized degree. She would never have to work late hours. Sushma's choice to work at Captivate emerged from a relation of care for her mother; she chose a job that would protect the public face of her family, maintaining them as respectable members of the middle class.

Absent these material infrastructures of middle-class life, at Captivate women often fostered the relations of care that would establish their life and work in the entrepreneurial sector as livable and respectable. Several times I heard the workplace and colleagues described through the narrative and affective construction of "family." The family was summoned in differing and ambiguous ways, and I came to realize that this was necessarily so. As ahistorical, ambiguous, and amorphous, the "work family" was a gesture to ties of kinship and care rather than the specific contours of middle-class heterosexual life. It is an indication of how care creates interdependencies among workers, challenging the liberal conception of the self as an individual and autonomous one. Thinking with and through care situates it as a feminist epistemology from where to interrogate the fantasy of sovereignty (Meyer 2024), and in my fieldwork, the fantasy of entrepreneurial autonomy. Relations of care extended to colleagues, care for one's own family as with Sushma, and presented a sort of ethical orientation to the world.

At her sunny two-level home built on top of her landlord's house, Susan, my manager at work, showed me her terrace garden of potted plants. She had also written a book on ecologically conscious weddings and sometimes volunteered as part of a local group that cleaned up neighborhoods on the weekends. She lived near the office and clocked long hours. When we met, she explained why:

> By this stage [a few years after working there] Captivate was my life. I live and breathe it. I breathe the passion of the individuals in the office: the family. I always say Captivate is like a family . . . one big diverse global family. We don't always know each other that well because we live in different countries, but we share the same values and passion. (Interview with Susan, October 2013)

Sipping tea in Susan's house, her words about the work family conveyed the sense of text on a corporation's official web page: a semblance of worker unity and satisfaction projected through smiling faces. And yet as she described her past work and her attachment to Captivate, I could understand how work came to be experienced as meaningful by producing it as nested within relations of care. Convened in this way, it lends work value by seemingly pulling it apart from its role in profit production to locate it as meaningful. A work family allowed Susan a sense of belonging in India despite being an expatriate, and she could imagine herself in a multiracial family with Indian, Spanish, English, and Scottish workers all together. At festive events, Captivate employees often invited others to their homes; small gatherings of employees, all dressed in regional finery, would gather to celebrate and eat a large meal together. Work thus becomes a practice of meaning making and world making that transcends the self.[14]

I read the trope of the work family as a narrative device; it indexes Susan's place within a collective whole even while ambiguously obscuring the hierarchies within it that allowed her to claim patronage by the company and belonging to it. Inherent in this mobilization of family is its production within market relations, nested within it as a relation of care. Conventional accounts of the family and market mark them as distinct, a relationship that Sareeta Amrute notes as "interdigitation rather than opposition" (2016, 159–60). Thinking of "family" as such an imbricated grouping allows us to consider how the idea of family and the practices of making one might move in and between the contours of a conventional heteronormative family. Thus, Susan could think of a family that cements her belonging in Captivate as an expatriate worker and visitor in India, she could extend the very conventional families of her colleagues to include herself in them, and she could imagine her work as meaningful through the trope of family. The market and the family move in and out of each other so that they are familiar but also being remade. And so perhaps from this unlikely site of the entrepreneurial office, we might queer the family and untether it from its conventional form.

Queer theorists remind us that most attempts to queer the family retain its structure and centrality. For example, Carly Thomsen notes that attempts to move "beyond" the family by thinking of it in terms of care rather than biology still gesture to the family through the imagination of "fictive family" and the assumption of invisibilized labor to maintain its relations. As Lee Edelman (2004) has called for us to "Fuck the Child" and abandon the commitments to politics that are predicated on reproductive futurity, Thomsen (2021) asks if we need, in fact, to "fuck the family." What I explore here is the unexpected disfiguration of the heterosexual family with these capitalist settings: it is cited and reiterated but in such different ways that it loses any central coherence. Central to why it is specifically the *family* form that so many interlocutors held onto is perhaps their reliance on the "family" as granting respectability and a future of multiracial and multireligious relations of care—a desirable alternative to thinking of the self as an employee generating profit and commerce.

These relations of care that are expressed through narratives of family at Captivate shape the possibilities of worker mobilization as they soothe and place individuals within a community.[15] The incident

I began this chapter with—Apu and her friends wanting infrastructural support and then changing their minds—indicates one such moment in which employees realized and articulated the absence of the company's care toward them. As Apu and others empathized with the stress of senior management, they simultaneously distributed care among themselves to shoulder the burden of what was absent and to become the missing infrastructure themselves.

Such moments of ambiguity were not uncommon at Captivate. Workers continually negotiated their sense that Captivate was the best job they could have, secured with their feeling that they could demand more benefits or expect more from the company. What I find crucial is how the situation ended: with workers sharing rides home. The company "family" fostered interdependencies, and workers relied on each other to manage the situation. Not all workers shared rides home and, as I show later, not all workers were offered rides home by colleagues. Instead these forms of care were extended unevenly: to specific office friends, to those who lived close by, and to those from the same community. Thus through the offer of care and the types of care offered, new infrastructures of work were formed. As Virginia Held writes, "Care has the capacity to shape new persons with ever more advanced understandings of culture and society and morality" (2005, 32), thus care does not merely reproduce material and biological realities while what is new and creative and distinctly human must occur elsewhere. In the absence of company care, new socialities and relations are produced.

Employees who had begun working with Captivate when it was first launched explained that they worked long hours, from 9:00 a.m. often until midnight, with no formal timing. As they built teams and generated business, work hours were determined by when work was completed. In this context, the narrative device of "family" might be read as legitimating close and caring interactions between unmarried men and women by convening them through the logics of the heterosexual family.[16] As a media columnist in a national daily explains, a familiar tactic in India to publicly remove the possibility of a sexualized relationship is to deploy a familial term with a stranger of the opposite sex (Krishna 2015). Calling someone a "brother" by tying a sacred thread on them during the annual Raksha Bandhan festival, for instance, can categorize a relationship as familial, precluding a romantic liaison. Yet these references to "family" convene vital relations of care that extend beyond a family unit. Maria de la Bellacasa writes, for example, that "standing by the vital necessity of care means standing for sustainable and flourishing relations, not merely survivalist or instrumental ones" (2012, 198).

Relations of care embed people in long-term dependencies and friendships. I frequently observed men who had their own bikes waiting for women to complete their work to drop them at home. At Captivate, imagined as a small and intimate "family" space, the dangers and taboos associated with being outside home—at work with strangers—were navigated through the familiar imaginaries and rhetoric of the middle-class heterosexual family. They generated relations of care but also enabled who cares for whom and how. "Care organizes, classifies, and disciplines bodies" (Martin et al. 2015, 627); it is selective in its choice of object, choosing what to pay attention to and what it can neglect. Trafficking in the practices of the middle-class heterosexual family enabled women to expect rides home, but also enabled men to decide who would do late-night pickups for guests and determine which women obtained rides home. I frequently witnessed those from the same region giving each other rides while other young women waited long hours for a bus ride.

The trope of the family assembles relations of care that lend work and life meaning and foster mutuality and interdependence.[17] Yet these relations do not emerge independent of the structuring forces of heteropatriarchy: care within the "work family" is thus "already distributed into racialized, postcolonial, economic, and transnational stratigraphies" (Murphy 2015, 722). Thinking of the family as an assemblage of relations of labor, care, and affect allows me to understand how the family functions as a mediating force, negotiating lives past and present and assembling the possibility of feminist futures. Lata's story elaborates on this.

LATA'S STORY: GROWING UP IN THE COMPANY FAMILY

Lata had moved to Bangalore from a small village where her parents worked in the informal labor market, selling produce for a daily wage. She studied for a bachelor's degree at a local college and then answered a job in a newspaper for a position that became her first job. While there, she made a contact who told her about a job in Bangalore. Her parents watched, somewhat helpless, as she boarded an overnight bus, took an entrance test for the position, and returned home. When she was offered employment, she moved to Bangalore. She was an important source of income: with three brothers, all apparently diffident and unambitious, Lata was a promising wage earner. Her parents allowed her to leave home, albeit with some reservations.

She described her first visit to Bangalore as one in which she alighted from the bus and "felt something in the air" that told her the city held promise. She had rented a small apartment in Bangalore, with two others, paying about $63 per person per month. A stranger to the city, she knew no one else and found a weekend spirituality class to give her free time some direction. There she met someone whom she fell in love with, and a year later she married him. By now her parents were reconciled to the idea that they could not restrain her wishes and ambitions. She helped them financially, called them every day, and maintained close family ties. Something terrible seems to have happened once she was married that Lata (and anyone else who knew her) would not talk about to me except to say regretfully, "Such a sad thing to happen to someone like her." She left her husband the day after their wedding and filed for divorce.

She told me this story—with key details missing—when we were lounging on my bed in the apartment I shared with Naina one evening, making small talk. She told it lightly, as if we had discussed it in detail many times before. I did not want to tell her I had heard bits of it before, or that others in the office had mentioned it discreetly. "You didn't know anything about it, right?" she said, with a light laugh. I could sense she was proud of having so effectively concealed such a significant detail of her life from me—someone she spent so much time with. With startling clarity, she explained to me that Captivate had given her the financial independence to be able to make the decision to divorce. This is still a radical break for most middle-class Indian women, who will linger in an unhappy marriage on instructions from their parents to keep public reputations intact or from their own private sense of duty and forbearance. Lata told me how Pushkar—probably only a few years older than she was—trusted her. She described their relationship to me as though she were telling a story about her childhood: "When we were small [meaning when they first joined], he used to do lot of things on his own, which he passed on to me. He's [Pushkar] a very good mentor who can mold you, train you" (Fieldwork interview with Lata).

By referring to her past as when she was "small," Lata articulated a coming-of-age narrative in which she grew up in the company, nurtured by the founder. Despite the managing director's wish to establish a flat work structure and for employees to take the initiative for their own development, employees like Lata refused the terms of this relationship. Instead, referring to herself as "small" and to him as someone who could "mold" her imbricates them in a meaningful, parental bond. She told me that she accepted this job because Pushkar trusted her with financial matters just a week into her joining; she compared this with the lack of "trust" at her previous company.

Lata took the family metaphor further. When her ex-husband began stalking her on the phone, it was her "brothers" at work (as she called male colleagues) who called him and threatened to report him to the police. It was work "brothers" who visited her after midnight on some nights to make sure she was all right. They remained her close confidantes. Her family appeared in her story as mute spectators to a wedding and divorce that they attended and contributed to as much as they could financially and emotionally, but that ultimately involved a set of circumstances far removed from their own practices. When she described her divorce proceedings, she narrated how she was working on her laptop throughout the protracted trial. Even the decision to get divorced was enabled by applying company ethics to her personal life:

> You make a mistake; they will never say anything [the founders]. They encourage you to learn from it. I think that is what I applied in my personal life also. I knew I made a mistake and I wanted to learn from it. That's how I thought I should move out of it. Some things you learn in your professional life and you apply in your personal life also. (Fieldwork interview, Lata, Oct 2013.)

At Captivate, in Lata's telling, the work family not only was a new family; it was attuned to her life in intimate and telepathic ways, assessing her needs, anticipating her desires, and guiding her through them.[18] Thus the work of social reproduction—meaningful, essential forms of feminized labor, care, and value production—under startup capitalism occur through relations in the workplace. Lata's sentimental attachment to colleagues—glossing them as "family"—helped her to think through a set of circumstances from which her biological family was alienated. Her family would have insisted she stay on in her earlier marriage, making her work ultimately untenable and preventing her full and complete thriving.

In her second marriage, Lata did something I suspected she had done in her first too—she bought gold jewelry and gifts from Bangalore and handed them to her mother, who formally presented them back to her in the appropriate ceremonies. She explained to me that when her husband's relatives gossiped about what her mother had given, there would be the correct checklist to tick off. Her relationship to her natal family allowed her to express her affection by performing her role as a dutiful daughter, but it was through the work family that Lata could access a realm of sympathetic care and inspiration. It was not only important that the work family provide relations of care; this care enabled the social reproduction of capitalism through which Lata could survive and thrive in her job. Her ability to work according to the logics of DWYL was predicated on a stable and fulfilling intimate life that was supported by her colleagues' care. Their care was attuned to her own desire for a feminist future based on affirming her autonomy, pleasure, and bodily sovereignty.

FANTASIZING RESPECTABILITY: PERFORMING WOMANHOOD

Relations of care among Captivate employees extended to each other and themselves but also to the office's physical spaces. Employees decorated cubicles and office walls for festival celebrations and marked spaces of work as though they were family homes. Offices, labs, and factories might appear to be the sanitized spaces of industrial and postindustrial modernity, but they carried with them the markers of caste. Science labs in some Indian settings are spaces where caste Hindu practices are expressed and legitimated as "cultural." Thus Ayudha Puja—a festive "worship of machines"—is analyzed as a practice that "normalizes Brahmanical Hinduism within scientific culture through the inclusion of non-Hindus and through scientists' description of the festival as "cultural" rather than "religious" (Thomas and Geraci 2018, 95). At Captivate, the actual day of celebration of a festive event was entangled within caste relations but also within a larger set of pleasures and intimacies. But what if we were to decenter upper-caste actors from the story of how festivals are marked at offices? Rather than see the celebrations as the reproduction of dominant religious practices, I see them as a stage for unruly figures to perform desirable forms of womanhood.

Before Diwali, Sukhleen, who was on a human resource team dedicated to organizing team outings, recruited me to accompany her to buy festive decorations in Shivajinagar, a crowded central city neighborhood where such decorations were being sold at wholesale (bulk) rates. We set off on her tiny scooter, after she had wrapped her hair up in a cloth covering and held this in place with her helmet. I clambered on behind her, and we set off across pot-holed streets in the late evening after work.

On our way, quite near the office, Sukhleen pointed down a street. "That's my parent's house," she told me. Her father owned a mechanic's shop, and her mother ran a paying guest accommodation for young women who had moved to the city. Sukhleen did not speak to them anymore. When I first met her, she was wearing red bangles that ran high up her wrist, symbolizing her recent marriage. Sukhleen had fallen in love with a man outside her Sikh religion and had eloped to marry him, leaving her house at midnight one New Year's Eve when her parents had visited a nearby *gurudwara* (Gupta 2017). When they finally found her, she was already married; although there had been a rapprochement of sorts, she barely talked to them now. I was surprised to see that they lived so close to the office.

When we reached Shivajinagar, we found a parking spot for scooters and pulled over. Sukhleen seemed to know the area well, although it wasn't near work or where she lived. "I got married at the temple here," she told me, pointing down the street. "Want to see?" We walked to it, avoiding traffic and puddles from the recent rain. The temple was a small one, a faded blue, with a single deity set back from the road. We looked at it for a while and then continued onward to the deals and discounts available deeper in the neighborhood. Sukhleen knew the vendors she wanted to shop at, so we walked past the men shouting out offers to us.

Across mounds of colored powder and stacks of firecrackers we selected some clay *diyas*, colored powders, and an assortment of firecrackers for our personal use from three different sellers. At the end, Sukhleen loaded a massive plastic bag onto her handlebars and stuffed smaller ones under the seat of her bike. If we were to analyze the celebration of Diwali solely through the lens of how spaces of modernity like the office are rendered "Hindu," we would miss the ways in which the significance of the festival was dispersed across several days, combining evenings out in preparation for it and a blend of pleasurable commerce, the gendered labor of preparing for it, and the celebration on the day of the festival. For Sukhleen, the opportunity to perform a sort of idealized caste womanhood through the careful selection of colors and lights and organizing the festival celebration at the office allowed her to establish her respectable gendered status in a way her own biological family had not yet done. Shopping for Diwali and participating fully in its festivities allowed Sukhleen to chart her own figuration of idealized womanhood.

By 8:00 a.m. on Diwali morning, Surekha, another employee, in jeans and a T-shirt with the sleeves rolled up, was kneeling on the office floor drawing a design across the entrance. She had found a tricolor pattern on the internet and referenced it on her phone as she drew. Bent over the white tiled office floor, she marked outlines in chalk and had us fill them in with colored powders. The circular pattern was arranged around a brass lamp that someone had brought from home. Gradually others came in and joined her.

At age twenty-six, unmarried and living and working on her own, away from home, for Surekha the office space offered a canvas to etch a domain of expertise. Many of those bent over the lamp that morning were upper-caste Hindus but did not lead lives embedded in the expectations of caste endogamy and middle-class propriety. Studies of corporate culture suggest that occasions such as "sari day," when celebrated in a transnational corporate office, offer sites at which to translate diverse Indian practices into a mobile set of global "Indian" norms

Figure 12. Rangoli decoration at Captivate Travels office celebration, 2013. Photo by author.

(Radhakrishnan 2011). Captivate's own employee base is far from the South Indian middle-class ethos of most IT companies. As an entrepreneurial company that does not require or demand specific technical skills and training, its workers are from different regions, castes, and religions.

Surekha was living an unconventional life, routinely neglecting her family's wishes that she get married and "settle down" into family life. Yet she wanted to partake in celebrations by remembering festive practices she had learned in her own family. The office celebration allowed her the opportunity to participate confidently and independently in reproducing her learned skills, while enhancing them through Google searches for complex designs. Bent over the *rangoli* pattern, passing around the phone to replicate the pattern pulled up on it, this was a technological mediation too—although not recognized or valued as such.

Diwali at Captivate allowed some employees like Sukhleen the opportunity to explore the city and immerse themselves in the sensorial commerce of the festival. She could perform herself as an ideal woman, reproducing religious and cultural practices in a way that her parents would not grant her. Hindu others, like Surekha and those who joined her on the floor, drew on their childhood experiences of growing up celebrating Diwali at home to create new social community among colleagues at the office. They performed womanhood but also challenged gendered labor in ways that aligned with their sense of themselves as professionals in a transnational entrepreneurial company. Their happiness at work was achieved by forging new and desirable versions of themselves and unlikely forms of community expressed through the office celebration of Diwali.

UNEVEN INFRASTRUCTURES OF CARE

On Diwali day, we were expected to come to the office in traditional Indian clothes. I had a few saris at home and finally decided on a narrow blue *bandhni*-print sari with its matching blouse to wear to the office. I watched some videos for how to best drape it and finally decided to let its *pallu* fall naturally, as I had seen my friends do with theirs.

As I walked into the office on Diwali morning, I could sense that it was a festive day right from the entrance. Little clay *diyas* had been lit along the reception counter and colorful thermacol ones were attached to the walls. Everyone was dressed in special clothing: saris for the older women and salwar kameezes for the younger ones. The men were in *mundus*, a formal shirt draped over them. People smiled and greeted me, nodding and smiling indulgently in acknowledgment of my clumsy efforts to drape a sari. I arrived at my cubicle and put down my handbag; Sneha, who sat behind me, swiveled around in her chair, aghast. She immediately offered me her honest and uncensored opinion of my efforts. "What's wrong with you?" she wanted to know.

"You look like a local!" She got up from her seat to take charge. When the social infrastructure of the office was threatened by the possibility of breakdown or dysfunction, it was quickly repaired and corrected.

Unlike Ritty Lukose's (2009) description of Keralan women, for whom being "local" is also to be rooted in local understandings of appropriate gendered behavior—a signal of virtue and belonging—in the transnational enterprise, "local" was used to chastise me. In case there was any doubt as to how she used the word, she explained further that I looked like a "woman on the bus"—a working-class woman, someone whom she imagined as disheveled and unkempt. I had left my sari fold loose and unpinned as women in my family and all my friends did, but the threat of a fallen *pallu* was to her a sign of being out of place in a professional environment. An upper-caste woman from the professional class would drape her pallu by pinning it in place.

Sneha's efforts to quite literally pull me into a place signaled her mastery over professional and class-appropriate behavior, a performance more about her expertise than about my own failure to master the norms around clothing.[19] In keeping with the notion of the company of family at Captivate is the corresponding expectation that all members will uphold family values and decorum. In these performances of sari wearing and *dupatta* draping, a specific meaning of the family is filled in: it is an institution reproducing middle-class, bourgeois values in which women's correct public femininity upholds their family's honor.

Historically the moral discourse of the Indian middle classes posited the gender relations and sexual mores of the patrilineal and patriarchal family system as core to "Indian family values," maintaining middle morality within the terms of Brahmanical culture and nationalist ideology (Upadhya 2016, 273–74). Sneha's evocation of middle-class respectability as distinct from working-class presentation echoes the devaluation of manual labor by the middle classes (see Qayum and Ray 2009).

I was hastily propelled to the tiny office restroom, where Sneha pulled safety pins out of her black coin purse and attached them to the errant runaway folds of my sari, attempting to pin me in place. Held tightly in place, I had now attained a sufficiently "professional" office look. Sneha had performed the care work of repair and maintenance, adjusting me to fit in with the others at work. Employees continually adjusted their own clothing, performing a form of what Susan Leigh Star and Anselm Strauss (1999) term "articulation work." Articulation is "the art of fitting, the myriad (often invisible) activities that enable and sustain even the most seemingly natural or automatic forms of order in the world" (Jackson 2014). Apu also reminded me how articulation work is sometimes ceaselessly performed when I photographed her a few weeks later. "Wait!" she said when she saw my camera. "Let me look a bit more professional!" and then proceeded to adjust the dupatta of her salwar kameez to neatly cover her chest.

While the literature on global workplaces as families has focused on the discursive ability of cultural and corporate discourses to discipline workers (Kondo 1990) or on people's turn to work as a substitute for the satisfaction derived from family life (Hochschild 2001), in Bangalore the entrepreneurial workplace is produced through the infrastructures of care that I analyze in this chapter. These are social infrastructures, mediated and galvanized through friendship, class, and caste but not in deterministic ways. For example, many employees at Captivate came to know of the company through others whom they went to college with; employees recommended and provided references for each other to get a job there. Apu heard of the job through her mother, who had heard about it from a friend, Ahana's mother. These networks not only cohered caste communities; Apu and Ahana were from different religious, caste, and class backgrounds, yet their mothers knew each other and extended the forms of care that would enable their daughters to receive an opportunity to work at a professional office. These friendships—sometimes birthed in college, sometimes through their parents—are infrastructures of care. They enabled each other to be recommended for jobs and extended to how they supported each other in everyday work: sharing rides on monsoon nights and maintaining a closeness and affection that allowed work to unfold smoothly.

Articulation work is performed continually, as employees adjust each other's clothing and cohere in social groups to partake of the pleasures of the city. Understanding the work "family" as a social infrastructure is thus to also pay attention to how these groups are produced through networks of care and communication, repairing and rejuvenating themselves by directing care to themselves as the travel consultants did, or to each other's well-being as young employees did for office rides and in personal crises. Thus the startup adage Do What You Love is provincialized to adapt to local networks of care and commitment: an affective charge that animates social infrastructures. These are slow infrastructures, articulating with failed public transport, erratic opportunities to perform as middle-class professional women, and propagating opportunities for middle-class work to those outside elite networks.

THINKING ABOUT FAMILIES AND CARE WITH UNRULY SUBJECTS

Infrastructures of care animate the work of social reproduction and make it possible for employees to chart meaningful work relations and social and intimate lives under startup capitalism. I read the many references to "family" as work as a narrative device that centers the uneven conditions of work and capacities of care through which employees make meaning of the classed and gendered worlds of the startup economy and offer support to each other. These forms of care and sustenance produce a willing, available, and steady workforce that startup capitalism relies on for its forms of creative work and DWYL mantras.

Yet care is not innocent of larger structures of power, as Michell Murphy (2015) argues. Positive affects can work through these structures rather than against them. It is noteworthy in this context that care for the material spaces of office life was expressed through the celebration of Diwali and an office Christmas party rather than a Muslim festival, or that articulation work drew bodies in line with caste Hindu practices of respectability. The conjoining of care with hegemonic practices was made visible through ruptures in the "archive of happiness" (Ahmed 2010) at work. Just as each family contains the unruly figure, the dissident body, the feminist killjoy at the dinner table, so too is the fantasy of a coherent Captivate family ruptured by the individual life histories of its members.

Sneha tied my sari and disciplined me sartorially into middle-class respectability even as she disarticulated from such respectability in her own life. As a young divorcee with a preteen child, she moved to Bangalore to live on her own with her daughter to make the salary needed for fees and a middle-class life. Some months after we first met, she was forced to ask her parents to move to Bangalore to help her, and all four of them crammed into a tiny one-bedroom apartment located in a narrow lane adjacent to a slum. Susan dated erratically, trying dating sites and apps, all the while negotiating living far from her own family. Lata was divorced and trying to find a new partner, to start a new life. All around me, articulations in one register were disarticulations in another.

Relations of care enabled new friendships and hopes that deviated from management's instructions about work practices and behaviors. For instance, analyzing Diwali celebrations at the office not only during the actual celebration at work but by extending my lens into what came before it, I came to understand Diwali as an opportunity for forged intimacies at work and possibilities to explore the city as an unruly subject.[20] A substantial literature on care work has focused on migrant women's care for their employers' offspring (Parreñas 2004). Martin Manalansan (2008) queers care work by challenging its heterosexual logics and shifting the focus to Filipina drag queens who also perform care work. By situating work families as relations of caring between unruly subjects, I similarly disentangle care from its role in (re)producing the heterosexual family to consider how it might produce and sustain unlikely lives and unconventional ways of living.

Queering the family through an attention to the lives of workers at Captivate—the lover, the rebel, the divorcee, the single mother—pushes us to ask how tropes of "love" and the "family" are assembled to reference infrastructures of care. Thus, attachments to work are not only marshalled for capitalist profit through the affective labor demanded at work but also enable social infrastructures through which the city is navigated and pleasure is embodied and protracted. Calling forth the family is thus not a reinforcement of heterosexual marriage norms but an arrangement of uneven relations of care. Ideas about love and the family are artfully deployed and inhabited to produce new forms of community and social life. These are the promiscuous pathways through which startup capitalism is conducted through bodies, spaces, and affects.

Reading the management graph presented earlier in the chapter alongside Surekha's rangoli pattern, we might witness how creativity and care emerge in a register other than the imperative to DWYL for capitalist profit. Rupturing dominant expectations of what happiness looks, sounds, and feels like, Captivate's employees generate new experimental socialities and subjectivities. Emergent forms of care allow unruly subjects to engage institutional frameworks like the family and corporate mantras of happiness and love but also to reorient their meaning and purpose. Social reproduction—understood as the invisible, back-end labor of maintaining the workforce—is now enacted in the semipublic space of the office and in the spaces of city streets, adventure activities, and nightclubs. Looking beyond for-profit happiness, we see how current conditions of startup capitalism draw on the invisibilized and continuous labor of creating the missing infrastructures of care that sustain the illusion that we can all do what we love.

6

TESTING THE FUTURE

Experiments in Everyday Life

<hr/>

I FIRST HEARD about El Calafate, Argentina's elite travel destination, at a small hostel for women in North-West Bangalore.[1] It was a Sunday, and I had taken a bus from my mother's apartment to visit Archana, a young employee who joined Captivate at the same time I did. Archana and her new colleagues joined entrepreneurial companies like Captivate often as a first generation of professional labor. As I interviewed people at the office, I asked them about their parents' paid work; their mothers typically worked as nurses, daily wage labor, or in government companies. In this chapter I show how the desire for experimentation among workers is essential for the larger techno-capitalist experimentation that technologists at companies like Captivate seek to implement. While the elite workers of India's digital economy have typically been known to reproduce the dominant norms of Brahminical patriarchy, thus achieving no substantive gains for gendered freedom, as Sarasvathy Raju (2013) argues, this chapter shifts to nonelite workers to demonstrate an economy of experimentation and self-remaking among them.[2] Following labor as method, I trace worlds of work across sites of experimentation that include leisure, fitness, and adventure.

The bus lurched past leafy streets and showrooms for Levi's jeans and Titan sunglasses. Occasional small homes wrestled for space between airy, spacious stores. Aggressive signs in front of small bungalows marked the rapid urbanization of the neighborhood: "Park here and I will kill you" read one. "Park and Die" read another. At the bus stop, Archana was waiting for me, her hair still damp from her weekly hair washing, dressed in a T-shirt and casual cotton pajamas. As we walked over to her hostel, a middle-aged man stopped to say hello—the hostel owner. Archana quickly told him I was interested in moving there. He asked me if I had a job, and when I told him I did, he waved us on. Visitors are not allowed at Archana's hostel, so I had to be snuck in this way, as a prospective, respectable tenant.

Finally, we arrived at a broad two-story building. We made our way up a small staircase, past a washbasin out in the corridor where a young woman was brushing her teeth. We reached a room where several young women lay on bunk beds, poring over textbooks ahead of an upcoming medical exam. We could only access Archana's room through this outer room.

"Hi," Archana said to them. And then, pointing to me: "This is my boyfriend." They all laughed. "So this is your secret visitor?" one of them said, jokingly. She moved aside on the bed to make space for us, but Archana told them all that we would go into her room, accessible only through this outer one. In the final inner room—Archana's—two bunk beds were at angles to each other. A small dresser with photographs of Hindu gods pasted on it covered part of one wall, and in a corner a few steps led up to a tiny bathroom from where we could hear someone washing clothes.

Archana shoved aside a pile of washed and unfolded clothes to make space for me on her bed. I asked her to tell me about working at Captivate. She began by telling me about her favorite destinations to recommend to the elite guests for whom she prepares travel itineraries. El Calafate was at the top of the list. "Of all the places I have heard about," Archana said, 'El Calafate is my favorite. . . . [O]nly our most adventurous guests travel there."

I had never heard of it before, so I later went home and looked it up on the Captivate website. It was classified as a "nature" destination, a "dream come true": "Deep in southern Patagonia lies El Calafate, a region of ice-fields, frozen lakes, wide-open spaces and vast estancias. . . . For those who enjoy the great outdoors, tranquility and being as far away from the trappings of modernity—El Calafate will be a dream come true."

Archana lived across the world from the scenic landscapes of El Calafate. She had arrived in Bangalore only a few months before our interview, after several earlier attempts to live and work there. When she graduated from a local college in her hometown in North Karnataka, Archana got a job selling cell phone plans at a local store. She registered her resume on a job portal and got some interest from Bangalore-based technology companies. For her first campus interview, Archana took a bus and came to the city. She stayed with a cousin at a local hostel much like the one she lived in now, and they both decided to go to the interview together. The interview was on a corporate technology campus on the fringes of the city, and they took two buses to get there; her cousin's local knowledge and confidence were essential.

As the interviews progressed, dusk came on, and it turned dark. Archana told me that she and her cousin began worrying about how they would get home—buses were few and far between, and their hostel was well over an hour's journey away. Finally, they decided they had no choice but to abandon the interview and head home. But after this disappointment, just a few months later the job portal Archana had registered on turned up another job, this time at Captivate.

At her interview, team leads at Captivate asked Archana about the vacations she had been on herself. She told me glibly that she had invented imaginary vacations, although she had only traveled with her family to meet relatives who lived in a nearby town. When she got the job, Archana was assigned to a team that built specialized itineraries for guests to South America. Her aim was to become a "destination expert," the term for those who excel in knowing and understanding the details of hotels and routes on their teams. She was informally mentored by Apu, about the same age as she, who sat beside her at work. This mentorship allowed Archana to learn from Apu not only how to route trips but also how to navigate the itineraries of everyday middle-class life in urban India.

As an employee of a global and entrepreneurial travel company, Archana routinely participated in new experiences: office lunches at hip cafés in the startup neighborhood of the office; meals at fast-food restaurants that friends treated her to; and—the highlight thus far—an off-site trip on which employees went rafting, stayed overnight at a resort, and splashed around in an infinity pool overlooking lush coffee estates.

Such moments of exhilaration and adventure marked Archana's work in an ambitious entrepreneurial environment where companies train their efforts to compete in global markets. Managers at Captivate hired a young and flexible workforce who were expected to learn quickly, adapt to innovative technologies, and demonstrate their fitness for the job through subjective and embodied modes of refashioning—such as being willing to raft and swim. Thus, the cognitive work here— of populating travel itineraries and updating logistical information online—was also concrete (Amrute 2016, 29) and materialized through everyday work practice.

But by the end of my ethnographic fieldwork at Captivate Travels, the mood among employees was decidedly sober, even bitter. Around 30 percent of the workers in the Bangalore office had been replaced by new forms of robotics and automation—the effects of new innovations by the consultant technologists. Archana and others lost their jobs with little notice. Others anxiously feared they would be next. These are forms of racialized and feminized labor that are precarious; routed to the India office; and assigned to workers deemed replaceable even as they are expected to infuse everyday work with energy, enthusiasm, and happiness.[3]

How do workers make sense of the exhilarating promise of creative work and simultaneous reality of precarious labor in the startup economy? How are these feelings related to the labor of startup capitalism? This chapter outlines a form of experimentation that does not just theorize techno-capitalism as producing experimental subjectivities. Instead, I show how experimentation is embodied and materialized through everyday work practice and dreams of the future—it is felt through *experimental time*. The experimental time of startup capitalism requires precarious and feminized work to flourish. Feminized labor, as I have mentioned before, is not just "women's work," but rather, following Kathi Weeks (2017), the conditions of women's work that are now the generalized conditions of all work.

In the startup office—a laboratory of techno-capitalist innovation—I enlarge our attention from the rich feminist literature on experimental subjectivities to show how experimentation unfolds temporally. First, it reworks labor as experimental future making. Second, experimental time emerges as a fantasy space allowing workers to inhabit other bodies and subjectivities during work. Finally, in the third section of the chapter I show how young workers become the "test subjects" of an experiment in innovation as they are invited to participate in testing the forms of automation that finally replace them. Experimental time is also created and inhabited by technologists who remake themselves from back-end workers and cyber coolies into desirable, creative innovators. Thus while other studies of entrepreneurialism suggest that workers continue to love work in the hope of better conditions in the future, here I understand the future as a condition of inhabiting the present. The future is lived in this current moment as an experimental possibility that does not necessarily yield long-term structural change.

LABOR AS EXPERIMENTAL FUTURE MAKING

One day I sat with Apu, a trip adviser, to understand how exactly trip itineraries were crafted. Following global labor chains, Apu in Bangalore was planning a trip in South America for a guest from Australia, a single woman traveler. Apu traced lines along computer-generated maps: "So she'll land in Buenos Aires. . . . [S]he's coming from Australia, so she'll be tired . . . so we'll give her two nights here." She selected a hotel for her guest and offered an activity—"visit to the Argentine side of Iguazu Falls"—and then the next stop, Mendoza. "Here she can do wine tasting. There are lot of outdoor activities also—horse riding, rafting, bicycling. Then after the outdoor activities she can have a one-hour massage," Apu said. She entered options on an itinerary: a map linking places, foods, activities, hotels, and modes of travel that together offered a unique experience.

"She'll be tired, no," Apu mused as her cursor hovered on the screen. Her guest had just been offered day-long treks into two national parks driving her own vehicle. "[W]e'll give her one more day here, then she can go to Santiago"—an option was ticked off on the screen—"then the next day she can return from another route so she sees something more." The red line was dragged along the map, and the planning for this twenty-nine day adventure, estimated at a little over US$30,000 in 2013, continued.

As Apu experimented with the itinerary, chopping and changing options for the desired outcome—"a relaxing once-in-a-lifetime travel opportunity"—she anticipated and crafted pleasure for her Australian guest. This was a form of "anticipation work": "a forward-looking frame to capture practices in the present that cultivate our expectations of the future, design pathways into those imaginations, and maintain those visions in the face of a dynamic world" (Steinhardt and Jackson 2015, 443). Significantly, Apu was not shaping her own future but rather anticipating another's future and, in the process, cultivating her own sense of experimentation.

The conditions of Apu's labor also produced aspirational futures in the present moment—experimental ones—through which young women imagined themselves in other bodies, temporarily inhabiting the elite worlds of leisure and adventure travel of their guests around the world. Given patriarchal restrictions on women's travel for pleasure and their own economic dependence on their larger families, Apu and her colleagues could not travel or be as mobile as their guests, but they immersed themselves in the photographs and labor of travel. I understand this as a form of experimental future making that produces real and pleasurable results in the present moment.

Although Apu's labor was invisible to her guests, she saw their photographs when they sent thank you emails back to Captivate. She might also read about their experiences and adventures, which were published frequently on the company blog. Routinely, the photographs that Captivate guests sent of themselves and their families on holiday were circulated in the Bangalore office. Apu and her friends commented on the special pose someone adopted for a selfie or the clothes that a mother-daughter duo wore on their trek. Apu also sent her guests rich and colorful images: each final itinerary that she typed up was an image-heavy document, bursting with textual information and colorful photographs of hotel rooms, monuments, and landscapes.

This back and forth of images enabled the circulation of desire and fantasy in the Bangalore office, enabling young women to enter transnational labor chains as consumers and travelers, creating new pleasures within the digital labor of back-office work.

The continual interaction with these photographs and itineraries shaped Apu's own possibilities for cultivating experimental adventures. One afternoon, she leaned over the low cubicle wall separating our desks at work and offered her cell phone to me. She had pulled up an image of two people I did not think I knew. She pointed out one of them—her mother—and the other was Apu herself. They both wore big hats and sunglasses in selfies with pouting smiles. Apu's working-class family never took vacations; their trips outside home were to visit relatives nearby. Yet recently she had successfully transformed the brief minivan ride to another part of Bangalore into a vacation-type photoshoot, inhabiting an experimental time that fashioned other possible selves.

Archana too fashioned varied selves after work. One day she noticed the sign for a contemporary dance class flash below her on her bus ride to work. The signboard advertised B-boying, hip-hop, and breakdance lessons.[4] She scribbled down the first half of the phone number quickly as the bus passed; on the way back home along that same route in the evening, she jotted down the other half of the number. She enrolled in the class to learn hip-hop.

Her class was in a densely crowded area, next door to an expanded stall that sold coconuts. I attended one evening class. The street was empty except for a young man walking a dog that strained at its leash. Her class was on the top floor of a narrow building, one flight above a working-class gym advertised by a massive poster of a muscular man posing with his flexed biceps foregrounded. The air in the stairwell was tepid with the smell of sweat. The top-floor terrace, barely covered by strips of wood and tarpaulin, had been remade as a dance studio.

At the more expensive dance studios in other neighborhoods in Bangalore, middle-class fitness enthusiasts arrived straight from work and use the facility's showers and changing rooms to wear their exercise clothes. Here at Archana's lesson in this lower middle-class neighborhood, participants came dressed for class in street wear—more appropriate for the kind of urban street culture they were practicing. After a brief warm-up, two women students dragged out thin sheets of foam to use as dance mats for floor moves. The young male instructor began teaching complex routines. Everyone learned quickly, and then they moved on to "face-offs": two or three of them performing what they had just learned with the rest watching.

Archana told me that she initially wanted to join salsa class because she had seen it on TV, but "salsa ke liye partner chahiye hota hain, na [for salsa, you need a partner, no?]," she explained, so she started with hip-hop class on Saturdays. I asked her, "Why salsa, because they have it in South America?" since Archana worked on Captivate's South America team. But she corrected me: "No, vahan pein belly dance karte hain na [No, over there—South America—they have belly dance, no]." She had no particular reason for choosing this form of dance except that she spotted the sign on her bus route home and she loved to dance. I am in touch with Archana now, and she no longer dances. She lives in Europe with her husband, who is part of a project with a software company. She has a small baby and is a full-time carer, staying connected with friends and family via WhatsApp and an active presence on Instagram.

Experimental time for workers like Apu and Archana was not only a frame encountered through the travel, leisure, and consumption at work but equally a way to apprehend and shape possible futures and selves.[5] At Captivate, the workplace offered experimental mediations to shape labor as a form of temporal work. The circulation of images, emails, and descriptive text of elite holidays combined with the materiality of a growing urban leisure culture to mediate the possibilities of experimental time. Archana's participation in her dance class might not have totally reshaped her being and subjectivity, but it offered her pleasurable immersions in transnational urban subcultures and a chance to play with experimental time and future making.

EMBODYING EXPERIMENTAL TIME IN UNCERTAIN ENVIRONMENTS

The neighborhood of the Captivate office was known as a "startup" neighborhood because of the number of entrepreneurial offices based there. It was filled with cafés, restaurants, and pizza parlors at which customers could try new foods and shape socialities. Captivate's management tried to stay connected with this urban environment through planned outings: bowling evenings, weekly visits to local cafés and restaurants, and ordering food delivered to the office.

One afternoon the CEO realized that all the company-sponsored lunches had featured Indian food. Each week, a different team selected what kind of food to order in, and they invariably settled on Indian food. He exploded in exasperation: "C'mon guys, try something new! We're a global company!" After his directive, the team who chose lunch that week selected Mexican from a nearby café. When the deliveryman appeared with the food, people looked anxious. Employees unpacked the lunch in the common cafeteria where we all ate together, guiding each other through new foods, encouraging each other to try a new dish.

When we went out to nearby cafés, we similarly performed the labor of steering each other through unfamiliar environments. Sitting with my team in a new German café in Bangalore one afternoon, anxiety was palpable as the waiter approached us. Team members faltered over how to pronounce the names of desserts on the menu—"mouse?," "mousse?"—and had to check their criticism of the bland food: pizza without spice or a burrito that tasted like a *roti* gone wrong. These are the "uncertain environments" in which adventures in experimental time unfold. In his work on gastropolitics in Mumbai, Harris Solomon

Figure 13. Neighborhood where Captivate Travels office is located, 2013. Photo by author.

Figure 14. Captivate Travels employees dubiously examining the new Mexican food ordered for office lunch, 2013. Photo by author.

notes that pizza parlors act as social laboratories for experiments in creating the common symbolic ground of consumption (2014, 24–25). Drawing on Adriana Petryna's work on experiments as operative environments for redistributing resources, he shows that experiments at material sites of food consumption also craft competencies and regimes of value among gastro-publics (see generally Solomon 2014, 24).

In our typical encounters with new cafés through work at Captivate, we found that menu options were unpredictable, and you could never know where you were supposed to sit or stand or what food accompanied another.[6] Uncertainty refers to one's ability to access genres of acceptable behavior and to prepare oneself for immersion or engagement with new social worlds of consumption and leisure. On the day I visited Archana's dance class, for instance, she was not able to attend. She told me later that she only went to every other class: her single set of exercise clothes that she handwashed never dried in time for class in Bangalore's moody monsoon weather. Experimental time is thus marked with uncertainty and stoppages as hesitant subjects acquire the modes of navigating them and slowly learning to take pleasure in or express distaste of them.

These possibilities for pleasure continually place the bodies of an aspirational middle class in environments that remind them they are out of place.[7] For example, one afternoon Lata urged two of us from the office to accompany her to a nearby store selling cell phones because she wanted to buy a new one and was hesitant about interacting with the store staff. We had just stepped out of the office when a sudden and unexpected monsoon deluge enveloped us. We stumbled through the rain looking for shelter, but all we found were the upmarket stores that surrounded our office. I wanted to duck into one of them, but Lata and Albert, our other colleague, hesitated. They would be reluctant to step inside this store even normally, let alone to use it so obviously as a space of shelter to avoid a downpour. We argued for a bit, getting soaked all the while, and finally in exasperation I ran in, knowing they would follow. They did, but almost immediately Albert was mistaken for a salesperson: "Do you have this in a Medium?" a woman asked him, waving a *salwar kameez* on a hanger. It took only a few seconds for a body to be marked out of place; not only as a man in a woman's clothing store—there were several others—but as someone who was not understood as properly belonging there as a consumer.

Another time I was out with Lata she took me on her scooter to Safina Plaza, a nearby shopping complex that was a popular commercial destination before the burgeoning mall culture of the 2000s. There was a large handicrafts sale going on, and we were both keen to see if we could score some good handloom material that could later be tailored into salwar kameezes. Local craftsmen from around India had set up stalls, selling reams of cloth, saris, jewelry, and flip-flops. Lata was comfortable in this indoor bazaar environment as a consumer. She wandered around open tables looking for things to buy her husband's family for an upcoming trip to their home, ready to haggle with salespeople.

After we picked up some cloth, we got hungry and decided to eat a *kaati* roll from a nearby fast-food chain. We picked up two rolls and noticed that a large central faux lawn area had outdoor seating with cane chairs and tables arranged on it. There was nobody around, and the seating area was empty. We decided to sit there, but even as we settled on the chairs, Lata became overcome with a fear that we would be asked to leave. We got up and asked the fast-food restaurant's manager if people actually sat there. He told us they did, but even so, after we sat down again, we began preparing what to tell the security guard whom we expected to remove us. Even as we ate, we continually anticipated the shrill whistle of the guard asking us to leave—and thereby publicly embarrassing us—at any moment.

Such incidents with Lata and others from the office mark the hesitancies, anxieties, and failures of inhabiting experimental time. If startup capitalism places a premium on the modes of experimental time that might yield new innovations and produce global subjects, it also creates the disjunctures and frictions through which bodies are rendered out of place. Public cultures of shopping, eating fast food, and relaxing in outdoor spaces are the settings in which experimental time might yield new sensorial pleasures. These experiences are also marked by feelings of vulnerability and public exposure that cause discomfort. I finally saw Lata carefree and at ease when I visited her in the state where she grew up, where I attended a conference during my fieldwork. She had planned a visit with her husband so we could all spend time together before I left to return to graduate school in Atlanta. We went to the local beach one evening, and her husband bought us peanuts to eat as we walked along the shore. She was completely at ease, taking photographs and fooling around. I had almost never seen her this relaxed in Bangalore except for the rare occasion when we ran errands to buy clothes from a local street vendor.

Such uncertainties that mark experimental time necessitate forms of care and support that workers can offer each other. On Apu's birthday, I received a discreet text message inviting me to a pizza lunch that she was hosting for a few close friends at a nearby café. I turned to her when I received it, and she silently mouthed, "Please come! Tomorrow!" Birthday lunches and treats for raises at the office were always small, discrete groups since one person paid the bill for everyone.

On the assigned day, we quietly left the office and walked to Pizza Hut, a nearby pizza parlor that offered fixed lunch combination plates. Outside the wide glass windows the fledgling Bangalore metro rail trundled past occasionally. A billboard advertised diamond wedding jewelry. As everyone settled down, Apu turned to Archana, who was listlessly turning the menu pages. "You can order the Friday discount lunch deal," Apu told Archana decisively. "You can choose the drink between a Sprite and a Coke, and you can choose which appetizer, either the chicken wings or the garlic bread option." Apu had barely looked at the menu, but she knew what everybody would eat (and what she would be paying for, as the birthday host): the lunch combo at Rs. 95 (less than $2) a person.

Similarly, everybody already knew exactly what they wanted. They had been to this café several times before, and everyone always chose the same options. These were "safe" choices—consuming at a fast-food restaurant rather than at the restaurants with "set menu" options around us—pedagogical experiments as well as pleasurable ones, opportunities to learn how to eat and relish the food in a safe environment with others like you.

Captivate's workers fashioned themselves in the experimental time of startup capitalism as the company's CEO hopes that moving, inhabiting, and consuming in these urban contexts *during* office hours might enable competencies and fluency in the spaces of new bars, restaurants, and cafés to make his workers "global" subjects. These invitations into new worlds of consumption shaped how workers themselves oriented to the tastes and commerce around them. Yet environments were uncertain and often hostile to workers; as they tested, tasted, and navigated their way through unfamiliar sensoria and material spaces, they cultivated their bodies to understand the appropriate kinds of pleasure expected of professional middle-class urban subjects. Workers managed their anxieties and desires through forms of care and friendship for each other that charted their own itineraries through new middle-class environments.

MAKING THE EXPERIMENTAL

Occasionally the desirable future arrived materially in the present as Captivate Travels enrolled its employees as "test subjects" to viscerally inhabit the preferences of their intended customers. Indian employees were sent on a "test" trip (to Indian destinations only) upon completing two years at the company. As the company cofounder explained to me, "Participating in test trips . . . people get to see what it means to be in a [Captivating] hotel—that level of exposure and ability to see things from a guest perspective . . . is unique."

For most employees, traveling to a Captivate destination was their first time on an airplane. They laid the groundwork for a guest trip by staying in the hotels, traveling the routes, and participating in the activities that their guests would. These trips with colleagues to different cities in India were anticipated with excitement, and women prepared for them meticulously. They often required getting permission from unwilling husbands or fathers. Before Apu was to leave on one such trip, I noticed her furiously whispering audio messages via WhatsApp into her phone weeks ahead of time. She was persuading her brother, who worked as a taxi driver in Dubai, to in turn persuade her father that she should be allowed to go on a trip with her colleagues.

Although anticipated as pleasurable—a first airplane ride and hotel stay for many employees—on their return, workers adopted a far more clinical air to describe their experiences. In trip debriefs back at the office, employees recounted details of the hotel services and the viability of the options offered to their guests. Quite methodically, those who traveled described each step of their trip and rated and reflected on its suitability for the anticipated guest. Others took diligent notes. The experimental time afforded by the trip was calibrated and assessed by the relevant team.

Yet for many employees, the significance of these trips—with their attendant bargaining and negotiating with larger patriarchal family structures—lay in the opportunity to strategically craft themselves as legitimate workers. For these precarious workers from nonelite backgrounds, the experimental time afforded by these office trips and their leisure was a condition of fluency in professional environments. Young workers situated themselves within an anticipatory experimental framework—bracketing their own affective immersion in the travel to divine how imagined guests might respond or react.[8]

Workers also prepared themselves to be ready for experiments in new environments. A few months into my work with Captivate, employees were invited to an off-site trip on which we would go rafting and stay overnight at a resort overlooking coffee estates. The initial briefing at the office was filled with nervous anticipation: How can we raft if we cannot swim? What if we drown? What if our families do not allow us to go on the trip?

On the morning of our trip, we were to assemble at the crack of dawn outside the office. It was still dark when I left home, and I struggled to find an auto, arriving only minutes before the rented bus was ready to leave. Inside we squeezed among friends, everyone still sleepy eyed and in casual tracksuit pants and T-shirts. It was an office outing, but it felt different. We hugged our backpacks close to us and discussed how everyone had managed to get there with so little public transport available at that time of day. One of the managers asked if anyone was missing and began a head count. Sakshi was missing. Her friends called out from the back that she lived with her in-laws, who hadn't allowed her to make the trip, but that she would still try to catch the bus before it left the borders of Bangalore.

We set off on our way, the bus racing down near-empty streets, towering over smaller motorcycles and bicycles that we passed by. At a second stop in the city, we picked up a few more people, and a manager asked again about Sakshi. "She's still trying," her friends yelled out from the back of the bus. "She might still come!"

"We have to leave now," the manager replied, and the bus slowly began moving. As we picked up speed, a motorbike pulled up alongside the bus. Sakshi was seated behind her husband; she rode astride on the bike, her hair billowing in the breeze and a black overnight bag balanced on her lap. She waved for the bus to stop. Her friends in the back cried out to the driver, and Sakshi was soon able to clamber onto the bus.

Later, sitting beside me on the last seat, she told me her parents-in-law, with whom she lived, had not consented to her going on an overnight trip with a mixed group of strangers. She and her husband told them she was going to her mother's house. She had to drop her overnight bag out a back window so as not to raise the alarm when she left the house. Her husband—who worked at Volkswagen as a salesperson—then raced across town with her till they caught up with the bus. The excitement of this initial incident seemed to mark the whole trip, indicating what was at stake in participating in this brief weekend of experimental time. It was a window of opportunity to explore varied modes of embodiment, sociality, and freedom.

At our first stop a few hours out of town, the managers handed out small snacks and showed us a small changing room to get dressed ahead of the rafting expeditions. Most of us emerged in rolled up pants and T-shirts to meet the rafting crew, who taught us how to strap on our life jackets. When the time came, the rafting organizers guided us onto inflated rafts, and most employees began protesting, and they were overwhelmed by the prospect of this adventure. People intertwined hands, held onto each other, and struggled together against the wind and water through the multiple levels of the rapids. Men gallantly held onto women, and the officious demarcations of space and bodies in the office hastily collapsed as the rapids surrounded us. We were invited by the event organizers to jump into the water at a placid spot, and some of us did, but for most of the group, in cut-off pants and wet T-shirts, intimately holding onto each other was excitement enough.

Through the weekend we immersed ourselves in other such entirely unpredictable activities; wading fully clothed to float in an infinity pool, trying our hands at basketball at the resort court, and staying up all night to chat with those who had been strangers on other teams just a day before. We returned to Bangalore after two days of sharing rooms, exchanging snacks and stories, and singing all through the bus ride.

Figure 15. Captivate Travels employees enjoying an off-site trip, 2013. Photo by author.

Off-site trips like this one have been described by anthropologists as corporate efforts to train flexible bodies. In a particularly evocative image from Emily Martin's (1995) ethnography *Flexible Bodies*, she finds herself slumped forward in a body harness, suspended from a tree during a training workshop for corporate employees. Martin uses this moment to return to a central question the ethnography poses: What does it means to be a person today (Martin 1995, 213)? She reminds us that the ideal for American corporate bodies (institutional and individual) is derived from a management approach called total quality management (TQM), which requires a constant adapting to environments in flux in order to survive (Martin 1995, 143–214).

I consider this expedition at Captivate as more than a management effort to train worker bodies and cultivate the flexibility and experimentation required for them to be appropriate workers in a "global company," as their CEO phrased it. For workers themselves, the expedition was a crucial marker of the anxieties, pleasures, and possibilities inherent in experimental time. While these modes of bodily being and becoming might reflect a form of flexibilization staged by the corporation, they also point to the expedition as an experiment in the making. As employees encountered the rapids, the infinity-style swimming pool at the resort, and long evenings of song and dance on the bus, they shaped themselves as fun, outgoing, experimental subjects. On this trip they were not experiencing and anticipating pleasure for someone else; they tested a way of being for their own selves that they might or might not be able to inhabit after the trip. Middle-class futures were being tested in this present moment; it was a respite from the rules governing office behavior and decorum that now allowed forms of fantasy and play to unfold.

After the trip, new intimacies resulted. The bus ride and the night spent out, mostly awake and chatting, and the time spent splashing around in the pool changed the dynamics of the office itself. Members from different teams exchanged flirtatious looks across cubicle tops the next morning, and new groups emerged. In the startup environment of Bangalore, the bodies of Indian women simulate the correct responses to new food and experiences, thus indexing themselves as legitimate workers in the transnational entrepreneurial economy. A new form of class and gender experimentation is a disruptive moment in which non-elite, working-class labor becomes the site for embodied experiences of consumption, leisure, and adventure unfolding in experimental time.

JOB CUTS: TESTING THE AUTOMATED FUTURE

Workers at Captivate were often invited to share ideas about how to rethink work processes. Ahana, a Captivate worker, explained to me how she devised a template for a work process. It was then adopted, and she was exhilarated as she described the feeling that she had shaped something at Captivate. But despite these occasional feelings of worth and value among employees who were encouraged to love work and assume responsibility for it "as though it were their own," Captivate's management didn't view workers within the same regimes of value. Both Captivate's managing director and its chief technology consultant explained to me at various times during my research that the goal of the company was to retain creative work while automating all other kinds of labor—like the work of Ahana, Archana, and Apu.

The company's consultant technologist, Krishna, often worked in a corner of the office hunched over a laptop, with a small team gathered around him. Every few months he rolled out a new technology. He was testing new software that could automate Captivate's work of building itineraries. Seated among employees, I heard the groans and saw the discomfort with which employees received his emails. Perhaps the women sensed that all this experimenting would lead to fundamental changes in the company.

The job cuts, when they finally came, right after my fieldwork ended, made about 30 percent of Captivate's Bangalore team redundant. Krishna later described to me what he had achieved at a time when the company was not turning a profit and faced the risk of sinking:

> [W]ith (our in-house technology) the turnaround for an itinerary was about twenty-four hours and work between two teams. This is now reduced to thirty minutes and one team member.
>
> A few years ago when their [Captivate's] business went down, everyone acknowledged it but had no idea where to start. The company would have gone down; we took a huge risk with technology, a lot could have gone wrong and it was very expensive, there was a huge investment made. . . . I felt what I was doing was possible. Two teams vanished and we were 30% less people with 50% increased profitability. . . . There was a lot of restructuring and people left the company. (Fieldwork interview, Krishna, September 2018)

This description of workplace automation fulfills what technologists call revenue per minute, the aim of which is to employ the fewest people and to make the most use of their time and resources. What these narratives do not always show is how technological innovation emerges through social infrastructures and caste-related values that are attributed to different types of work. Krishna's own history and his enchantment with modern experiments in software point to how projects in innovation derive from the social and political worlds in which they are embedded.

Growing up in the neighboring state of Kerala, Krishna was born into a business family. "My hands got dirty at fifteen," he told me. "I come from a business family, I was helping my dad in the factory, he had a mechanical shop for kitchen equipment, it was his dream to automate human efforts to machines. For instance, grinding *dosa* batter, mixing *papads*. I was working as a delivery boy and intern in the factory; when the exams overlapped I would be on the road! My factory couldn't afford the taxi so I was (myself) a taxi service and delivered things using the private vehicle."

Krishna was introduced to computers when he was in school in the late 1990s; his first exposure to computers was with Windows 95 and computer classes on summer vacation. In his iteration of his life's events, he was engaged in manual, embodied, and unglamorous labor prior to his introduction to computers. Being introduced to computers was life-changing. He loved the experience of learning about computers in school enough to take computer engineering as his major in college, where he continually supplemented his knowledge by reading books about coding and writing small programs on his own.

When he graduated, he only wanted a job using open-source software: "At that time it was like men marrying men or something, it was unthinkable," he said. His college had invited Richard Stallman from the Free Software Foundation to speak to the students, and Krishna said that after the talk he thought Stallman "made complete sense. . . . I was drawn to Linux because it made learning available to everybody without stealing or hacking." Linux emerged among coders in

Bangalore as a radical alternative to capitalist practices—here in the postcolony, software engineers could build a global future.[9]

Krishna was entering the heady heyday of open-source computing in the 1990s; his need to immerse himself in free knowledge creation and sharing code was conversant with other aspects of his life. He joined an ashram "with the purpose of serving humanity," he said, and that journey brought him to the outskirts of Bangalore, where the Art of Living Foundation has a massive setup. Krishna had been reading the famous Chicago lectures of the Indian philosopher Vivekananada when he came across a line in which the philosopher urges his readers: "If there's a living master, drop everything and go meet him." Krishna did that. He dropped everything to meet someone he considered a living master: the guru Sri Sri Ravi Shankar at the Art of Living school in Bangalore. Here, among devotees in pale pink robes, he began using his computer skills to help the ashram—converting software to Linux and helping with any database-related work.

Krishna's interest in programming and his preference for this form of work over the work he was doing in his father's factory mark a caste-ascribed valuation of the work of the mind over that of bodily labor.[10] As a sensory, affective labor regime sedimenting value, it is caste that links laboring bodies with low-status work; the need for the higher spirituality of philosophers and the work of the intellect is the practice of Brahmanical supremacy. Elaborations on freedom from manual work and routine are also the freedom from caste-based work; innovators are clear they do not want to be confused with software "coolie" work, understood as racialized labor.

When outsourcing first began in India, the euphoria over newly available jobs was soon offset by cynicism about the kind of work that was being sent to India. When Thomas Friedman, the *New York Times* journalist, visited India to research his book on globalization, *The World Is Flat*, he met a company CEO who reassured him that Indians would never take away American jobs of value; what was being sent to India was the low-end work that Americans would not want to do. Thus liberated from "bullshit jobs" (Graeber 2018), they could focus on the skill upgrading required for more intelligent and creative work. The cultural critic Harish Trivedi (2003) called this kind of work that was being sent to India after the globalization of the 1990s cyber coolies work, an extension of the legacies of colonialism that determine the type of work performed by laboring Indian bodies.

Krishna said to me: "I realize that I'm doing something similar to Dad—he was also an innovator craving for managed innovations—I hate this role of 'product management' which has such a distinction from innovation but I started work when the division wasn't clear to me. I'm not engaged in being a software coolie or a product manager."

Describing himself as "not a software coolie," Krishna's words become crucial to understanding how attempts at automation are not driven only by profit or the need for sustainability, although those are the ostensible reasons he gave for automating processes. Instead, he calibrated forms of work along a continuum of what is creative and valuable and what is routine and expendable. Krishna emphasized technology as key to Captivate's future; the company's founders clearly shared this belief because he was now part of senior management. "Technology," as Lilly Irani argues, "does cultural and financial work, mobilizing subjects, citizens, value, and visions of progress" (Irani and Sengul-Jones 2015).

Technologists' investments in robotic futures are haunted by the specter of coolie work that has both defined Asian labor and located its relationship to the West as one of extraction in which colonized bodies have provided the labor to sustain colonial capitalism. I am using coolies in the sense of Moon-Ho Jung, who writes: "Coolies were never a people or a legal category. Rather, coolies were a conglomeration of racial imaginings that emerged worldwide in the era of slave emancipation, a product of the imaginers rather than the imagined" (2008, 5). *Coolie* is the term that I use here from a lineage of racialized Asian workers, typically indentured labor, who worked as "mobile slaves" in the Americas (Yun 2008). As a racial image, the figure of the coolie invokes the servitude of workers moving in circuits of colonial capitalism but still indentured and affixed to their owners; they sometimes called themselves "unfree laborers" (Yun 2008, xx).

Mythri Jegathesan notes that geographically the coolie was dispersed and moving across European and Asian empires as early as 1581; it was first noted in the archive ambiguously and later with more precision as menial, subhuman labor (2019, 12). In her ethnography of Hill Country Tamils in Sri Lanka's tea plantations, she rightly marks the relationship between the figure and racial imaginary of the coolie with mobility and movement: "Integral to these former concepts of coolie is movement—the physical move from homeland to industrial landscape, the capitalist move from person to payment, the calculated move from labor to commodity, and the oppressive move from human to subhuman" (Jegathesan 2019, 12).

Another kind of emphasis on movement is crucial to understanding how contemporary technologists in Bangalore distance themselves from the racialized and demeaning labor of "coolie" work that has been tagged onto back-end software outsourcing to India. Here, the capacity for professional mobility marks work as valuable; Krishna narrated his labor in order to differentiate it from historical relations of colonial capitalism. He explained to me how he relinquished prestigious jobs at major corporations that are the marker of middle-class success and upward mobility in urban India:

I also wanted to explore what it meant to work for a large company and so I worked for a bit for Adobe and Yahoo and discovered that people were always talking about how bad lunch is or how bad their manager is; I knew I couldn't go back to corporate. I have to find some way not to work for someone. My biggest frustration was not being close to the business leader—to know their perspective is a lot more liberating. For instance [he turns to the floor beside us], if this floor is dirty I need to ask the owner why and he may tell me the reason and tell me his future plan. [For example, I will get an automated robot to clean the floor,] but if I ask the man who mops the floor he will just be able to clean it and not tell me why it is dirty or what to do about it. If I'm not close to the problem statement, I can't work. I need to work with someone who knows what they are solving. (Fieldwork interview, Krishna, September 2018)

Krishna's quest for liberation and freedom was articulated in and through various social and philosophical practices including seeking out yoga, philosophical traditions, and coding Linux software for free. The relations binding these different lifeworlds constitute what Christopher Kelty (2008) terms "recursive publics": a moral field in which technological publics are recursively constituted through their music, leisure, and coding. Innovators and design workers in technology can also be thought to move in what Lilly Irani develops as the emic concept of the "scene" wherein members of a design studio "saw a scene as a context of partners, shops, and work spaces that lent inspiration, resources, and credibility to their own individual studio" (Irani 2019, 83). Members circulate figuratively in and through differing forms of cultural, entrepreneurial, and creative production, building on what Tim Ingold describes as "knots formed by lines of people's practices" and what Turner might describe as the "cultural infrastructure for the production of innovation" (both quoted in Irani 2019, 113). Thus the scenes are social life made productive, in Irani's words; through these scenes, people become more than their work for multinationals (2019, 112).

For Krishna and other technologists whom I met in Bangalore, "scenes" of yoga, Linux, and entrepreneurial creativity were creating a form of experimental time in which they attributed value to their labor and distinguished themselves from salaried employees, back-end workers, or even managers tied down by bureaucratic infrastructures. For Krishna, it was the Hindu philosopher Swami Vivekananda's

Chicago lectures that were compelling; when he moved to Bangalore, it was to the globally attuned Sri Sri Ravishankar ashram, where devotees from across the world gathered at the carefully labeled Art of Living International Center, and the compulsion regarding the free software was via Richard Stallman, the American president and founder of the Free Software Foundation. Every weekend when Krishna participated in, and led, yoga sessions, he integrated his practice into an understanding of work itself:

> The basic thumb rule is that "if you breathe well, you can think better," I encourage everyone who works with me to take up some fitness to handle the emotions. There are a lot of emotions in working with startups, many different people come to the table and they don't always understand each other. Some are thinkers, some are doers, there is nothing called "I know it," there is always experimentation, so you reduce the time and minimize the risk since time is equal to money. The challenge is that thinkers talk and bring points to the table, which can be confusing for doers, in collaborations there are a lot of emotions in a high energy work environment so we need some inner engineering, we need to be committed to physical exercise because when you do that your emotions wash away or you get the time (when you're running or swimming) to reflect on a mistake or to say sorry. (Fieldwork interview, Krishna, September 2018)

It is telling that the physical exertions of the body are not related to labor but to self-care and elevated selfhood, which are caste-based understandings of the essence of Brahmanical life. However, this is not only caste politics or caste capitalism writ large. Krishna was also describing a form of mobility that allowed him to draw on one world to enrich another: these affects were sutured in and through his embodied experiences. He was deeply interested in assuming a mastery over Indian practices that receive transnational validation—his fluency with the aesthetics and embodiments of yoga was experienced as a form of liberating freedom.

This is a conceptualization of the fully human as a distancing from caste work and gained via a sense of mastery over the encounter between East and West. As Julietta Singh argues, "Engaging the logic of mastery that had long since governed over the colonies was critical to restoring a full sense of humanity to the colonized subject, to building a thoroughly decolonized postcolonial nationstate, and to envisioning less coercive futures among human collectivities" (2018, 3). As an entrepreneur, technologist, and innovator, Krishna Iyengar felt freed from the belittling suturing in place that comes from offshore work. He was now empowered by work consultancies and the ample funds that allowed him to travel abroad and back. His mastery over yoga and software were carefully chosen fields that allowed his transnational movement and helped him acquire validation and legitimacy.

In the time since my fieldwork, Krishna's technology has been implemented, and most of the itinerary can now be built automatically. When Captivate's Travel Consultants chat with their guests, they can directly generate itineraries using the software. The painstaking work of assessing a client's exhaustion, choice of route, and activity is now approximated by the software, rendering the work of Bangalore-based employees like Ahana and Archana unnecessary.

THE ROBOTIC FUTURE

As workers, Ahana and her colleagues joined the innovation efforts at Captivate and aligned themselves with the "we" of the company, taking pride in devising new processes and shaping work culture. Yet this sense of belonging and ownership of work obscures the differential value of workers.[11] Given the relations of care and kinship that had been generated among workers, the layoffs were experienced as a personal betrayal.

Unlike other conditions of precarious labor, such as in India's informal sector (Sanyal 2007), there was a particular intensity and quality to the precarity that Captivate workers experienced in the aftermath of the layoffs. Worker responses to the loss of jobs were framed in privatized terms. One woman explained to me that she was removed from work because her particular manager was unsympathetic. "She does not understand how difficult it is for me to commute two hours on a scooter on such bumpy roads," she explained, attributing her retrenchment to the fact that she often worked from home. Others cultivated a resentment of the technologist Krishna that they often expressed publicly. These affective ties to work—the very conditions of labor in the startup economy—also distill how people understand the effects of automation and their current precarity.

The case of layoffs at Captivate offers one way in which to understand how the raced and feminized labor of startup capitalism sustains its proliferation and its visions for the future of work. While Captivate is a small and entrepreneurial company, its example of how labor is demarcated and how affect is mobilized is not unique. Across the varying conditions of startup capitalism, workers are promised that they are being offered creative or flexible work that is deeply meaningful. Uber drivers are promised great profits if they work just that one extra hour. Amazon MTurk workers are offered work in their homes and in flexible time. At Gimlet Media, an ambitious company based in New York, Black producers were continually encouraged to work, promised that when their podcasts achieved desirable ratings, they would be made permanent.[12]

The overarching feature of these examples of startup capitalism at work is how experimental time is mobilized toward corporate profit. By holding out the promise—and the fiction—of how work might be rewarding and profitable for vulnerable workers, startup capitalism creates the conditions of precarity that sustain its own profits. The promises of creativity and flexibility are the affective ties that bind contractors, temp workers, and employees to the conditions of work—they work in the continual hope that their next Uber ride will yield a great profit or the next task on MTurk will be the one to have made the long work hours worthwhile.[13] And yet it never seems to happen. Veena Dubal's (2020) powerful work on startup capitalism in the United States shows, in fact, that significant gains of the New Deal (namely the end of piecework and the institution of a minimum wage) have been ceded under startup capitalism as workers enter the wage market per task/ride.

Yet at Captivate Travels, I did not find that worker experiments reinvested in the hope of a better future. Experiments in sociality and time were oriented to fashioning new possibilities in the present. Workers found pleasure in the daily modes of pleasurable middle-class consumption that is a part of the workday, and they used the opportunities at work to experiment with fitness, leisure, and adventure.

IN EXPERIMENTAL TIME

Innovation at work in the entrepreneurial economy is framed as an "open experiment"—all are welcome to join. A feminist orientation toward innovation specifies the terms of this labor. A gendered and racialized workforce is created as companies invite young and vulnerable workers to be trained by them and then to inhabit jobs that are framed as creative, exciting, and meaningful. The promises of future making within the worlds of startup capitalism appeal especially to young women inhabiting the experimental time between the end of formal education and their later commitments to affinal kin, parents, and reproductive labor. Even for married women, experimental time is fluid and potent, a realm that can be inhabited through the consumption and leisure of middle-class life that unfolds at work. Thus mobilized, heterosexual domestic arrangements make this in-between experimental time of work under startup capitalism especially meaningful and pleasurable.

For technologists and innovators, automation promises entry into a world of work that is creative and meaningful—this is not the back-end coolie work of racialized imaginaries of workers in Bangalore. Automating to achieve the maximum human potential creates the figure of the human as one who is spared manual labor and racialized work. The technologist is the mobile figure of creative, global labor, circulating in new elite coworking spaces and transposing the norms of Brahmanical work into the startup world.

Meanwhile, it is the women from low-income families who are the first professionals in their households to form a class of precarious workers who are replaced by technological change. They are the surplus feminized labor of capitalist work and become enrolled in the space of the office as an experimental laboratory. Operating in uncertain environments of leisure and adventure, they experience the sensations of being bodies out of place, of anxiety and trepidation, as they are prepared to be the forms of work and middle-class leisure that signal the global company. Yet these precarious lives are also central to work productivity and capitalist profit. Their deeply embodied labor anticipates and predicts the leisure of affluent consumers, indexes the company as global and middle class, and knots the allure of startup work into their own commitments to the company. As professional employees, young women are especially suitable candidates to be enrolled in experiments to test and perfect new technologies. They contribute their care and affective attachments to growing the company and enabling its profits through both their ideas and their participation in innovation.

Unlike India's large informal sector, in which workers exist on contracts, work project to project, and may frequently be unemployed—that is, the informal sector that Kalyan Sanyal (2007, 209) terms the "need economy" or "the ensemble of economic activities undertaken for the purpose of meeting needs"—at Captivate, workers were invited to join an experiment in innovation. They experimented with new systems, suggested new processes, and tested itineraries both physically and imaginatively. The workers whom I have introduced here did not perform frontline care or servitude like call center workers. They were a part of the experiment themselves, tinkering and changing life and labor, theirs and others, within the unfolding of experimental time. Workers were encouraged to be entrepreneurs, aspiring to be middle class, imagining themselves as travelers, caring for the company as though it were their own.

The concept of experimental time is thus crucial to understanding new gendered figurations of labor and anticipatory futures in the transnational startup economy. In this chapter I have taken inspiration from the rich literature in feminist science and technology studies (STS) that establishes the gendered and racialized use of Black and brown women's bodies to situate experiments in medicine and pharmacology.[14] Feminist STS points us to the experiment as "[a] subjective orientation toward the world and toward society in everyday practices . . . [m]oving beyond the realm of the laboratory and clinic into the larger field of material culture and consumption" (Towghi and Vora 2014, 2). I have shifted emphasis to ask how the experimental time of startup capitalism maps futures of labor.

I suggest that affective investments in startup capitalism allow experimental time both to be the time of testing new innovations and to enable forays and experiments in inhabiting new middle-class modes of leisure and consumption. This chapter makes clear that experimental time is not only the blatant exploitation of precarious workers; instead, I traced how it enables forms of pleasure and future making that allow experimental time to be embodied and inhabited, however temporarily. What attachments and collectives are made possible by inhabiting such time that is insistently in the present?

CONCLUSION

Feminist Itineraries for the Future

FEMINISTS HAVE long struggled with how to account for the persistent and draining effects of doing underpaid and undervalued gendered labor. Their primary responses to work have been to demand equal access to waged work, revalue unwaged work (see Weeks 2011, 12, 13; Federici 1975; Nadasen 2015, 2017), and, under capitalism in the South, interrogate how the central promises of work have been differently embodied (Sekharan and Tandon 2021; Islam 2022). The feminist political philosopher Kathi Weeks suggests that a project of freedom must examine the politics of work itself. Writing with a focus on the United States, Weeks asks: Why has work assumed such central importance in our lives? Why do we accept that we live for work? How has it become so naturalized as to effectively privatize work, such that we strive to do what we love? In these contexts, she examines the possibilities of resisting work itself such that our imaginations of freedom do not *reinvest* in productive work. Her compelling vision offers freedom as a resistance to work, a site from which to imagine and question the command and control that work exercises over the spaces and times of life (Weeks 2011, 23).

While Weeks's project offers a compelling political vision of a feminist future *beyond* and *outside* work, this book has turned to the South as both a material space and an epistemic one, to ask what different meanings work takes on here. You have read detailed ethnographic accounts of everyday work life in this book, of how entrepreneurial strategies are embodied and navigated, and how freedom is imagined, as well as accounts of the dispersed effects of office life in the Startup city and of experimentation as both a sociotechnical venture and a form of class longing essential to producing the ideal workforce for startup capitalism. So what kind of concept is the South to think with? Its use seems to be disappearing as the conditions of particular geographies are not stratified uniformly across national borders; cities and regions are differently resourced and defy the easy distinctions of "North" and "South" (Simone 2014, 31). And yet Abdoumaliq Simone acknowledges, "Still, cities of the apparent South continue to feel different. Perhaps there is no way around the absence of a precise account" (2014, 31). This book offers such a precise account of the specific and the particular, asking what we might learn about emergent forms of startup capitalism from a particular place and time. We have temporarily joined the world of the workers at Captivate; traversed the Startup Festival; visited entrepreneurs in their homes and networking meetings; and approached entanglements of gender, labor, and capital historically and through a postcolonial lens. Through this very particular account, the South appears as a space of urban experimentation (see also Simone 2014), a marking of experimental time, and an embodiment of sociotechnical forms of experimentation. The South is a space of difference from which to dislocate dominant imaginaries of entrepreneurial value as that which can travel and scale homogeneously by instead asking how value is produced through the differences of class, caste, gender, and religion. The South is a site for the kinds of experimentation with labor and technology that undergird the possibility for global techno-capitalism to flourish.

But the South is also a space from which to query dominant theories of capitalism that assume industrialization and employment: What happens when surplus populations are skilled but have no jobs (Ossome 2022; Sanyal 2007)? How are people able to survive? Within active deindustrialization and surplus populations, people do not survive on living wages alone but through relations to land, extended networks, and the support of households that extend beyond the nuclear (Naidu and Ossome 2016; Ossome 2022). Building on this expansive view of social reproduction, I offer a view of the South as additionally a space of survival and thriving through distributions of care and friendship that both name and queer social reproduction. Thus the South is a space for masculinist projects of entrepreneurship and postcolonial nation building through techno-science projects that *also* shows us how the marginalized sustain and survive under them.

Labor as method is my invitation to theorize the space and time of labor and, from there, to map new imaginaries for feminist futures of work from the South. I follow Kuan-Tsing Chen's formulation of Asia as method when he writes that a methodology specific to the colonial third world is needed: "Local history, in dialectical interaction with colonial and other historical forces, transforms its internal formation on the one hand, and articulates the local to world history and the structure of global capital on the other hand. In many contexts, colonial history mediates the histories of the local and the global" (2010, 66).

To follow this formulation in thinking of labor as method suggests then that labor is not a prefabricated category of analysis and experience but is shaped by the relations between colonial pasts and the present movements of global capital. Labor is fabricated through its entanglements with religion, caste, class, and gender. It is a derogatory term in the nationalist view that techno-scientific planning will produce a nation of *innovators* rather than workers. But it is an aspirational category when workers strive to join the middle classes and achieve status as professional employees.

Chen's work speaks to the vision of a triumphalist Asia in which techno-scientific innovation will produce a new and developmentalist nation, ready to effect change and affirm its place as a global leader in entrepreneurship. As India's first prime minister after independence, Jawaharlal Nehru, emphasized, science and technology projects could overcome the effects of colonial extractivism by showing a new nation's ability to harness knowledge power for developmental projects (Prakash 1999; Amrute and Murillo 2020). Currently in India, state-led planning toward digitized financial transactions, a universal ID, and a mandate to encourage entrepreneurship in India through the Make in India policy are all figurations of the symbolic space of technological labor in the postcolonial South. As Sareeta Amrute and Luis Felipe Murillo (2020) assert, the South can be understood as a "historic block, an epistemic formation, a political compass, and a poetics of relation." Labor as method weaves through the temporalities of colonial pasts and shiny startup futures by staying close to varied forms of labor and their movements through time and space. As capitalism mutates and reinvents itself, so too do the conditions under which it thrives, showing it to be less a logic and more comprehensible through the analogies of sluice gates and vagabond movements (Hattam 2022; Katz 2001).

Throughout this book, feminist futures are fashioned through projects that craft multiracial, cross-class, and transnational friendship and kin relations; they center desire outside the heterosexual family and queer social reproduction; they cobble together infrastructures of care; and they offer experimentation as a demand for the present as pleasurable. These insistent reformulations of time make the present count in the face of a precarious and unknowable future. The feminist futures unfolding in the second half of this book work with existing vocabularies and practices of flexibility, love, and experimentation to offer an undoing from within. Workers refuse the promises of linear startup time that speculates on future profitability. Instead, by remaking flexibility, fragmenting love as a hegemonic feeling, and embodying the call to experimentation, they fashion the possibilities for survival and even joy in their inhabitation of the present conditions of work. These feminisms are contingent, provisional, and often compromised because they work within the larger structures of neoliberalism and nationalism. But in their everydayness they offer a vital vantage point to understand the vagabond topographies of startup capitalism and its fundamental dependence on feminized and racialized labor.

Sneha worked at Captivate and lived with her parents and daughter in a small neighborhood cut off from major bus routes. It was difficult to reach her apartment and for her to leave because the streets are too narrow for autos to reach. Her interaction with others in the office was limited because just venturing out of her neighborhood was both challenging and expensive. When the office planned an event that Sneha really wanted to attend, she sometimes asked if she could stay the night at my home and attend it with me. We often planned a weekend together, but as a single parent (she was divorced) she was busy with her daughter's school, homework, and extracurricular schedule. Our plans rarely materialized. One festival weekend, her parents took her daughter to visit their hometown in a nearby state; this was our opportunity to finally spend a weekend together. Her primary request was that we visit a pub.

When our weekend began, I picked her up from the bus station, and we took an auto back to my house. Sneha wanted to wax her legs and buy a strapless bra in preparation for the evening expedition. Finding a beauty parlor to do this was harder than I expected. It was a state holiday for a religious festival, and the busy road that I lived next to was empty; most shops were shut. We walked across several streets looking inside buildings and in back alleys until we finally found an open beauty parlor.[1]

Once we entered, the usually confident and self-assured Sneha fell behind me. There was a male manager taking bookings, and she waited for me to ask him about the services she wanted. She fingered the rate card and pored over it for a few minutes while we all waited in silence. I wasn't sure what her budget was. Finally, she turned to me. "Very expensive, no?"

I agreed. We left and kept walking. I was sure that nothing would be open, but she persisted in her plan, finally prevailing upon me to walk down a leafy residential street. It opened out onto a small stretch of commercial buildings, and surprisingly she found an open parlor. I leafed through a magazine outside the curtained off space, waiting for her to finish. As I waited, the night lights began to come on in the street, and I knew our plans for a night out were getting cut short. When she finished, we began the hunt for a bra shop, seeking a special strapless bra.

I took her to a lingerie store on the next street: it was squeezed into a tiny building with counters bursting with products from Bangkok. We wobbled up a tiny spiral staircase, following a young male salesperson. Upstairs in a room that just about fitted a counter and a makeshift wooden changing room, I asked the salesman for a strapless bra. This store followed the older sales practice of lingerie sales in which customers interact across a counter with the salesperson. They assess your size and your needs and hand you what they think is best. In the cramped space of the lingerie store, this practice was most space effective. In the newer malls, display practices reflect the emphasis on choice and the sexualization of the female body that accompanied globalization in India (John and Nair 2001). Customers in malls wander around display shelves and racks, handling and selecting goods. At this tiny store, Sneha's body was subjected to the gaze of the salesman as he decided her fit.

"32," he declared, moving to pull boxes from the racks.

"No, 36," Sneha said, turning to me.

"36," I relayed to him.

We were all inches apart from each other in the small space; he was behind a counter rummaging through bra boxes.

"I can tell you that for a strapless it's definitely going to be a 32," he said to me, irritated. I looked at Sneha.

"36," she said again.

"OK, it makes no difference to me," he said, shrugging and switching boxes. He handed her a bra.

She went into the tiny changing room behind us and pulled the thin plywood door shut. The bra salesman was an amateur photographer and asked to see the SLR (single-lens reflex) camera I was holding. He quickly scanned my past photographs, commenting on light and clarity and telling me about the model of camera he wanted to buy. Sneha came out in a few minutes. "It's not fitting," she said to me. "I told you," the bra salesman said to me, handing me back my camera and bending into his pile of boxes. He emerged with another box and handed it to her. He turned to me, "Trust me, I know these things."

Sneha's entry into the small bra shop was simultaneously an entry into a public world in which her body was rendered visible. She was hypervisible as the only customer in this small salesroom. Negotiating with the salesman was a dispute over how to calibrate her own body: its contours, depths, appearance, and ratios. Wanting to enter the public world of Bangalore's nightlife required subjecting her body to scrutiny, both the pleasurable inhabitation of the pub to come later that evening and the labor and awkwardness of preparing for it, in this other public encounter.

After Sneha made her purchase, we walked back to my apartment, where she took a shower, washed her hair, and put on a red dress with the strapless bra, although the dress had sleeves and didn't need a strapless bra. She asked if she could leave her wallet behind at my apartment because she thought it would be too dangerous to carry it out to the pub at night: What if someone stole it? Sneha was unfamiliar with what to expect from the streets of the city at night. She imagined them as a dangerous space, far from the safety and predictability of her home-office routine. She did not want to immerse herself completely in it, and mediated her participation by leaving her wallet behind, although the pub I picked for us to visit was a four-minute walk from the apartment.

The pub was marked by shiny red lights above it. The bouncer opened the door for us, and we walked into a largely empty room with a cricket match playing on an overhead television and casually dressed, middle-aged men desultorily watching it from the few occupied tables. We seated ourselves and browsed the menu, and I asked for a fresh lime soda for Sneha and a beer for myself. Sneha sat self-consciously in her red dress with her newly blow-dried hair, and I fiddled around with my camera taking photographs of the drinks and the food. In about an hour, we had finished and decided to take a walk around the block before heading home.

It was windy, with a full moon slipping in and out of cloud cover. Sneha and I walked down the busy street, stepping across the strewn litter, until the people and the shops tapered off. The vacant grounds of a public boy's school led into my residential neighborhood shaded with trees that blocked the streetlights. Sneha strolled leisurely, enjoying the quiet night and the empty streets.

I had expected and anticipated an exciting night—meeting strangers perhaps or exchanging phone numbers with new friends—but what had passed felt underwhelming: the languor of the corner pub, a sports game we were not watching, and then a leisurely walk home through streets I knew intimately as my neighborhood. I remember this evening because it emblematizes the comfort I came to share with Sneha, and so many other women I worked alongside. I knew we could spend hours together doing nothing, chatting aimlessly for hours on end and creating small events that took weeks to plan.

Yet I could never be sure what this evening meant for Sneha. How much planning and thought must have gone into arranging child care and making her way to my apartment with many buses? How did she mark the trepidation and anxiety of needing to prepare for an evening out, navigating city streets and spaces of consumption as a confident member of the middle class? Walking aimlessly through central city streets late at night, alongside young single women, passing by sex workers and bar dancers at work—was this the excitement she had prepared for?

This evening has further stayed in my mind because it captures the many registers through which the promises of experimental time are sensed, embodied, and navigated beyond the workplace. It reminds me that global capitalism is most obviously visible in work practices and through the disseminated ideologies of techno-utopianism, but these are materialized through the mundane and everyday social relations of friendship, care, and desire that weave in and out of the formal office. The promise of startup capitalism—that all work will be fun and creative, automating the mundane—remains a fiction. Yet that horizon structures expectations of work for those across the economy.

Strolling down a street late at night is a simple enough pleasure, yet to be in public, roaming, walking, at leisure, and at ease is an evasive and rare occurrence for many women like Sneha. Her work world is defined by the possibilities offered by the startup economy, but her after-work hours are spent rooted to her domestic life. I knew that the next day Sneha's parents would return with her young daughter, and she would be at home and unavailable on weekends. These moments remind me of how the desire to resist work might not be a compelling one for workers like Sneha, for whom work offers an entry into a set of possibilities and friendships not found elsewhere.

When I had first met Sneha and asked what she did in her leisure time, she had told me, "washing clothes, eating, sleeping!" She was rooted to her home in all of these activities, and when I visited her, I was rooted to the activities with her: helping to hang clothes out to dry on the terrace or idly watching TV with her parents and daughter, all of us squeezed into a single bedroom. It took me two hours to get to her home, and she almost never had the time or energy to take the multiple buses to get to my apartment. Through work there were moments of incremental readjustments of life's registers and new horizons for what Sneha could imagine possible for herself.

LONGUE DURÉE FIELDWORK

In the years after my fieldwork, I was back in Bangalore for a postdoctoral research project and was in touch with people I had done initial PhD fieldwork with. Those who had left Captivate because of the job cuts had other jobs, some in travel agencies and some with other small companies in Bangalore. Jyothi had left Captivate to follow her interest in languages and work with the Goethe Institute. She was still unmarried but better able to handle her work, given that the seams between work and life were more in her favor in the new job.

Susan, my "manager" on the marketing team at Captivate, left it to return to Scotland, where she continues working in communications and as an editor but now freelance.

Apu doesn't go to hip-hop classes anymore. While she was in Bangalore and living in a hostel, she had begun communicating by text with a college friend from her hometown. They later got married, and he was obtained in an IT job in the Netherlands, where they now live. Apu now has a small boy and takes care of him. On Instagram she posts pictures of her brief holidays in Europe with her family and friends, a stark contrast to my first interview with her, in which she told me how she invented having been on a vacation at her entrance interview with Captivate.

Lata left Captivate because work became untenable for her. She was not explicitly asked to leave, but her requests for flexibility during the COVID pandemic and care work for her family were not received kindly. She was hurt that a company she had spent a decade with would treat her "like any other employee." She moved to work part-time, married again, and had two children with her new husband. She bought an apartment that she rented out in one part of her town and lived in her husband's apartment, across town, closer to where he worked at an IT company. When I was in Bangalore during my postdoctoral position, Lata asked for help from me in circulating her CV as an accounts professional. She wanted to start working freelance. When I returned after a gap of three years, after COVID lockdowns had been lifted, she had what seemed to be her dream job working for a major global corporation, with an office in a shiny glass WeWork building in the city center. She said on some days she worked out of UB City Mall, a skyscraper modeled on the Empire State Building, in Bangalore's most expensive real estate district.

Krishna, the technologist who had engineered the job cuts, was promoted to chief technology officer at Captivate but then left after several years with the company to lead projects at another UK-based travel company.

Shonali and Supraja are still very close friends, although they don't live together anymore. Shonali married a man in the army and is now posted around the country; she has a small daughter to whom she has transferred her love of popular dance. Supraja went home to her parents for several years during COVID and then returned to Bangalore to work with the large travel agency Thomas Cook. She began to take her artwork more seriously and now sells intricate patterns and sketches and wants to do this full time.

During COVID, many of my interlocutors at Captivate worked from home, and the travel industry took a major hit. Many Captivate employees kept their jobs, although they described to me a tension around going to work and not being sure if their jobs were secure. Unable to travel back to Bangalore between 2020 and 2022 owing to my visa, I developed a small collaborative video project to piece together how work and life were impacted by the pandemic. During a January term class, my students at Middlebury College worked with Captivate employees whom I had done fieldwork with to produce short and collaborative video essays on workers' everyday lives.

These comprised various forms of "found footage" that employees would send the students via WhatsApp: photos, videos, and extracts from social media. Students also conducted interviews over Skype and Zoom and extracted the video from these, editing together video collages of interview material and footage to produce short essays on workers' lives. The narrative was driven by the women themselves; they decided what story to tell and shared footage accordingly. I continued making these short video essays in 2023, and I see this form as an instantiation of what labor as method looks like when pursued in a nontextual form. As video, photo, and excerpted interview, labor as method offers these short filmic essays as open-ended and exploratory trips into city spaces, workspaces, and intimate life that center workers. They try to open conversations around work futures and experimental time(s) in postcolonial Bangalore.

EXPERIMENTAL TIMES

This book has drawn on what I call labor as method to navigate multiple worlds of work across sites and temporalities. The turn to startup capitalism in Bangalore produces the entrepreneur as a valiant figure who must be prepared for a new life of "risk-taking." Ethnographic work into startup festivals and in accelerator labs and at networking meetings shows how this production of risk as value is only new for a certain subject: the upper-caste Brahmin man. Thus the central figure of startup entrepreneurship is not the neoliberal and unmarked homo economicus, but a particularly caste-framed, classed, masculine subject. This entrepreneur is further produced through [his] fluid movements across the experimental times of late-night Skype and Zoom calls, networking at bars and pubs, and ability to immerse himself in the sociospatial worlds of startup entrepreneurship.

At the fringes of this economy of startup capitalism are those who traffic in other temporalities: of caste life, of gendered social reproduction, and of middle-class, gated community living. Women entrepreneurs are continually read as "failures" as their movements in space and time defy entrepreneurial time and value making.

Moving from the scale of startup capitalism to a particular midsize company that embodies entrepreneurialism, we encounter experimentation in everyday life. Managers seek employees who can "try something new!" and experiment with their food, leisure, and adventure as a sign of their potential to produce value at work. The startup mantras of love, flexibility, and risk are remade from managerial and entrepreneurial discourse into everyday possibilities for pleasure and care. In fact, everyday worlds of work rely on forms of collective care and friendship as the basis for experimental startup capitalism to function and flourish.

Throughout, this book challenges the fictions of startup capitalism: it assesses the dreams of the startup city, the imperative on risk, the dream that everyone can DWYL, the focus on experimentation, and the insistence on a singular vision of flexibility as freedom. Understanding the turn to entrepreneurialism as an invitation to experimentation, I showed the divergent meanings that result from an ethnographic and feminist reading of contemporary global capitalism.

What is a feminist approach to the study of capitalism? While narratives of neoliberalism emphasize the entrepreneurial individual,

I suggested in chapter 2 that participation in contemporary forms of public life has always required crucial and contingent realignments of space and time that enable gendered publics. Tracing a long history of such gendered publics, I showed how they are not outside of but constituted through dominant ideas of nation and capital. And yet women's incremental bids for freedom and collective belonging in a gendered public have achieved confidence, freedom, and influence within the terms of neoliberalism and nationalism.[2] Thus a feminist approach to global startup capitalism shows how futures are navigated through small readjustments to how gendered bodies circulate in public spaces.

In India, startup entrepreneurship is "taught" to wider publics through state and private efforts such as startup festivals, weekend workshops, and the integration of leisure and fitness into everyday life (see also Freeman 2015; Amrute 2016). The startup economy self-represents as a meritocratic and welcoming space that gathers the "maverick" entrepreneurs, "quixotic" innovators, and "unpredictable" creative minds who love what they do. Middle-class professionals and technology entrepreneurs imagine the startup self as the individual who challenges the formal caste- and class-governed norms of doing business locally. Entrepreneurs are expected to be risk-taking and adventurous.

My fieldwork showed that the ideals of risk, unpredictability, innovation, and genius that assemble the startup economy are not self-evident. I argue that they are specific, material, and affective signifiers that attach to bodies along the lines of gender, class, and caste. Chapter 3 showed the entrepreneur's production through the correct and desirable mobilizing of the structural and performative conditions of difference. By examining the lives and labor of women who were peripheral entrepreneurs, I analyzed their pitches for future investments and their unacknowledged labor. Desirable feminist futures of creative enterprise were enacted along the everyday calendrics of care work, home work, and reproductive labor. Networking events might take place at home and in the apartment building and at times squeezed out of housework. These future-making projects that I mapped at the outskirts of the city shape a detailed registry and record of uncompensated, gendered labor struggling to be valued and recognized. While most of these entrepreneurial ventures did not receive the funding they wished for, I understand these not as failures but as the irreconcilability of heterosexual time and entrepreneurial time.

By exploring women entrepreneurs as those on the fringes of startup capitalism, I showed how their bodies were associated with reproductive labor and often deemed incapable of fundable investment. Even events to focus attention on women's exclusion from entrepreneurial narratives only served to reinforce gendered norms; thus the category of "woman entrepreneur" itself presented gender as both a problem and a solution, an impossible category to work through. Feminist futures thus are not failed business projects but detailed inventories of past work done and labor demanded from family.

In part 2, I shifted attention from the key figure of entrepreneurship to understand how [he] shapes everyday worlds of work. What do we make of the dream of management discourse that work is a freedom from routine that enables us to be more productive? I showed how freedom for entrepreneurs is the flexibility of unorthodox office timings and free movement through time and space. The phrase "I'm not a software coolie!" stayed with me long after its casual utterance on a WeWork terrace. This statement grounded my analysis of entrepreneurial ambitions as particularly postcolonial desires to remake the racialized subject of labor from one who is associated with indentureship to one who commands and controls their own time and labor.

Among workers, flexibility was an anti-colonial impulse, a desire for class belonging, and a set of gendered relations shot through with debt and obligation. I traced how these varied inhabitations of flexibility position it as a sort of boundary object that emerges as both managerial discourse and through histories of racialized desire and class possibility and mobility. Thus, a feminist understanding of future making does not ride along with entrepreneurial visions of flexibility as freedom but queries how these visions seek to remake the laboring subject through historical and social relations of labor and capital.

Fieldwork at Captivate Travels opened up the lifeworlds of everyday experimentation through which the entrepreneurial economy is made. The key injunctions of entrepreneurship—flexibility, love, experimentation—are provincialized at Captivate as workers generate new socialities and friendships under their sign. For example, the hope that all workers are able to DWYL is circulated by entrepreneurs and company management as a key register through which to reproduce happiness to generate profit. Refusing this forward-looking frame, workers refracted and diffused the direction to "Be Happy" at work into complex and collaborative relations. Thus, "Love" is remade into forms of caring and social reproduction through the production of work as "family" and colleagues as "kin." As these relations of care leave the heterosexual family and travel amid lower-caste and -class workers, they offer new ways to imagine how workers navigate the precarity of quickly automating jobs. Such relations of care sustain and replenish the workforce, offering us a model of social reproduction outside the domestic family unit: an arrangement of queer social reproduction enabled by startup capitalism's austerity and precarity. This is a queering as a fabrication that refuses Western technological teleology to instead dream up and practice something better (McElroy 2020, 3). A central hope of entrepreneurship is remade from the vision of profit-driven production of happiness into the unruly deviances of office friendships and desires.

As a central condition of life in the South, experimentation marks the historic planning of colonial cities as domains of experimentation with spatial design (Simone 2014, 31) and their populations as experimental subjects—for microfinance, family planning, and clinical trials—that are first conducted locally and then scaled to be replicated globally (Gupta 2019b). These histories and geographies of difference situate how the spirit of startup entrepreneurship shapes the possibilities of work in Bangalore. What it means to experiment shifted dramatically between the technologists and entrepreneurs, for whom experimentation was a call to automate and more thoroughly personalize technology. For workers from lower-caste and -class groups, experimentation enabled them to call into being play and world making. Rather than orient themselves toward the telos of reproductive futurity and family making, they immersed themselves in the desires and pleasures of consumption and romance, muddling expectations of middle-class respectability.

As state projects and private capital chart future markets in India, new subjects and aspirations are enabled and imagined (Cross 2015; Searle 2016). At Captivate, it is the workplace that offers experimental mediations to shape labor as a form of temporal work. The circulation of images, emails, and descriptive text of elite holidays combines with the materiality of itinerary building and planning to mediate the possibilities for future (re)making (Gupta 2019b, 123). As Leya Mathew and Ritty Lukose write, "In the context of [India's] liberalisation, the deepening of consumer culture is spawning all kinds of value transformations, potential selves and futures to normalise aspiration as a form of social belonging" (2020, 694–95).

Feminist futures of labor urge us to forge a politics of place and people in which we control the means of production and design for a collective future while keeping space for the unlikely ways in which the present is also queered and the future fantasies of startup capitalism are already disrupted by workers' everyday practices: "The distance between imagined futures and the constrained present provides fertile ground for imaginative work in the fleeting spaces of selfies, job descriptions and career-planning workshops" as Mathew and Lukose note (2020, 698). This is a politics that requires a shared solidarity between Sneha—a precarious worker, single parent, and caregiver—with the other workers we have encountered in the pages of this book.

This is a solidarity across class: perhaps the hardest kind of solidarity given the attractions, enticements, and ambitions that coalesce around classed consumption and leisure that I have shown as integral to startup capitalism throughout this book.

I imagine walking out of the pub with Sneha into a city of our imagination. Outside, one of Bangalore's central commercial city streets comes to life after its afternoon stupor. A disco thuds music from deep inside a building; strobe lights occasionally shine out of the windows and light up the sidewalk as we pass by. Young women spill out of its discreet door in shorts and sleeveless tops, laughing on their way back home or to somewhere new. One of them might be Sophie Das, whom we met in the introduction, the protagonist of Anjum Hasan's *Neti Neti*, making her way home with friends, aware that her landlord would note the time of her return and that she would have to be up in time for work on one day that weekend, transcribing video for her employer.

On the street, auto drivers line up by the sidewalk, hassling us to take a ride with them. We shake our heads and walk on. Behind us is one of the city's first pubs that has no bouncers, no decorous middle class, no IT workers: the antithesis to Sadhwani's 1980s dream of respectable middle-class consumption. At this pub, college students, artists, and musicians all hang out drinking cheap beer, stumbling to find a table in its dark interiors. Patrons climb up the spiral staircase, suddenly finding themselves under a partially open terrace, cooled instantly by Bangalore's night breezes. This is the pub that dancers from a neighboring dance bar had once spontaneously jumped into in the early 1990s when their bar was raided by the police on charges of being illegal, an incident I detailed in chapter 2. They rushed down the stairs before the bar patrons could make out what was happening, still in their elaborate embellished skirts and blouses, heavily made up.

At the corner of Brigade Road is an intersection that hums with traffic by day. At this time of night, traffic is scarce. The busiest part of the street is the entrance to a dive bar at the corner, where a queer public of sex workers, gay men, queer women, activists, and the urban lower middle class gather on the dance floor upstairs. At the bus stand across the street, a group of sex workers wait for the bus to Majestic, the central bus terminus. At Majestic they might find new queer connections, possibilities for sexual labor, or perhaps the memories of the confusion and abjection that marked their initial entry into Bangalore; perhaps the bus depot would be a site of rebirth and self-making.[3] *Experimental Times* reads startup capitalism through an exploration of space, figures, and social relations to understand its production across scales. It offers a feminist reading of experimental time that takes seriously the possibilities of collective life and reimagining of social relations that are always woven through work.

Notes

INTRODUCTION

1. Throughout the book I use Bangalore as the city name, although it was officially changed to Bengaluru in 2014 following sustained activism by local politicians and writers arguing for a rejection of the Anglicized Bangalore. My choice stays true to the practices of those I interviewed: none of them used Bengaluru, suggesting that their use of Bangalore marks a certain global aspiration and not merely a failure to register a new nomenclature.

2. Carol Upadhya (2016) describes the rhythms of project time in *Reengineering India*.

3. Yet science studies scholar Renny Thomas (2020) draws on fieldwork in the Indian Institute of Science with scientists and engineers to query these projects of modernity. Interviewing those who are responsible for building the so-called modern India as a space of merit and talent, he found that caste very much shapes everyday life in scientific institutions. Although it is not explicit, it emerges through food, ritual celebration, and networks of collaboration,

and it becomes so naturalized that scientists don't see it as "caste practice" but as modern scientific practice.

4. Feminist anthropologists have mapped the feminization of labor, showing how the racialization and gendering of work works in favor of global capital. For example, Carla Freeman (2000) shows how the feminization of work produces new characteristics of "pink collar work" in Barbados, Aihwa Ong (2010) details the possibilities of resistance and agency among factory workers in Malaysia, and Caitryn Lynch (2007) and Jan Padios (2018) show how the expectations around work tie into colonial relations. This feminization and racialization is not only transnational, as with contemporary Foxconn factories in China that rely on migrant workers (Chan 2013), but is also within the nation (Nakamura 2011).

5. This is key to how Neda Atanasoski and Kalindi Vora bring debates on the future of work to bear on the figuration of the "human"; they assert that "engineering projects that create the robots and program the AI are predetermined by techniques of differential exploitation and dispossession within capitalism" (Atanasoski and Vora 2019, 4), and thus it is "insufficient to point to the ways in which human racialized and gendered labor underwrites techno-utopic fantasies," so we need to instead turn to who or what counts as human (Atanasoski and Vora 2015).

6. Thank you to Marc Boeckler for grasping exactly my usage through this reference.

7. I use [he/his] in brackets to identify the entrepreneur in order to signify the default masculinization of this figure.

8. Veena Dubal writes powerfully about how the gains of the labor movement have been ceded under the guise of "flexible" work: "Silicon Valley capitalists have brought back piecework, using legal gray zones and digital machinery to accelerate the amount of work that goes unpaid. . . . [W]hile the companies might have created new ways for people to earn income, workers in the gig economy today labor for longer and earn far less" (Dubal 2020). See also Medappa et al. (2020) on the power exerted by gig companies over their workers in Bangalore.

9. As Jodi Melamed explains, "We often associate racial capitalism with the central features of white supremacist capitalist development, including slavery, colonialism, genocide, incarceration regimes, migrant exploitation, and

contemporary racial warfare. Yet we also increasingly recognize that contemporary racial capitalism deploys liberal and multicultural terms of inclusion to value and devalue forms of humanity differentially to fit the needs of reigning state-capital orders" (2015, 77).

10. Startup India is a flagship initiative of the government of India, intended to build a strong ecosystem for nurturing innovation and startups in the country that will drive sustainable economic growth and generate large-scale employment opportunities. Through this initiative the government aims to empower startups to grow through innovation and design.

11. The "knowledge for all" program was done through a body known as the Knowledge Commission, which emphasized the importance of knowledge in "leapfrogging social and economic development" (Radhakrishnan 2007, 143). Banu Subramaniam writes about how science and religion have been mobilized toward a nationalist Hindu vision in contemporary India: "Rather than characterize Hinduism as ancient, nonmodern, or traditional, the Hindu nationalists have embraced capitalism, Western science, and technology as elements of a modern Hindu nation" (2019, 266).

12. The anthropologist Ravinder Kaur (2020a) marks a specifically Hindu vision of the future in which Brand India campaigns create the nation-state itself as an enclosure of capitalism invested in a majoritarian quest of recovering a "golden past" bled free of Muslim figures.

13. These are also key concerns of Miya Tokumitsu's book examining what she calls the "Do What You Love" economy, which has foundationally shaped my thinking here (Tokumitsu 2015), and Sarah Jaffe's (2020) book examining the precarity of neoliberal work. It also crucial to the debates on social reproduction and care that I take up more specifically in the chapter "Do What You Love."

14. See also Gupta (2019). Lilly Irani was instrumental in pointing me toward ways to develop this idea.

15. In "border as method," Mezzadra and Neilson explain, "on one hand, we refer to a process of producing knowledge that holds open the tension between empirical research and the invention of concepts that orient it. On the other hand, to approach the border as a method means to suspend, to recall a phenomenological category, the set of disciplinary practices that present the objects of knowledge as already constituted and investigate instead the processes

by which these objects are constituted. It is by rescuing and reactivating the constituent moment of the border that we try to make productive the vicious circle Balibar identifies" (2013, 17).

16. By July 1991, when postcolonial India responded to a fiscal crisis by formally undertaking Bretton Woods–led reforms—"also known as economic liberalization"—public-sector industries were closed in favor of privatization and large-scale structural readjustment. Reforms were "outward looking," aimed at integrating India into a global market by de-restricting domestic production, loosening constrictions on foreign trade, reducing tariffs, and reforming company law to enable majority shareholding by foreign corporations in their Indian subsidiaries and new ventures (Gupta and Sivaramakrishnan 2011).

17. Bangalore was well-known for large public-sector companies in industries such as aerospace, watches, and industrial parts. The HMT museum traces some of these histories.

18. In addition to liberalization, there were other factors producing a new middle class: Prime Minister Indira Gandhi's salary hikes were enabled by the 1973 Pay Commission, the long-term effects of the Green Revolution were being felt, and foreign remittances from Indian laborers in the Gulf grew this class (Mazzarella 2005). The new middle class was defined and identified by their location within circuits of consumption and production differentiating them from an earlier Nehruvian socialist model of growth; see Menon and Nigam (2007, 3).

19. More information on the Burroughs computer can be found at http://www.computinghistory.org.uk/det/2969/Burroughs-B25/.

20. For a discussion, see Chen (2010, 68). Elsewhere, writing about decolonialism, Julietta Singh (2018) notes that the impulse toward mastery dominates both colonialism and anti-colonialism.

21. Although the notion of the "middle class" in India has a lengthy genealogy, it peaked with the economic liberalization that facilitated foreign direct investment (FDI) and trade, freed businesses from the license permit Raj that Prime Minister Nehru had inaugurated after independence, and eased banking regulations to encourage spending (Baviskar and Ray 2011).

22. Arlene Davila writes about malls in Latin America not as homogenized spaces but rather as sites of speculative possibility, what she calls "settlement institutions" that link neoliberal systems of production, consumption, and

imagery (Davila 2016, 3). This mall too functioned as a site of speculation in which potential entrants to the startup world could be cultivated and attracted through visual cues and the promises of new ways of linking work and leisure as pleasurable. Thus the location of the launch event at a mall was not coincidental or convenient but gestures to the blurring of work and pleasure that the startup industry is invested in.

23. In more recent work, Swethaa Ballakrishnen (2020) studied management consultants, elite lawyers, and litigators for more traditional law forms in India to understand the reasons behind social mobility and unprecedented levels of gender parity experienced by women lawyers in transactional law firms. Ballakrishnen found that an education from a national law school, combined with the as yet unestablished gender norms for a new industry and the support of family and domestic help, enabled women to rise to senior positions early in their careers and to maintain this advantage as they negotiated family leave and other recalibrations of time and workday.

24. "Inappropriate Indians," as Kareem Khubchandani (2020, 34) might term them when he refers to those who refuse the heteronormativity of the Indian techie.

25. Kathi Weeks (2011) offers a powerful feminist critique of work that asks us to imagine liberation outside of work. Why must we so resolutely invest in the idea and realm of work as a site for our liberation, Weeks asks; the politics of work is invariably a plea to differing conditions of work, or less work, or the demand for better-compensated work.

26. Asiya Islam (2021, 101) shows how participants from the lower middle class in her ethnographic study used different words to refer to the relevance and significance of what they were doing: "jobs" referred to short-term work, "career" to long-term professional engagement, and "labour-type" to manual work that some of their parents were employed in.

27. I found especially helpful Nat Raha's (2021) essay "A Queer Marxist Transfeminism" in mapping these debates and Hil Malatino's (2020) *Trans Care* as an exploration of how forms of care and labor outside the heterosexual family unit are integral resources for trans survival.

28. At another site of the transnational labor economy, elite women lawyers might also be thought of as living within "experimental time." In a sociological study of lawyers in India, Swethaa Ballakrishnen (2020) notes how elite lawyers

structure pleasurable pursuits into their work day: golf in the mornings and tennis in the evenings. Jyothsna Belliappa's (2013) important work on gender and class in Bangalore suggests that with professional work and consumption, larger joint family and kin systems are reworked but not dismantled.

29. Bonnie Urciuoli (2008) writes about the training and retraining of the self to compete in ever-changing neoliberal markets.

30. In a piece on women's entrepreneurship, I have detailed how efforts to equip women with entrepreneurial skills attempt to fit them into a masculine world that demands relentless hours, mobility across sites of entrepreneurship, and the unlimited time commitment to scale a business (see Gupta 2021). Women's entrepreneurship is not recognized as valuable because women are not recognized as entrepreneurial. They are seen by funders as homemakers, with their primary allegiance to the domestic realm. I explore these questions in chapter 3.

1. LABOR AS METHOD

1. In his analysis of the middle classes in India, Steve Derné (2008) identifies the difference between the locally oriented middle class and the transnational middle class. Life for the former has not changed drastically with the globalization accompanying economic liberalization, he argues: their ideas about marriage, family, and modernity remain largely the same. The dramatic changes assumed to have accompanied middle-class growth in India are mostly true for a 5 percent English-speaking population for whom the material effects of globalization have enabled cultural change and altered patterns of consumption.

2. GENDERED PUBLICS

1. See Lata Mani (1998) for an overview of the debates on *sati*. Anagha Ingole (2023) astutely reads against these dominant historiographies with her analysis of texts by three non-Brahmin women from the nineteenth century, showing how they refuse the terms of anti-colonial discourse through which Indian womanhood has been mapped thus far.

2. This is a process that Third World feminist Chela Sandoval (2000, 58) terms "differential consciousness": it functions like the clutch of an automobile,

she writes, selecting, engaging, and disengaging gears for the transmission of power. Sandoval was writing in the context of dominant US feminisms, but her consideration of how feminist subjects move between ideologies is a powerful example of the real-world navigations of power that understand how subjects are enmeshed within and shaped by dominant ideologies.

3. Who better to theorize this expectation of familial love and duty than Silvia Federici? She writes in *Revolution at Point Zero*: "The literature of the women's movement has shown the devastating effects that this love, care, and service has had on women. . . . We refuse then to retain with us and elevate to a utopia the misery of our mothers and grandmothers and our own misery as children!" (Federici 2020, 30).

4. I understand intimate publics in Lauren Berlant's sense of the term: "[L]aboratories for imagining and cobbling together alternative construals about how life has appeared and how legitimately it could be better shaped not merely in small modifications of normativity" (2011, 184).

5. See also Mrinalini Sinha (2006) on gender as a superior site for distinction; see also Henrike Donner (2008, 42). Donner writes that as colonial legislation permeated spheres of family life including age of marriage, sati (or widow immolation), and age of reproduction, women's bodies were dragged into these debates as a part of colonial modernity (43).

6. Partha Chatterjee (1987) writes of India's nationalist struggle in which freedom fighters mapped India's superiority through the bodies of middle-class women whom they described as moving between public and private spheres, navigating both modernity (signified as participation in the public world) and tradition (marked by the sanctity and spirituality of the middle-class home).

7. Susan Seizer writes of Tamil film actresses who perform in special drama acts that take place outdoors that they "*expand* the category of good woman to include themselves" (Seizer 2005, 97). For Seizer it is the private rooms and spaces that are erected and appropriated by traveling artistes that create spaces for the production of "good women." Categories of private and public are made mobile, as new subjectivities and freedoms also create new spaces.

8. The cultivation of confidence has a rich literature in feminist studies. Writing about the cultivation of confidence through personality development programs for Bahujan students in contemporary India, Savitha Suresh Babu notes that emphasizing confidence works as a strategy to mark the caste

differentials through which young people access the middle-class market economy. Thus while most analyses of confidence-building programs and activities suggest their deployment toward neoliberal frames of self-improvement, for Bahujan students, they work as historical memory (Suresh Babu 2020, 745).

9. Scholars of postcolonialism explain that nationalism was imagined via the trope of the family to depend on the "prior naturalizing of the social subordination of women and children within the domestic sphere" (McClintock 1993, 64).

10. Ritty Lukose (2009, 86–89), writing of how gender is fashioned in Kerala, notes how young women are produced as "demure moderns" through forms of disciplining: harassment and anger.

11. Meenakshi Thapan (2004) writes of the global frameworks legitimizing gendered consumption. On the pages of a leading women's magazine, *Femina*, the New Indian Woman was shaped through a discursive and image-heavy orientation toward global consumption. Not only was her body well-groomed and desirable; it was also a product for consumption in the global marketplace.

12. See also Kelty (2008, 28) for a link between open source software cultures in Bangalore and heavy metal, pub-going masculine subcultures.

13. Toby Beauchamp writes about surveillance mechanisms that do not just police the transgender subject but in fact discipline and produce gendered subjects (2019, 8).

14. Mary John (John and Nair 2001) explicitly points to the desiring consumer of the neoliberal economy as a careful creation constructed in distinction to the inhibited consumer of India's earlier socialist and state-controlled model of economic planning

15. The Indian IT-BPO sector is the largest private sector employer in the country, with direct employment of about 2.23 million professionals, and is the largest private sector employing women (see Bhattacharyya and Ghosh 2013).

16. These local conditions combine with the ascendant rationale of global flexible specialization (see Harvey 1991) since the 1970s, by which firms find the most economically viable destinations for some aspects of their production. Early waves of this kind of offshoring occurred in manufacturing, and flexible specialization mapped onto gender and race, as Third World women performed feminized jobs for low pay (Fernandez-Kelly 1984; Ong 2010; Salzinger 2003).

17. Equality Labs, *Caste in the United States* (2018).

18. Unlike countries where call centers often serve domestic markets and employ fewer than one hundred people in old warehouses and makeshift back-end offices, countries like India, Ireland, and Canada are known as subcontracting nations and have significant infrastructure and state support to run large operations; see Basi (2009) and Batt, Holeman, and Holtgrewe (2007).

19. In fact, it is not only call center jobs that are singled out in this way; women employed in manufacturing jobs navigate the consequences of being "too public," visibilized when they go to work everyday and are seen outside the workplace, spending their own money. Caitryn Lynch's (2007) study of young feminized labor in Sri Lanka's manufacturing industry notes that these women were called "juki girls," a derogatory term referencing the Japanese brand of sewing machine ("juki") that they worked on. She writes that women's financial independence, their urban circulation without paternalistic and patriarchal supervision, their class mobility, and their employment are all forms of mobility (spatial, class, employment) that threaten men's roles as workers, providers, and protectors of women (Lynch 2007).

20. See Krishnamurthy (2004), and for a comparison with similar discourses in the Philippines, where many technology jobs have now been further shifted, see Padios (2018).

21. What Meredith McGuire (2011) parses as the training in "how to sit, how to stand."

3. PRODUCING THE ENTREPRENEUR

1. Pat O'Malley (1996) clarifies this, writing that risk-management techniques articulate with neoliberalism via prudentialism: a "technology of governance that removes the key conception of regulating individuals by collectivist risk management and throws back upon the individual the responsibility for managing risk."

2. The sociologist Gowri Vijayakumar writes that "risk is defined in relation to race, gender, sexuality, and geopolitics" (2021a, 3). Being marked at risk (in her study of AIDS) both builds on and reinforces existing relations of hierarchy and exclusion.

3. The anthropologist Ajantha Subramaniam has powerfully traced the historical life of caste in Indian technology and engineering education, which

feeds the current information technology industry that my interviewee is attempting to remake. She writes about India's premier engineering college, the Indian Institute of Technology (IIT): "The majority of IITians come from upper-caste families of bureaucrats, school-teachers, and academics where capital has long been held in education. While most were already children of the professional class, the value of their accumulated capital has suddenly spiked due to the reorganization of late twentieth- and early twenty-first-century capitalism around the 'knowledge economy.' At the same time, the role of caste and state in producing the IITian has been obscured in favor of his or her portrayal as a socially disembedded individual with an innate capacity for technical knowledge" (Subramaniam 2015, 293).

4. Indian enterprise has traditionally been rooted in family networks and histories of business experiences that enable communities to obtain credit and mobilize capital. These thick networks also offered sources of information and markets for products and provided implicit guarantees against trade default and opportunistic behavior (Damodaran 2008). Businesses that gained strength from their communities before growing and entering formal state-regulated markets thus had significant resources through which to differ and displace risk.

5. Yet new forms of technoscientific innovation cannot erase what came before them: today's techies might just as readily celebrate Ayudha Puja, in which prayers and offerings are placed before machines, signaling the diverse routes through which Hinduism comes to be "culturized" (Thomas and Geraci 2018) and thus redefining it as cultural practice.

6. This is not the entrepreneurial American ideal of the "self-made man" who takes risks, ventures into uncharted territory, and carves out his own rugged individuality—the precursor to the present-day US internet entrepreneur (see Kimmel 2012). Instead, this figuration keeps intact the privileges of forms of difference, attempting to rework them within a global startup environment.

7. I often met entrepreneurs for late morning interviews, and they appeared red-eyed and exhausted, explaining to me that they had been up all night with a collaborator across the ocean.

8. Lilly Irani (2019) makes the distinction between "jugaad" and "innovation" in the chapter "Can the Subaltern Innovate" in her book *Entrepreneurial Citizens*. Irani shows how innovation is produced through the support of

reproductive labor, kin networks, and the scalability of an idea. Here I am interested in showing how forms of caste, class, and gender capital are translated and transformed into the production of the risk-taking startup entrepreneur.

9. Being and becoming a startup entrepreneur requires generating hype in the pitch. For Kaushik Sunder Rajan, writing about genomic startups, cultures of innovation are driven by vision and hype, which are not a waste but an extremely productive mechanism of value generation in a speculative marketplace. "Hype is a discursive mode of calling on the future to account for the present—hype *is* reality, or at least constitutes the discursive grounds upon which it unfolds," writes Rajan (2006).

10. Lilly Irani (2019) explains the place and role of reproductive labor in her discussion of the inventor of Indian refrigerator Mitti Cool.

11. The association of circulation with masculinity and capitalist penetration shapes a particular valuation of financial behavior as well. In her analysis of Wall Street women working in the 1990s, Melissa Fisher (2012) describes "predatory market machismo" as the value of mastery over speed, distance, and density. Fisher understands market machismo in concert with a wider move in the US financial sector toward acquiring shareholder value over all other considerations. This led to aggressive risk-taking behavior, she says, as bankers expanded client bases, sealed deals, and sped up transactions—cementing predatory market machismo as the hegemonic masculinity in finance (Fisher 2012, 99). Cynthia Enloe (2014) and Caitlyn Zaloom (2004) similarly describe how the embodiment of masculinized imaginaries, discourses, and practices of aggressive risk-taking constitute the core of financial capitalism. Karen Ho's (2009) ethnography of wall street shows how shareholder value is compromised through practices that value risk-taking in and of itself; the more the risk taken, the greater the value of the deal. Thus risk is created through projections of rapid growth via the conquering of space, the devotion of time, and a reliance on speed.

12. In Walter Benjamin's Arcades Project, the figure of the flaneur traipsed along Parisian boulevards, soaking in the sights and sounds of urban life. The figure of the flaneur is typically associated with white middle-class masculinity, but Martin Manalansan (2015) reworks the flaneur through a queer of color method, to experience the nightlife and street life of New York city as ambiguous and embedded in various forms of community, as a person of color.

13. Lata Mani (2014) discusses this neoliberal urge in "Sex and the Signal-Free Corridor."

14. Lilly Irani (2019) discusses how innovations are differentiated from local forms of experimentation—"jugaad"—in *Chasing Innovation.*

15. Karen Ho (2009) describes the process by which investor firms recruit on elite college campuses; she notes the practices through which men crowd and cluster around the speaker, making themselves seen and heard while others hang back, on the fringes of the group.

16. Chapter 5 in Ballakrishnen (2020) shows how caste advantage is mobilized as elite women lawyers outsource reproductive labor to paid help in Mumbai.

17. I contrast this with the elite lawyers of Ballakrishnen's (2020) study, who turn to help recognizing that their client-facing jobs require an in-person presence. Similarly, writing of neoliberal feminism, Catherine Rotterberg (2019) notes that neoliberalism produces the universal subject capable of doing anything they put their mind to; this is a postgender discourse. Introducing the narrative of "work-life balance" reintroduces gender to narratives of neoliberalism and pulls women back into the folds of reproductive labor through the language of choice and agency.

18. In her fieldwork on Bangalore's IT entrepreneurs, Simanti Dasgupta (2015) shows how their self-representation of themselves as businessmen invokes tropes of nation-building. IT entrepreneurs do not see themselves purely as profit oriented, but imagine their expertise in corporate settings to be usefully translatable into issues of local civic governance (water, roads, garbage maintenance). This is a masculine translation of business profit into technocratic norms of governance, quite distinct from what I found with women entrepreneurs, who continually iterated their gendered exclusions and commitments.

19. As Kalindi Vora (2015) points out in her writing on call center workers, labor is considered "reproductive" when it is oriented toward maintenance and upkeep of technological infrastructures rather than innovating or creating new products.

4. THE OFFICE

1. Saying "Switzerland" was an apt indicator at Captivate that an employee was a recent hire. For decades, Switzerland has been the idealized vacation

destination for middle-class Indians whose exposure to "exotic" Western locales has been via Bollywood films that use the Alps as backdrops for song numbers. Employees who had been at Captivate more than a few months would almost never say "Switzerland" (not a Captivate destination), but were more likely to be far more specific, with a destination on an African safari route or in the Amazonian jungle.

2. And yet a young employee who was conversational and informal, offering frank feedback to the company, did not last in the office longer than three months.

3. In Carol Upadhya's (2008) ethnography of information technology workers, she too finds employees reluctant to adopt a casual tzone, preferring instead to address their superiors as "Sir" or "Ma'am."

4. Veena Dubal's (2020) work maps this speculative promise of flexible work, but here I am referencing a study by the Center for Internet and Society on the platform Urban Company in India (Tandon and Sekharan 2021).

5. I frame the masculinity at work here as a specifically startup masculinity because control over time is not a universal sign of masculinity. Craig Jeffrey's (2010) ethnography of time in North India, for example, shows how young men postpone graduation and engage in masculine practices of "timepass" by waiting for the right opportunities to ensure their class status and security upon entering adulthood and work.

6. For Arendt (2017), the excesses of the body need to be consigned to the private realm so that courageous, heroic action can be performed in the public realm, allowing subjects to come into being within spaces that are not colonized or contaminated by the burdens of the body, the social, and the private. Melissa Gregg (2018, 97) describes this in *Counterproductive*.

7. Kalindi Vora (2015) traces a longer history of freedom and labor, noting the imperial conditions under which a category of indentured labor was materialized to service British sugar plantations in its colonies. While not enslaved labor, these workers muddy our understanding of choice and coercion when we study how they came to be constructed as mobile and surplus labor based on gendered and racialized forms of work (see Vora 2015, 27).

8. Vora (2015) terms the repetitive work of BPOs and backend software as reproductive labor because it sustains the infrastructure of global software corporations.

9. Bonnie Honig (1995, 221) notes that the performative character of the public self is marked in explicit contrast to the constative and sedimented nature of the private self, incapable of action in the public realm. As Linda Zerilli (2005) elaborates on Arendt, to set aside the social and its necessities (meaning welfare, housing, food) is to claim freedom outside of a means-end relationship or a moral claim that the social could benefit the political. In this vein, to be truly free is to be freed from the claims of embodiment and of bodily necessity.

10. For example, as Renny Thomas's (2020) work among elite scientists in Bangalore's Indian Institute of Science shows, contemporary discourses on meritocracy channel upper-caste privilege to define normative work and educational environments and practices within them.

11. Anthropologists mark the specific ways in which formal professional work enables the construction of middle-class subjects. Professional work offers pedagogical lessons in how to be middle class, reminds employees of their new status, and offers opportunities to continually distinguish professional work from other types of labor in the office. In Carla Freeman's (2000) ethnography, workers in an offshore informatics factory in Barbados were tutored in expectations regarding dress, including how to deodorize and how to distinguish themselves from women workers on plantations, as office work offered a key site for middle-class self-making. On Wall Street it is high heels, sneakers, and clothes that signify where one is placed in the worlds of finance and what class position one occupies (Ho 2009). At orientation sessions for software workers, they enter hotel rooms amazed at the coffee machines and on-site facilities, excited about the prospects of entering a new middle class promised by their corporate jobs (Upadhya 2016).

12. For a rich discussion of the value of flexibility lying in the boundaries of work, see Richardson (2024).

13. As Kathi Weeks (2011) points out, the allure of contemporary work is that it is glossed as fun and offered to workers as a promise to join a "company family" and thereby reproduce the bourgeois heterosexual family. The affective labor required to maintain this unit is concealed and underpaid, as workers complete their jobs driven by feelings of love, duty, and obligation. Such fabrication of work in affective terms bleeds it of its political possibilities.

14. My interviews with Captivate workers resonate with feminist readings of Hannah Arendt's work on freedom. For example, Ahana's understanding of

freedom outside the frame of identity is in keeping with Linda Zerilli's reading of Arendt: an action that is itself a practice of freedom. For Zerilli (2005, 14), such freedom refuses to invest in a subject's agency, temporarily quelling the ethos of individualism and autonomy privileged in the subject-centered frame. Yet as I show in the conclusion, there is a more powerful elucidation of freedom than that proposed by these philosophers. Captivate's workers show us how freedom itself cannot be imagined outside the social lives of class, caste, gender, and nation.

15. Emily Martin (1995, 208) describes this need for employees to be skilled as a kind of flexibility that makes them more hirable in the job market: the more replaceable the labor, the more flexible it should be, like biological systems that have to survive in nature.

16. As Kiran Mirchandani explains, "Professionalism . . . mutates in meaning as it crosses national borders" (2012, 73). While professionalism is often understood to enact control through disciplinary techniques (see also Mirchandani 2012, 82), here Sanjay found that it gave him specific tools to succeed.

17. Kiran Mirchandani (2012, 13), for instance, describes how workers at call centers explain their work as adhering to a system but simultaneously maintaining a "personal touch" while attending to timed calls. Sanjukta Mukherjee (2008, 57) describes as "alienation" the atomized work and deskilling in contemporary software applications in India.

5. LOVE IN THE OFFICE FAMILY

1. Malini Ranganathan (2015) explains Bangalore's routine flooding through assemblage theory that traces how lakes and stormwater drains shape the city's aquatic ecology.

2. In *Living a Feminist Life*, Sara Ahmed (2017, 48–49) talks about happiness as a straight path that leads one in the right direction.

3. Feminist labor activists have long insisted on parsing love from labor and claiming their work as work rather than as spontaneous and natural or as leisure. For instance, Premila Nadasen (2017) writes about the activist Dorothy Bolden, who worked to denaturalize Black women's labor as emanating from their "love" for the families of those who employed them. She organized African American domestic labor in the 1960s within the National Union for

Domestic Workers. One of the organization's major strategies was to establish their work as skilled and respectable through events such as Maids Honor Day and skilling programs, thus professionalizing and formalizing their work as labor. The Wages for Housework program in the 1970s, founded by Selma James and Maria della Costa, similarly insisted on wages for housework not to "struggle to enter household relations but because we have never been out of them," as Silvia Federici (2012, 15) writes. The demand for wages is a political and revolutionary act to mark the essential labor that capitalism invisibilizes by casting it as borne from love or embedded in spontaneous affect.

4. Scholars of technology have analyzed how the fetish describes a particular relation between the labor involved in the production of a commodity and its circulation in digitally mediated worlds that are shaped by histories of colonialism and threats of job loss (Mirchandani 2012, 7). Lisa Nakamura (2011) extends the idea of a fetish to describe the "digital fetish": "a commodity that enjoys some of the special and exalted social status of a non-commodity."

5. This is what Mythri Jegathesan (2019) might term a "poeisis of desire" as she charts the multiple and overlapping fields of desire among her interlocutors, Hill Country Tamils, who labor on tea plantations.

6. For instance, see Negron (2018) on technology organizing in the workplace.

7. For example, Kalindi Vora notes that "an important component of call center work is directing agent's efforts away from subjective self renewal into producing a call center persona" (2015, 45). Building on A. Aneesh's sociological study of technology work, she finds that the "data form"—a form/specter/projection of data that is compatible with customer needs—of the call center agent is more useful in finding jobs and creating value than the "real" or nondata form. The role of the nondata form is to reproduce the life of the data form (Vora 2015, 53). My research under the conditions of startup capitalism suggests that the data forms and nondata forms are not distinct; the customer-facing roles at Captivate hire people based on "fit" require workers to have rich and full lives that produce both middle-class selves enjoying leisure and work-as-play as well as extracting value for the company.

8. This is similar to what Jan Padios terms "relational labor" in the context of Filipino call center work: "the labor required to positively identify with, signal proximity to, and effectively communicate with others, particularly in ways that meet the demands of capital" (2018, 9). For Padios, such labor

emerges from the affective histories of empire and colonialism that structure the relationship between the Philippines and the United States.

9. Vora (2015, 59), who reads the good life with Marx, whereas I am referring to it more in keeping with Millar (2018), as eked out from within conditions of precarity and developed in and through forms of labor.

10. This feminist analysis of surrogacy is a crucial analysis of how racialized and gendered labor underwrites the reproduction of the capitalist class through an extension of the colonial conditions of unfree labor. Women in India are placed under surveillance in separate living quarters as they carry the children of the commissioning clients for whom they are surrogates (Vora 2009, 270). For Vora, commercial surrogacy involves both biological and affective labor, but also produces value through more than just labor.

11. Silvia Federici and Maria Dalla Costa and others propagating Wages for Housework have demanded compensation and recognition for the unpaid social reproduction of housework (not for the housewife) that is crucial to maintaining the labor force. Beth Capper and Arlen Austin have a wonderful microsyllabus on these issues: "Wages for Housework and Social Reproduction: A Microsyllabus," The Abusable Past, n.d., https://www .radicalhistoryreview.org/abusablepast/wages-for-housework-and-social -reproduction-a-microsyllabus. Their own work reminds us that WfH sought to dismantle the social reproduction of capitalism's central unit rather than to bolster it with wages. "Rather than a stable location, the house was understood, on the one hand, as a political-economic modality that regulated racialized, gendered, and sexual labor across multiple sites that included, but was not confined to, the heteronormative familial household and, on the other, as a mutable and contested form that, if imagined collectively, might yield an altogether different organization of sexuality and social reproduction" (Capper and Austin 2018, 446).

12. For instance, Fernando and Cohen (2014) detail this imperative. Ritty Lukose maps it on the body through a practice of "oudhukum," in which the gendered body folds in upon itself; Lukose (2009) is describing young college-going women who need to signal their belonging in a small college town. In the transnational IT sector, Smitha Radhakrishnan (2011) maps respectability as the modulation of "appropriate Indianness" as her interlocutors (middle-class women employed in IT) navigate transnational work environments.

13. Sharmila Rudrappa's (2012) interviews with surrogate mothers in Bangalore similarly show how they chose this form of work over the garment factory work they would otherwise have been employed in. They named the continual task-based labor, sexual harassment at work, and low pay as reasons for preferring surrogacy despite the hardships of labor, hormonal injections, and surveillance. Women were continually calibrating their needs and assessing their risks, framing surrogacy as creative and meaningful work. Interviewees at Captivate similarly named the need for respectability as motivating their decision to do this work (Rudrappa 2012).

14. Anthropologists have read the production of the workplace within the safe and contained boundaries of "family" life as a mediation of the "cultural struggle" (Ong 1991, 281) that accompanies the movement of young women away from family life into employed labor. Companies appealing to young women to join their professional workforces may also fabricate the trope of the company "family" in order to entice women to work in a safe, comfortable, and desirable environment—the "Data Air Family" in Carla Freeman's (2000, 181) study of informatics processing in Barbados. What I mark here are the relations of care that create interdependencies and enable survival despite precarity.

15. Kathi Weeks (2017) writes powerfully about how the idea of "love" at work conceals hierarchies to create work as a middle-class space in which all workers are happily ensconced within the family.

16. Narratives of company as family conceal women's part-time and low-paid status even though their bodies are crucial aspects of the interpellation of the company as family (Kondo 1990). Yet workers do not embody these narratives without negotiating them, and women workers sometimes take advantage of, and deploy, these narratives of family for the unexpected benefits it offers them (Kondo 1990; Lynch 2007).

17. For Jane Collier, Michelle Rosaldo, and Sylvia Yanagisako, the family is understood as a "part of a set of symbolic oppositions through which we interpret our experience in a particular society" (1992, 35). As they explain, ideologies of "The Family" are not isolated from people's experiences; their interest is in how "people come to summarize their experience in folk constructs that gloss over the diversity, complexity, and contradictions in their relationships" (Collier, Rosaldo, and Yanagisako 1982, 35).

18. Arlie Hochschild's (2001) thesis on US workplaces traces the changing boundaries between home life and work; she notes that professionals seek out support and companionship at work, making these the new families and communities.

19. Repeatedly, anthropologists of gender have been tutored in respectability politics—guided on how to cover their chests and walk with downcast eyes (Lukose 2009) and how to move in public spaces (Gilbertson 2014).

20. Sareeta Amrute might term a "politics of pleasure" this practice in which leisure offers the time to try on some of the possible lifeworlds one might inhabit (Amrute 2016, 140), such that spaces of leisure are also profound spaces of pleasure (144).

6. TESTING THE FUTURE

1. This chapter is based on my article in *Feminist Review* (Gupta 2019).

2. Here I take inspiration from a special issue on bodies and experimentation in South Asia edited by Towghi and Vora (2014), and more specifically from Harris Solomon's work crystallizing the idea of the experiment: "If one aspect of the experiment refers to individual attempts to engage novelty, then a second constellation of meanings I explore here involves the careful attempts to enroll the body, the senses, and the self into consumer public cultures" (2014, 21).

3. As I explained in the introduction, I understand this labor as racialized, as it is built on hierarchies of labor value that decide whose work can be automated. Typically this is work that is striated according to caste-based visions of labor distribution.

4. Gabriel Dattatreyan's (2020) ethnography of artistes in Delhi has rich discussions of B-Boying.

5. As state projects and private capital chart future markets in India, new subjects and aspirations are enabled and imagined (Cross 2015; Searle 2017).

6. Meredith McGuire's (2011) essay "How to Sit, How to Stand" charts a genealogy of embodied middle classness and how it is learned through an ethnography of a new middle class in Delhi.

7. Minna Säävälä's (2010) description of an outing by her interlocutors to a middle-class park in Hyderabad exemplifies some of these conflicting desires and anxieties.

8. The construction of laboring subjects who divine the taste of elite consumers marks the hierarchies between diviners of pleasure and those who enjoy it, as Harris Solomon (2014, 25) attests.

9. Christopher Kelty (2008) has a wonderful ethnography of Linux in *Two Bits*. He shows how the significance and practices associated with Free Software have spread exponentially along with the circulation of the internet through a shared "social imaginary" within which publics play with and modify practices related to access and availability of knowledge and power.

10. I reflect on the emergence of the postcolonial robot through histories of caste, class, and infrastructure in "Postcolonial Assembly Protocols for Unnamed Automation Projects" (Gupta 2020, 1–14).

11. Kathi Weeks (2017) writes about this—the affective bond between managers and workers conceals the class hierarchies and precarity at work.

12. C. C. Paschal's writing on Gimlet is found at C .C. Paschal, "Here Is My Experience of Gimlet: Https://T.Co/Dx08pwGoQv," Tweet, @chiquitapaschal (blog), March 8, 2021, https://twitter.com/chiquitapaschal/status/1368728088545 263617.

13. Miya Tokumitsu (2015) describes this as part of the economy of hope galvanizing the entrepreneurial economy.

14. Feminist analyses of technology have also mapped the movements between technology and human development (Suchman and Bishop 2000), the imbrications of technology and difference (Wajcman 1991), and the ways in which narratives of difference are galvanized through technological infrastructures and practices (Philip 2016), showing how "gender-in-the-making" shapes an experimental way of life (Haraway 2003, 228).

CONCLUSION

1. What is also known as a salon in other areas of the world.

2. A wonderful book that came out after my manuscript was with the press and thus too late for substantive engagement is Srila Roy's (2022) *Changing the Subject*.

3. This sentence draws on research by Gowri Vijayakumar (2021a, 2021b).

References

Ahmed, Sara. 2010. *The Promise of Happiness*. Durham, NC: Duke University Press.

———. 2017. *Living a Feminist Life*. Illustrated ed. Durham, NC: Duke University Press Books.

Amrute, Sareeta. 2016. *Encoding Race, Encoding Class: Indian IT Workers in Berlin*. Durham, NC: Duke University Press.

Amrute, Sareeta, and Luis Felipe R. Murillo. 2020. "Introduction: Computing in/from the South." *Catalyst: Feminism, Theory, Technoscience* 6 (2). https://doi.org/10.28968/cftt.v6i2.34594.

Anantharaman, Manisha. 2014. "Networked Ecological Citizenship, the New Middle Classes and the Provisioning of Sustainable Waste Management in Bangalore, India." In "Sustainable Production, Consumption and Livelihoods: Global and Regional Research Perspectives," special issue, *Journal of Cleaner Production* 63 (January): 173–83. https://doi.org/10.1016/j.jclepro.2013.08.041.

Arendt, Hannah. 1998. *The Human Condition*. 2nd ed. Chicago: University of Chicago Press.

———. 2017. "The Freedom to Be Free." *New England Review* 38 (2): 56–69. https://doi.org/10.1353/ner.2017.0037.

Aryn, Martin, Natasha Myers, and Ana Viseu. 2015. "The Politics of Care in Technoscience." *Social Studies of Science* 45 (5): 625.

Atanasoski, Neda, and Kalindi Vora. 2015. "Surrogate Humanity: Posthuman Networks and the (Racialized) Obsolescence of Labor." *Catalyst: Feminism, Theory, Technoscience* 1 (1). https://doi.org/10.28968/cftt.v1i1.42.

———. 2019. *Surrogate Humanity: Race, Robots, and the Politics of Technological Futures.* Durham, NC: Duke University Press Books.

Austin, Arlen, Beth Capper, and Tracey Deutsch. 2020. "Wages for Housework and Social Reproduction: A Microsyllabus." *The Abusable Past* (blog). April 27, 2020. https://www.radicalhistoryreview.org/abusablepast/wages-for-house work-and-social-reproduction-a-microsyllabus.

Baas, Michiel. 2007. "Bangalore @Night: Indian IT Professionals and the Global Clock Ticking." *Etnofoor, After Dark* 20 (2): 59–72.

Bairy, Ramesh. 2016. *Being Brahmin, Being Modern: Exploring the Lives of Caste Today.* London: Routledge.

Ballakrishnen, Swethaa S. 2020. *Accidental Feminism: Gender Parity and Selective Mobility among India's Professional Elite.* Princeton, NJ: Princeton University Press.

Basi, J. K. Tina. 2009. *Women, Identity and India's Call Centre Industry.* London: Routledge.

Bastani, Aaron. 2020. *Fully Automated Luxury Communism: A Manifesto.* London: Verso.

Batt, Rosemary, David Holman, and Ursula Holtgrewe. 2007. "Call Center Workers in International Perspective." *Perspectives on Work* 10 (2): 21–23.

Bauman, Zygmunt. 2007. *Consuming Life.* Malden, MA: Polity Press.

Baviskar, Amita. 2002. "The Politics of the City." http://www.india-seminar .com/2002/516/516%20amita%20baviskar.htm.

Baviskar, Amita, and Raka Ray. 2011. *Elite and Everyman: The Cultural Politics of the Indian Middle Classes.* New Delhi: Routledge.

Bayat, Asef. 2013. *Life as Politics: How Ordinary People Change the Middle East, Second Edition.* Redwood City, CA: Stanford University Press.

Bear, Laura, Karen Ho, Anna Tsing, and Sylvia Yanagisako. 2016. "Gens: A Feminist Manifesto for the Study of Capitalism—Cultural Anthropology." http://www.culanth.org/fieldsights/652-gens-a-feminist-manifesto-for-the -study-of-capitalism.

Beauchamp, Toby. 2019. *Going Stealth: Transgender Politics and U.S. Surveillance Practices*. Durham, NC: Duke University Press.

Beauvoir, Simone de. 2007. *The Second Sex*. London: Vintage/Ebury.

Bedi, Tarini. 2007. "The Dashing Ladies of the Shiv Sena." *Economic and Political Weekly* 42 (17): 1534–41.

Bellacasa, María Puig de la. 2012. "'Nothing Comes without Its World': Thinking with Care." *Sociological Review* 60 (2): 197–216. https://doi.org/10.1111/j.1467-954X.2012.02070.x.

Belliappa, Jyothsna. 2013. *Gender, Class and Reflexive Modernity in India*. London: Palgrave Macmillan.

Benjamin, Ruha. 2019. *Race after Technology: Abolitionist Tools for the New Jim Code*. Cambridge, UK: Polity.

Berlant, Lauren Gail. 2011. *Cruel Optimism*. Durham, NC: Duke University Press.

Bettie, Julie. 2003. *Women without Class: Girls, Race, and Identity*. Berkeley: University of California Press.

Bhagat, Chetan. 2007. *One Night at the Call Center: A Novel*. New York: Ballantine Books.

Bhattacharyya, A., and B. N. Ghosh. 2013. "Gender Inclusivity in Information Communication Technology: Some Policy Indications." *International Journal of Humanities and Social Science Invention* 2 (3): 61–65.

Biao, Xiang. 2011. *Global "Body Shopping": An Indian Labor System in the Information Technology Industry*. Princeton, NJ: Princeton University Press.

Birla, Ritu. 2008. *Stages of Capital: Law, Culture, and Market Governance in Late Colonial India*. Durham, NC: Duke University Press.

Boellstorff, Tom. 2007. "When Marriage Falls: Queer Coincidences in Straight Time." *GLQ: A Journal of Lesbian and Gay Studies* 13 (2–3): 227–48. https://doi.org/10.1215/10642684-2006-032.

Boltanski, Luc, and Eve Chiapello. 2007. *The New Spirit of Capitalism*. Translated by Gregory Elliott. London: Verso.

Bosworth, Kai. 2023. "What Is 'Affective Infrastructure'?" *Dialogues in Human Geography* 13 (1): 54–72. https://doi.org/10.1177/20438206221107025.

Bourdieu, Pierre. 1986. *Distinction: A Social Critique of the Judgement of Taste*. London: Routledge.

———. 1987. "What Makes a Social Class? On the Theoretical and Practical Existence of Groups." *Berkeley Journal of Sociology* 32: 1–17.

Braverman, H. 1974. *Labor and Monopoly Capital: The Degradation of Work in the Twentieth Century.* New York: Monthly Review Press.

Brennan, Denise. 2004. *What's Love Got to Do with It? Transnational Desires and Sex Tourism in the Dominican Republic.* Durham, NC: Duke University Press Books.

Capper, Beth, and Arlen Austin. 2018. "'Wages for Housework Means Wages against Heterosexuality': On the Archives of Black Women for Wages for Housework and Wages Due Lesbians." *GLQ: A Journal of Lesbian and Gay Studies* 24 (4): 445–66. https://doi.org/10.1215/10642684-6957772.

Chatterjee, Partha. 1987. *The Nationalist Resolution of the Women's Question.* Occasional Paper no. 94. Calcutta: Centre for Studies in Social Sciences.

Chan, Jenny. 2013. "A Suicide Survivor: The Life of a Chinese Worker." *New Technology, Work and Employment* 28 (2): 84–99. https://doi.org/10.1111/ntwe.12007.

Chen, Kuan-Hsing. 2010. *Asia as Method.* Durham, NC: Duke University Press.

Collier, Jane, Michelle Rosaldo, and Sylvia Yanagisako. 1992. "Is There a Family? New Anthropological Views." In *Rethinking the Family: Some Feminist Questions*, rev. ed., edited by Barrie Thorne and Marilyn Yalom, 25–39. Boston: Northeastern University Press.

Cross, Jamie. 2015. "The Economy of Anticipation: Hope, Infrastructure, and Economic Zones in South India." *Comparative Studies of South Asia, Africa and the Middle East* 35 (3): 424–37.

Damodaran, Harish. 2008. *India's New Capitalists: Caste, Business, and Industry in a Modern Nation.* London: Palgrave Macmillan.

Danewid, Ida. 2023. *Resisting Racial Capitalism: An Antipolitical Theory of Refusal.* LSE International Studies. Cambridge: Cambridge University Press. https://doi.org/10.1017/9781009127707.

Dasgupta, Simanti. 2015. *BITS of Belonging: Information Technology, Water, and Neoliberal Governance in India.* Philadelphia: Temple University Press.

Dattatreyan, Ethiraj Gabriel. 2020. *The Globally Familiar: Digital Hip Hop, Masculinity, and Urban Space in Delhi.* Durham, NC: Duke University Press.

Dávila, Arlene. 2016. *El Mall: The Spatial and Class Politics of Shopping Malls in Latin America.* Oakland: University of California Press.

Derné, Steve D. 2008. *Globalization on the Ground: New Media and the Transformation of Culture, Class, and Gender in India.* Los Angeles: Sage.

Donner, Henrike. 2008. *Domestic Goddesses: Maternity, Globalization and Middle-Class Identity in Contemporary India*. Urban Anthropology Series. Aldershot, UK: Ashgate.

Dubal, Veena. 2020. "Digital Piecework." *Dissent* (blog). Fall 2020. https://www.dissentmagazine.org/article/digital-piecework.

Edelman, Lee. 2004. *No Future: Queer Theory and the Death Drive*. Series Q. Durham, NC: Duke University Press.

Elyachar, Julia. 2010. "Phatic Labor, Infrastructure, and the Question of Empowerment in Cairo." *American Ethnologist* 37 (3): 452–64. https://doi.org/10.1111/j.1548-1425.2010.01265.x.

Enloe, Cynthia. 2014. *Bananas, Beaches and Bases: Making Feminist Sense of International Politics*. 2nd ed. Berkeley: University of California Press.

Equality Labs. 2018. *Caste in the United States: A Survey of Caste amongst South Asian Americans*.

Federici, Silvia. 1975. *Wages against Housework*. London: Power of Women Collective.

———. 2012. *Revolution at Point Zero: Housework, Reproduction, and Feminist Struggle*. Oakland, CA: PM Press; Brooklyn, NY: Common Notions: Autonomedia. http://public.eblib.com/choice/publicfullrecord.aspx?p=1011442.

———. 2020. *Beyond the Periphery of the Skin: Rethinking, Remaking, and Reclaiming the Body in Contemporary Capitalism*. Oakland, CA: PM Press/Kairos.

Fernandes, Leela. 2006. *India's New Middle Class: Democratic Politics in an Era of Economic Reform*. Minneapolis: University of Minnesota Press.

Fernandez-Kelly, Maria Patricia. 1984. *For We Are Sold, I and My People: Women and Industry in Mexico's Frontier*. SUNY Series in the Anthropology of Work. Albany: State University of New York Press.

Fernando, Weerahannadige Dulini Anuvinda, and Laurie Cohen. 2014. "Respectable Femininity and Career Agency: Exploring Paradoxical Imperatives." *Gender, Work & Organization* 21 (2): 149–64. https://doi.org/10.1111/gwao.12027.

Fincher, David, dir. 2010. *The Social Network*. Sony Pictures Releasing.

Fisher, Melissa S. 2012. *Wall Street Women*. Durham, NC: Duke University Press.

Fraser, Nancy. 2022. *Cannibal Capitalism: How Our System Is Devouring Democracy, Care, and the Planet—and What We Can Do About It*. London: Verso Books.

Freeman, Carla. 2000. *High Tech and High Heels in the Global Economy: Women, Work, and Pink-Collar Identities in the Caribbean*. Durham, NC: Duke University Press.

———. 2001. "Is Local: Global as Feminine: Masculine? Rethinking the Gender of Globalization." *Signs* 26 (4): 1007–37.

———. 2015. *Entrepreneurial Selves: Neoliberal Respectability and the Making of a Caribbean Middle Class*. Durham, NC: Duke University Press.

Gidwani, Vinay, and Priti Ramamurthy. 2018. "Agrarian Questions of Labor in Urban India: Middle Migrants, Translocal Householding and the Intersectional Politics of Social Reproduction." *Journal of Peasant Studies* 45 (5–6): 994–1017. https://doi.org/10.1080/03066150.2018.1503172.

Gilbertson, Amanda. 2014. "A Fine Balance: Negotiating Fashion and Respectable Femininity in Middle-Class Hyderabad, India." *Modern Asian Studies* 48 (1): 120–58.

Goldman, Michael. 2020. "Dispossession by Financialization: The End(s) of Rurality in the Making of a Speculative Land Market." *Journal of Peasant Studies* 47 (6): 1251–77. https://doi.org/10.1080/03066150.2020.1802720.

Gopakumar, Govind. 2020. *Installing Automobility: Emerging Politics of Mobility and Streets in Indian Cities*. Cambridge, MA: MIT Press. https://doi.org/10.7551/mitpress/12399.001.0001.

Govinda, Radhika. 2020. "From the Taxi Drivers' Rear-View Mirror: Masculinity, Marginality and Sexual Violence in India's Capital City, Delhi." *Gender, Place & Culture* 27 (1): 69–85. https://doi.org/10.1080/0966369X.2019.1567469.

Graeber, David. 2018. *Bullshit Jobs*. New York: Simon and Schuster.

Gregg, Melissa. 2011. *Work's Intimacy*. Cambridge, UK: Polity.

———. 2018. *Counterproductive: Time Management in the Knowledge Economy*. Durham, NC: Duke University Press.

Gupta, Akhil, and K. Sivaramakrishnan, eds. 2011. *The State in India after Liberalization: Interdisciplinary Perspectives*. London: Routledge.

Gupta, Hemangini. 2016. "Taking Action: The Desiring Subjects of Neoliberal Feminism in India." *Journal of International Women's Studies* 17 (1): 152–68.

———. 2017. "Modern Love." In *Gender: Love*, edited by Jennifer C. Nash, 227–41. Farmington Hills, MI: Macmillan Reference USA.

———. 2019a. "Testing the Future: Gender and Technocapitalism in Start-Up India." *Feminist Review* 123 (1): 74–88. https://doi.org/10.1177/0141778919879740.

———. 2019b. "The Corporeal Costs of Doing What You Love." *Feminist Media Studies* 19 (2): 295–97. https://doi.org/10.1080/14680777.2019.1573530.

———. 2020. "Postcolonial Assembly Protocols for Unnamed Automation Projects." *Catalyst: Feminism, Theory, Technoscience* 6 (2): 1–14.

———. 2021. "Feminist Multimodality: A Retrospective Account of an Exhibition on Speculative Urbanism." *Multimodality and Society* 1 (3): 281–99.

Gupta, Hemangini, and Kaveri Medappa. 2020. "Nostalgia as Affective Landscape: Negotiating Displacement in the 'World City.'" *Antipode* 52 (6): 1688–1709. https://doi.org/10.1111/anti.12674.

Hamilton, Jennifer A., Banu Subramaniam, and Angela Willey. 2017. "What Indians and Indians Can Teach Us about Colonization: Feminist Science and Technology Studies, Epistemological Imperialism, and the Politics of Difference." *Feminist Studies* 43 (3): 612–23. https://doi.org/10.15767/feministstudies.43.3.0612.

Hamraie, Aimi. 2017. *Building Access: Universal Design and the Politics of Disability.* 3rd ed. Minneapolis: University of Minnesota Press.

Haraway, Donna. 1996. *Simians Cyborgs and Women.* London: Free Association Books.

———. 2003. *The Haraway Reader.* New York: Routledge.

Harvey, David. 1991. *The Condition of Postmodernity: An Enquiry into the Origins of Cultural Change.* Cambridge, MA: Wiley-Blackwell.

Hasan, Anjum. 2009. *Neti, Neti: Not This, Not This.* New Delhi: Roli Books.

Hattam, Victoria. 2022. "Border Economies/Capitalist Imaginaries: Dispelling Capitalism's System Effects." *Borderlands Journal* 21 (1): 39–66. https://doi.org/10.21307/borderlands-2022-003.

Heiman, Rachel, Carla Freeman, and Mark Liechty, eds. 2012. *The Global Middle Classes: Theorizing through Ethnography.* Illustrated ed. Santa Fe, NM: SAR Press.

Heitzman, James. 2004. *Network City: Planning the Information Society in Bangalore.* New Delhi: Oxford University Press.

Held, Virginia. 2005. *The Ethics of Care: Personal, Political, and Global.* New York: Oxford University Press. https://doi.org/10.1093/0195180992.001.0001.

Ho, Karen. 2009. *Liquidated: An Ethnography of Wall Street.* Durham, NC: Duke University Press.

Hochschild, Arlie Russell. 1997. *The Time Bind: When Work Becomes Home and Home Becomes Work.* New York: Metropolitan Books.

———. 2003. *The Second Shift.* New York: Penguin Books.

Honig, Bonnie, ed. 1995. *Feminist Interpretations of Hannah Arendt.* University Park: Pennsylvania State University Press.

Ingole, Anagha. 2023. "Imagining a New Ethic of Sociality: The Non-Brahmin Educated Woman in 19th-Century Western India." *Economic and Political Weekly* 58 (13): 51–57.

Irani, Lilly. 2019. *Chasing Innovation: Making Entrepreneurial Citizens in Modern India.* Princeton, NJ: Princeton University Press.

Irani, Lilly, and Monika Sengul-Jones. 2015. "Difference Work: A Conversation with Lilly Irani." *Catalyst: Feminism, Theory, Technoscience* 1 (1).

Isaacson, Walter. 2011. *Steve Jobs.* Simon & Schuster.

Islam, Asiya. 2021. "Wilful Resignations: Women, Labour and Life in Urban India." In *Beyond the Wage,* 95–114. Bristol: Bristol University Press. https://bristol universitypressdigital.com/edcollchap/book/9781529208948/ch004.xml.

———. 2022. "Plastic Bodies: Women Workers and Emerging Body Rules in Service Work in Urban India." *Gender & Society* 36 (3): 422–44. https://doi .org/10.1177/08912432221089637.

Jackson, Steven J. 2014. "Rethinking Repair." In *Media Technologies: Essays on Communication, Materiality, and Society,* edited by Tarleton Gillespie, Pablo J. Boczkowski, and Kirsten A. Foot, 221–39. Cambridge, MA: MIT Press. https:// doi.org/10.7551/mitpress/9042.003.0015.

Jackson, Zakiyyah Iman. 2020. *Becoming Human: Matter and Meaning in an Anti-black World.* New York: NYU Press.

Jaffe, Sarah. 2020. "The Relational Economy." *Dissent* 67 (3): 12–17. https://doi .org/10.1353/dss.2020.0051.

Jayawardena, Kumari. 1986. *Feminism and Nationalism in the Third World.* New Delhi: Kali for Women.

Jeffrey, Craig. 2010. *Timepass: Youth, Class, and the Politics of Waiting in India.* Stanford, CA: Stanford University Press.

Jegathesan, Mythri. 2019. *Tea and Solidarity: Tamil Women and Work in Postwar Sri Lanka.* Seattle: University of Washington Press.

John, Mary, and Janaki Nair. 2001. *A Question of Silence? The Sexual Economics of Modern India.* London: Zed Books.

Jung, Moon-Ho. 2008. *Coolies and Cane: Race, Labor, and Sugar in the Age of Emancipation.* Baltimore, MD: Johns Hopkins University Press. http://ebook central.proquest.com/lib/middlebury/detail.action?docID=3318306.

Kaplan, Caren. 2000. *Questions of Travel: Postmodern Discourses of Displacement.* 3rd ed. Durham, NC: Duke University Press Books.

Karnad, Raghu. 2012. "City in a Bottle." *Caravan Magazine,* July 1, 2012. http://caravanmagazine.in/Story.aspx?StoryId=1467.

Katz, Cindi. 2001. "Vagabond Capitalism and the Necessity of Social Reproduction." *Antipode* 33 (4): 709–28. https://doi.org/10.1111/1467-8330.00207.

Kaur, Ravinder. 2020a. *Brand New Nation: Capitalist Dreams and Nationalist Designs in Twenty-First-Century India.* Stanford, CA: Stanford University Press.

———. 2020b. :Brand New Nation." Paper presented in the Transnational Asia speaker series, Houston, TX, October 9.

Kelty, Christopher. 2005. "Geeks, Social Imaginaries, and Recursive Publics." *Cultural Anthropology* 20 (2): 185–214. https://doi.org/10.1525/can.2005.20.2.185.

Khubchandani, Kareem. 2020. *Ishtyle.* Ann Arbor: University of Michigan Press.

Kimmel, Michael S. 2012. *Manhood in America: A Cultural History.* 3rd ed. New York: Oxford University Press.

———. 2015. *Angry White Men: American Masculinity at the End of an Era.* Reprint ed. New York: Nation Books.

Kondo, Dorinne K. 1990. *Crafting Selves: Power, Gender, and Discourses of Identity in a Japanese Workplace.* Chicago: University of Chicago Press.

Krishna, T. M. 2015. "Revisiting the Bond." *The Hindu,* July 4, 2015. http://www.thehindu.com/opinion/columns/t_m_krishna/tm-krishna-on-why-raksha-bandhan-is-not-thebonding-ofequals/article7382607.ece.

Krishnamurthy, Mathangi. 2004. "Resources and Rebels: A Study of Identity Management in Indian Call Centers." *Anthropology of Work Review* 25 (3–4): 9–18. https://doi.org/10.1525/awr.2004.25.3-4.9.

Landes, Joan B. 1988. *Women and the Public Sphere in the Age of the French Revolution.* Ithaca, NY: Cornell University Press.

———. 1995. "The Public and the Private Sphere: A Reconsideration." In *Feminists Read Habermas: Gendering the Subject of Discourse,* edited by Johanna Meehan, 91–116. New York: Routledge.

Latour, Bruno. 2005. *Reassembling the Social: An Introduction to Actor-Network-Theory.* Clarendon Lectures in Management Studies. Oxford: Oxford University Press.

Liechty, Mark. 2003. *Suitably Modern: Making Middle-Class Culture in a New Consumer Society.* Princeton, NJ: Princeton University Press.

Lukose, Ritty A. 2009. *Liberalization's Children: Gender, Youth, and Consumer Citizenship in Globalizing India*. Durham, NC: Duke University Press.

Lynch, Caitrin. 2007. *Juki Girls, Good Girls: Gender and Cultural Politics in Sri Lanka's Global Garment Industry*. Ithaca, NY: ILR Press/Cornell University Press.

Mahmood, Saba. 2005. *Politics of Piety: The Islamic Revival and the Feminist Subject*. Princeton, NJ: Princeton University Press.

Malatino, Hil. 2020. *Trans Care*. Minneapolis: University of Minnesota Press. https://www.upress.umn.edu/book-division/books/trans-care.

Manalansan, Martin F. 2008. "Queering the Chain of Care Paradigm." *Women's Studies Quarterly* 6 (3). http://sfonline.barnard.edu/immigration/manalansan_01.htm.

———. 2015. "Queer Worldings: The Messy Art of Being Global in Manila and New York." *Antipode* 47 (3): 566–79.

Mani, Lata. 1998. *Contentious Traditions: The Debate on Sati in Colonial India*. Berkeley: University of California Press.

———. 2014. "Sex and the Signal-Free Corridor." *Economic and Political Weekly* 49 (6): 26–29.

Mankekar, Purnima. 1999. *Screening Culture, Viewing Politics: An Ethnography of Television, Womanhood, and Nation in Postcolonial India*. Durham, NC: Duke University Press.

Mankekar, Purnima, and Akhil Gupta. 2016. "Intimate Encounters: Affective Labor in Call Centers." *Positions: Asia Critique* 24 (1): 17–43. https://doi.org/10.1215/10679847-3320029.

Maslow, Abraham H. 2022. *A Theory of Human Motivation*. Floyd, VA: Wilder Publications.

Massey, Doreen. 1994. *Space, Place, and Gender*. Minneapolis: University of Minnesota Press.

———. 2018. "Power-Geometry and a Progressive Sense of Place (1993)." In *The Doreen Massey Reader*, edited by Brett Christophers, Rebecca Lave, Jamie Peck, and Marion Werner, 149–58. Newcastle upon Tyne: Agenda Publishing. https://doi.org/10.2307/j.ctv5cg7pq.15.

Martin, Emily. 1995. *Flexible Bodies*. Boston: Beacon Press.

Mathew, Leya, and Ritty Lukose. 2020. "Pedagogies of Aspiration: Anthropological Perspectives on Education in Liberalising India." *South Asia: Journal of *South Asian Studies* 43 (4): 691–704. https://doi.org/10.1080/00856401.2020 .1768466.

Mathur, Anuradha, and Dilip Da Cunha. 2006. *Deccan Traverses: The Making of Bangalore's Terrain.* New Delhi: Rupa & Co.

Mauss, Marcel. 2000. *The Gift: The Form and Reason for Exchange in Archaic Societies.* New York: W. W. Norton.

Mazzarella, William. 2005. "Middle Class." Accessed September 3, 2012. https://d3qioqp55mx5f5.cloudfront.net/anthrolpology/docs/mazz_middle class.pdf.

McClintock, Anne. 1993. "Family Feuds: Gender, Nationalism and the Family." *Feminist Review* (44) (July): 61–80. https://doi.org/10.2307/1395196.

McDowell, Linda. 1994. "Missing Subjects: Gender, Power, and Sexuality in Merchant Banking." *Economic Geography* 70 (3): 229.

McElroy, Erin. 2020. "Corruption, Şmecherie, and Siliconization: Retrospective and Speculative Technoculture in Postsocialist Romania." *Catalyst: Feminism, Theory, Technoscience* 6 (2): 1–25. https://doi.org/10.28968/cftt.v6i2.32905.

McGuire, Meredith Lindsay. 2011. "'How to Sit, How to Stand': Bodily Practice and the New Urban Middle Class." In *A Companion to the Anthropology of India,* edited by Isabelle Clark-Decès, 115–36. Malden, MA: Wiley-Blackwell.

Medappa, Kaveri, Rajorshi Ray, and Mohammad Sajjan Hussain. 2020. "Confronting Precarious Work." *The India Forum,* 7 October 2020. https://www .theindiaforum.in/article/confronting-precarious-work.

Meehan, Johanna, ed. 1995. *Feminists Read Habermas: Gendering the Subject of Discourse.* New York: Routledge.

Melamed, Jodi. 2015. "Racial Capitalism." *Critical Ethnic Studies* 1 (1): 76–85.

Menon, Nivedita, and Aditya Nigam. 2007. *Power and Contestation: India Since 1989.* London: Zed Books.

Mertia, Sandeep, ed. 2020. *Lives of Data: Essays on Computational Cultures from India.* Vol. 39. Amsterdam: Institute of Network Cultures, Amsterdam. https:// networkcultures.org/blog/publication/lives-of-data-essays-on-computational -cultures-from-india/.

Meyer, Katrin. 2024. "Centring Care as a Practice of Politics." *GENDER.ED* (blog), June 4, 2024. https://www.gender.ed.ac.uk/blog/2024/centring-care -practice-politics.

Mezzadra, Sandro, and Brett Neilson. 2013. *Border as Method, or, the Multiplication of Labor*. Durham, NC: Duke University Press.

Mezzadri, Alessandra. 2019. "On the Value of Social Reproduction: Informal Labour, the Majority World and the Need for Inclusive Theories and Politics." *Radical Philosophy*, no. 2.04: 33–41.

Mies, Maria. (1982) 2012. *The Lace Makers of Narsapur*. 2nd ed. North Melbourne, Victoria, Australia: Spinifex Press.

Millar, Kathleen M. 2018. *Reclaiming the Discarded: Life and Labor on Rio's Garbage Dump*. Durham, NC: Duke University Press.

Mirchandani, Kiran. 2012. *Phone Clones: Authenticity Work in the Transnational Service Economy*. Ithaca, NY: ILR Press/Cornell University Press.

Mody, Perveez. 2008. *The Intimate State: Love-Marriage and the Law in Delhi*. New Delhi: Routledge India.

Mohanty, Chandra Talpade. 2003. *Feminism without Borders: Decolonizing Theory, Practicing Solidarity*. Durham, NC: Duke University Press Books.

Moi, Toril. 1991. "Appropriating Bourdieu: Feminist Theory and Pierre Bourdieu's Sociology of Culture." *New Literary History* 22 (4): 1017–49. https://doi.org/10.2307/469077.

Molé, Noelle J. 2011. *Labor Disorders in Neoliberal Italy: Mobbing, Well-Being, and the Workplace*. Bloomington: Indiana University Press.

Mosse, David. 2006. "Anti-Social Anthropology? Objectivity, Objection, and the Ethnography of Public Policy and Professional Communities." *Journal of the Royal Anthropological Institute* 12 (4): 935–56.

———. 2020. "The Modernity of Caste and the Market Economy." *Modern Asian Studies* 54 (4): 1225–71. https://doi.org/10.1017/S0026749X19000039.

Mukherjee, Sanjukta. 2008. "Producing the Knowledge Professional: Gendered Geographies of Alienation in India's New High-Tech Workplace." In *In an Outpost of the Global Economy: Work and Workers in India's Information Technology Industry*, edited by Carol Upadhya and A. R. Vasavi. New Delhi: Routledge.

Mukhopadhyay, Sukumar. 2002. "Globalisation and Indian Services Sector." *Economic and Political Weekly* 37 (40): 4097–98.

Murphy, Jonathan. 2011. "Indian Call Centre Workers: Vanguard of a Global Middle Class?" *Work, Employment & Society* 25 (3): 417–33.

Murphy, Michelle. 2013. "The Girl: Mergers of Feminism and Finance in Neoliberal Times." S&F Online. http://sfonline.barnard.edu/gender-justice-and-neoliberal-transformations/the-girl-mergers-of-feminism-and-finance-in-neoliberal-times/.

———. 2015. "Unsettling Care: Troubling Transnational Itineraries of Care in Feminist Health Practices." *Social Studies of Science* 45 (5): 717–37. https://doi.org/10.1177/0306312715589136.

———. 2017. *The Economization of Life*. Durham, NC: Duke University Press Books.

Nadasen, Premilla. 2015. *Household Workers Unite: The Untold Story of African American Women Who Built a Movement*. Boston: Beacon Press.

———. 2017. "Rethinking Care: Arlie Hochschild and the Global Care Chain." *WSQ: Women's Studies Quarterly* 45 (3): 124–28. https://doi.org/10.1353/wsq.2017.0049.

Nagendran, Harini. 2016. *Nature in the City: Bengaluru in the Past, Present, and Future*. New Delhi: Oxford University Press.

Naidu, Sirisha C., and Lyn Ossome. 2016. "Social Reproduction and the Agrarian Question of Women's Labour in India." *Agrarian South: Journal of Political Economy* 5 (1): 50–76. https://doi.org/10.1177/2277976016658737.

Nair, Janaki. 1998. *Miners and Millhands: Work, Culture and Politics in Princely Mysore*. Walnut Creek, CA: Altamira Press.

———. 2002. "Past Perfect: Architecture and Public Life in Bangalore." *Journal of Asian Studies* 61 (4): 1205–36. https://doi.org/10.2307/3096440.

———. 2005. *The Promise of the Metropolis: Bangalore's Twentieth Century*. New Delhi: Oxford University Press.

Nakamura, Lisa. 2011. "Economies of Digital Production in East Asia." *Media Fields Journal* (2). http://mediafieldsjournal.org/economies-of-digital.

Neff, Gina. 2015. *Venture Labor: Work and the Burden of Risk in Innovative Industries*. Reprint ed. Cambridge, MA: MIT Press.

Negron, Wilneida. 2018. "Ford Foundation Fellow: Tech Needs to Begin with People." Fast Company. November 20. https://www.fastcompany.com/90270299/want-to-build-tech-for-good-understand-peoples-needs-first.

Ng, Cecilia, and Swasti Mitter. 2005. "Valuing Women's Voices: Call Center Workers in Malaysia and India." *Gender, Technology and Development* 9 (2): 209–33. https://doi.org/10.1177/097185240500900203.

Nguyen, Lilly. 2018. "'This Is Not Who We Are': Freedom as Moral Affect and the Whiteness of Mutuality." *Catalyst: Feminism, Theory, Technoscience* 4 (1): 1–10. https://doi.org/10.28968/cftt.v4i1.29636.

Noble, Safiya Umoja. 2018. *Algorithms of Oppression: How Search Engines Reinforce Racism.* Illustrated ed. New York: NYU Press.

Norton, Jack, and Cindi Katz. 2017. "Social Reproduction." In *International Encyclopedia of Geography,* 1–11. John Wiley & Sons. https://doi.org/10.1002/9781118786352.wbieg1107.

O'Malley, Pat. 1996. "Risk and Responsibility." In *Foucault and Political Reason: Liberalism, Neo-Liberalism and Rationalities of Government,* 189–208. London: UCL Press Limited.

Ong, Aihwa. 1991. "The Gender and Labor Politics of Postmodernity." *Annual Review of Anthropology* 20 (1): 279–309. https://doi.org/10.1146/annurev.an.20.100191.001431.

———. 2006. *Neoliberalism as Exception: Mutations in Citizenship and Sovereignty.* Durham, NC: Duke University Press.

———. 2010. *Spirits of Resistance and Capitalist Discipline: Factory Women in Malaysia.* 2nd ed. Albany: State University of New York Press.

Ossome, Lyn. 2022. "Introduction: The Social Reproductive Question of Land Contestations in Africa." *African Affairs* 121 (484): 9–24.

Oza, Rupal. 1992. *The Making of Neoliberal India: Nationalism, Gender, and the Paradoxes of Globalization.* New York: Routledge.

Padios, Jan M. 2018. *A Nation on the Line: Call Centers as Postcolonial Predicaments in the Philippines.* Durham, NC: Duke University Press.

Parrenas, Rhacel. 2004. "The Care Crisis in the Philippines." In *Global Woman: Nannies, Maids, and Sex Workers in the New Economy,* edited by Barbara Ehrenreich and Arlie Russell Hochschild, 39–54. New York: Metropolitan/Owl.

Patel, Reena. 2010. *Working the Night Shift: Women in India's Call Center Industry.* Stanford, CA: Stanford University Press.

Patico, Jennifer. 2008. *Consumption and Social Change in a Post-Soviet Middle Class.* Stanford, CA: Stanford University Press.

Philip, Kavita. 2016. "Telling Histories of the Future: The Imaginaries of Indian Technoscience." *Identities* 23 (3): 276–93. https://doi.org/10.1080/1070289X.2015.1034129.

Piscione, Deborah Perry. 2014. *The Risk Factor: Why Every Organization Needs Big Bets, Bold Characters, and the Occasional Spectacular Failure.* New York: Palgrave Macmillan Trade.

Poon, A. 1993. *Tourism, Technology and Competitive Strategies.* New York: CAB International.

Prakash, Gyan. 1999. *Another Reason: Science and the Imagination of Modern India.* Princeton, NJ: Princeton University Press.

Pringle, Rosemary. 1989. *Secretaries Talk: Sexuality, Power and Work.* London: Verso Books.

Qayum, Seemin, and Raka Ray. 2009. *Cultures of Servitude: Modernity, Domesticity, and Class in India.* Stanford, CA: Stanford University Press.

Radhakrishnan, Smitha. 2007. "Rethinking Knowledge for Development: Transnational Knowledge Professionals and the 'New' India." *Theory and Society* 36 (2): 141–59.

———. 2009. "Professional Women, Good Families: Respectable Femininity and the Cultural Politics of a 'New' India." *Qualitative Sociology* 32 (2): 195–212. https://doi.org/10.1007/s11133-009-9125-5.

———. 2011. *Appropriately Indian: Gender and Culture in a New Transnational Class.* Durham, NC: Duke University Press.

Raha, Nat. 2021. "A Queer Marxist Transfeminism: Queer and Trans Social Reproduction." In *Transgender Marxism*, edited by Jules Joanne Gleeson and Elle O'Rourke, 85–115. London: Pluto Press.

Rajan, Kaushik Sunder. 2006. *Biocapital: The Constitution of Postgenomic Life.* Durham, NC: Duke University Press.

Raju, Saraswati. 2013. "Women in India's New Generation Jobs." *Economic and Political Weekly* 48 (36): 16–18.

Ramamurthy, Priti, et al. 2022. "Preface." *Feminist Studies* 47 (3): 479–91.

Ranganathan, Malini. 2015. "Storm Drains as Assemblages: The Political Ecology of Flood Risk in Post-Colonial Bangalore" 47 (5): 1300–1320. https://doi.org/10.1111/anti.12149.

Rao, Rahul. 2024. "Is the Homo in Homocapitalism the Caste in Caste Capitalism and the Racial in Racial Capitalism?" *South Atlantic Quarterly* 123 (1): 79–103. https://doi.org/10.1215/00382876-10920678.

Rheinberger, Hans-Jörg. 1997. *Toward a History of Epistemic Things: Synthesizing Proteins in the Test Tube.* Stanford, CA: Stanford University Press.

Richardson, Lizzie. 2024. "Automated Office Infrastructures and the Valuation of Work." *Environment and Planning D: Society and Space* 0 (0): 0263775823121 8799. https://doi.org/10.1177/02637758231218799.

Robinson, Cedric J. 2021. *Black Marxism: The Making of the Black Radical Tradition.* 3rd ed. Chapel Hill: University of North Carolina Press.

Rofel, Lisa. 2002. "Modernity's Masculine Fantasies." In *Critically Modern: Alternatives, Alterities, Anthropologies,* 175–93. Bloomington: Indiana University Press.

Rotterberg, Catherine. 2019. "Women Who Work: The Limits of the Neoliberal Feminist Paradigm." *Gender, Work, and Organization* 26 (8): 1073–82. https://doi.org/10.1111/gwao.12287

Roy, Srila. 2022. *Changing the Subject: Feminist and Queer Politics in Neoliberal India.* Durham, NC: Duke University Press Books.

Rubin, Gayle. 2011. "The Traffic in Women: Notes on the 'Political Economy' of Sex." In *Deviations: A Gayle Rubin Reader,* 33–65. Durham, NC: Duke University Press.

Rudrappa, Sharmila. 2012. "India's Reproductive Assembly Line." *Contexts* 11 (2): 22–27. https://doi.org/10.1177/1536504212446456.

Säävälä, Minna. 2010. *Middle-Class Moralities: Everyday Struggle over Belonging and Prestige in India.* New Delhi: Orient Blackswan.

Salzinger, Leslie. 2003. *Genders in Production: Making Workers in Mexico's Global Factories.* Berkeley: University of California Press.

Sandoval, Chela. 2000. *Methodology of the Oppressed.* Minneapolis: University of Minnesota Press.

Sanyal, Kalyan. 2007. *Rethinking Capitalist Development: Primitive Accumulation, Governmentality and Post-Colonial Capitalism.* New Delhi: Routledge India.

Searle, Llerena Guiu. 2016. *Landscapes of Accumulation: Real Estate and the Neoliberal Imagination in Contemporary India.* Chicago: University of Chicago Press.

Seizer, Susan. 2005. *Stigmas of the Tamil Stage an Ethnography of Special Drama Artists in South India.* Durham, NC: Duke University Press.

Sekharan, Abhishek, and Ambika Tandon. 2021. "Are India's Much-Lauded Startups Failing Their Women Workers?" Centre for Internet and Society, *Researchers at Work Blog,* December 6, 2021. https://cis-india.org/raw/are-indias-much-lauded-startups-failing-their-women-workers.

Sharma, Sarah. 2014. *In the Meantime: Temporality and Cultural Politics.* Durham, NC: Duke University Press Books.

Shylaja, S., and Sharada Jayagovind. 2003. "Quiet in Its Mission." *The Hindu,* March 24, 2003. http://www.thehindu.com/thehindu/mp/2003/03/24/stories /2003032401170200.htm.

Simone, Abdoumaliq. 2004. "People as Infrastructure: Intersecting Fragments in Johannesburg." *Public Culture* 16 (3): 407–29. https://doi.org/10.1215/089 92363-16-3-407.

———. 2014. *Jakarta, Drawing the City Near.* Minneapolis: University of Minnesota Press.

Singh, Juliette. 2018. *Unthinking Mastery: Dehumanism and Decolonial Entanglements.* Durham, NC: Duke University Press. http://oapen.org/search ?identifier=648165.

Sinha, Mrinalini. 2006. *Specters of Mother India: The Global Restructuring of an Empire.* Radical Perspectives. Durham, NC: Duke University Press.

Solomon, Harris. 2014. "Taste Tests: Pizza and the Gastropolitical Laboratory in Mumbai." In "Bodies and Experiments in Asia," special issue, *Ethnos* 79 (1): 19–40.

Srinivas, Smriti. 2001. *Landscapes of Urban Memory: The Sacred and the Civic in India's High-Tech City.* Minneapolis: University of Minnesota Press.

Star, Susan Leigh. 2010. "This Is Not a Boundary Object: Reflections on the Origin of a Concept." *Science, Technology, & Human Values* 35 (5): 601–17.

Star, Susan Leigh, and Anselm Strauss. 1999. "Layers of Silence, Arenas of Voice: The Ecology of Visible and Invisible Work." *Computer Supported Cooperative Work (CSCW)* 8 (1): 9–30. https://doi.org/10.1023/A:10086511 05359.

Steinhardt, Stephanie B., and Steven J. Jackson. 2015. "Anticipation Work: Cultivating Vision in Collective Practice." In *Proceedings of the 18th ACM Conference on Computer Supported Cooperative Work & Social Computing,* 443–53. New York: ACM. https://doi.org/10.1145/2675133.2675298.

Stevenson, Emily. 2023. *British Indian Picture Postcards in Bengaluru: Ephemeral Entanglements.* New York: Routledge.

Subramaniam, Banu. 2001. "Technoscientific Imaginations." *Feminist Studies* 27 (2): 526–31.

———. 2017. "Recolonizing India: Troubling the Anticolonial, Decolonial, Postcolonial." *Catalyst: Feminism, Theory, Technoscience* 3 (1). https://doi.org/10.28968/cftt.v3i1.28794.

———. 2019. *Holy Science: The Biopolitics of Hindu Nationalism.* Seattle: University of Washington Press.

Subramanian, Ajantha. 2015. "Making Merit: The Indian Institutes of Technology and the Social Life of Caste." *Comparative Studies in Society and History* 57 (2): 291–322. https://doi.org/10.1017/S0010417515000043.

———. 2019. *The Caste of Merit: Engineering Education in India.* Cambridge, MA: Harvard University Press.

Suchman, Lucy, and Libby Bishop. 2000. "Problematizing 'Innovation' as a Critical Project." *Technology Analysis & Strategic Management* 12 (3): 327–33.

Suresh Babu, Savitha. 2020. "Education for Confidence: Political Education for Recasting Bahujan Student Selves." *South Asia: Journal of South Asian Studies* 43 (4): 741–57. https://doi.org/10.1080/00856401.2020.1777692.

Thapan, Meenakshi. 2004. "Embodiment and Identity in Contemporary Society: Femina and the 'New' Indian Woman." *Contributions to Indian Sociology* 38 (3): 411–44. https://doi.org/10.1177/006996670403800305.

Thomas, Renny. 2020. "Brahmins as Scientists and Science as Brahmins' Calling: Caste in an Indian Scientific Research Institute." *Public Understanding of Science* 29 (3): 306–18.

Thomas, Renny, and Robert M. Geraci. 2018. "Religious Rites and Scientific Communities: Ayudha Puja as 'Culture' at the Indian Institute of Science." *Zygon* (1): 95–122. https://doi.org/10.1111/zygo.12380.

Thomsen, Carly. 2021. *Visibility Interrupted: Rural Queer Life and the Politics of Unbecoming.* Minneapolis: University of Minnesota Press.

Tokumitsu, Miya. 2015. *Do What You Love: And Other Lies about Success and Happiness.* New York: Regan Arts.

Towghi, Fouzieyha, and Kalindi Vora. 2014. "Bodies, Markets, and the Experimental in South Asia." In "Bodies and Experiments in Asia," special issue, *Ethnos* 79 (1): 1–18. https://doi.org/10.1080/00141844.2013.810660.

Trivedi, Harish. 2003. "Cyber Coolies or Cyber Sahibs?" *Times of India*, September 7, 2003. https://timesofindia.indiatimes.com/home/sunday-times/all-that-matters/Cyber-coolies-or-cyber-sahibs/articleshow/169677.cms.

Tsing, Anna Lowenhaupt. 2004. *Friction: An Ethnography of Global Connection*. Princeton, NJ: Princeton University Press.

Upadhya, Carol. 2007. "Employment, Exclusion and 'Merit' in the Indian IT Industry." *Economic and Political Weekly* 42 (20): 1863–68. https://doi.org/10.2307/4419609.

———. 2008. "Ethnographies of the Global Information Economy: Research Strategies and Methods." *Economic and Political Weekly* 43 (17): 64–72.

———. 2016. *Reengineering India: Work, Capital, and Class in an Offshore Economy*. New Delhi: Oxford University Press.

Upadhya, Carol, and A. R. Vasavi. 2013. *In an Outpost of the Global Economy: Work and Workers in India's Information Technology Industry*. New Delhi: Routledge India.

Upadhya, Carol, and Deeksha M Rao. 2022. "Dispossession without Displacement: Producing Property through Slum Redevelopment in Bengaluru, India." *Environment and Planning A: Economy and Space* 55 (2): 428–44. https://doi.org/10.1177/0308518X221073988.

Urciuoli, Bonnie. 2008. "Skills and Selves in the New Workplace." *American Ethnologist* 35 (2): 211–28. https://doi.org/10.1111/j.1548-1425.2008.00031.x.

Urry, John, and Jonas Larsen. 2011. *The Tourist Gaze 3.0*. 3rd ed. Los Angeles: Sage.

Vaghela, Palashi, Steven J. Jackson, and Phoebe Sengers. 2022. "Interrupting Merit, Subverting Legibility: Navigating Caste in 'Casteless' Worlds of Computing." In *Proceedings of the 2022 CHI Conference on Human Factors in Computing Systems*, 20. https://dl.acm.org/doi/10.1145/3491102.3502059.

Van Dijk, Meine Pieter. 2003. "Government Policies with Respect to an Information Technology Cluster in Bangalore, India." *European Journal of Development Research* 15 (2): 93–108.

Veblen, Thorstein. 2008. *The Theory of the Leisure Class*. Edited by Martha Banta. Oxford: Oxford University Press.

Vijayakumar, Gowri. 2013. "'I'll Be Like Water': Gender, Class, and Flexible Aspirations at the Edge of India's Knowledge Economy." *Gender & Society* 27 (6): 777–98. https://doi.org/10.1177/0891243213499445.

———. 2021a. *At Risk Indian Sexual Politics and the Global AIDS Crisis*. Stanford, CA: Stanford University Press.

———. 2021b. "Risk and Respectability: Reinventing Sexuality in State-NGO HIV Prevention Programs." *Qualitative Sociology* 44: 437–54. https://link .springer.com/article/10.1007/s11133-021-09490-3.

Visweswaran, Kamala. 1994. *Fictions of Feminist Ethnography*. Minneapolis: University of Minnesota Press.

Vora, Kalindi. 2009. "Indian Transnational Surrogacy and the Commodification of Vital Energy." *Subjectivity* 28: 266–78.

———. 2015. *Life Support: Biocapital and the New History of Outsourced Labor*. Minneapolis: University of Minnesota Press.

———. 2019. "After the Housewife: Surrogacy, Labour, and Human Reproduction." *Radical Philosophy*, no. 2.04: 42–46.

Wajcman, Judy. 1991. *Feminism Confronts Technology*. Cambridge, UK: Polity Press.

Walkerdine, Valerie. 2003. "Reclassifying Upward Mobility: Femininity and the Neo-Liberal Subject." *Gender & Education* 15 (3): 237–48.

Weeks, Kathi. 2011. *The Problem with Work: Feminism, Marxism, Antiwork Politics, and Postwork Imaginaries*. A John Hope Franklin Center Book. Durham, NC: Duke University Press.

———. 2017. "Down with Love: Feminist Critique and the New Ideologies of Work." *WSQ: Women's Studies Quarterly* 45 (3): 37–58. https://doi.org/10.1353 /wsq.2017.0043.

Wiegman, Robyn. 2002. "The Progress of Gender: Whither Women?" In *Women's Studies on Its Own: A Next Wave Reader in Institutional Change*, edited by Robyn Wiegman, 106–40. Durham, NC: Duke University Press.

Williams, Christine L., and Catherine Connell. 2010. "'Looking Good and Sounding Right': Aesthetic Labor and Social Inequality in the Retail Industry." *Work and Occupations* 37 (3): 349–77. https://doi.org/10.1177/0730888410 373744.

Wright, Andrea. 2021. *Between Dreams and Ghosts: Indian Migration and Middle Eastern Oil*. Stanford, CA: Stanford University Press.

Yang, Mayfair Mei-hui. 1994. *Gifts, Favors, and Banquets: The Art of Social Relationships in China*. Ithaca, NY: Cornell University Press.

Yergeau, Melanie. 2012. "Disability Hacktivism." Hacking the Classroom. http://www2.bgsu.edu/departments/english/cconline/hacking/#yergeau.

Young, Iris. 2005. *On Female Body Experience: "Throwing Like a Girl" and Other Essays*. New York: Oxford University Press.

Yun, Lisa. 2008. *The Coolie Speaks: Chinese Indentured Laborers and African Slaves in Cuba*. Asian American History and Culture. Philadelphia: Temple University Press.

Zaloom, Caitlin. 2004. "The Productive Life of Risk." *Cultural Anthropology* 19 (3): 365–91.

Zerilli, Linda M. G. 2005. *Feminism and the Abyss of Freedom*. Chicago: University of Chicago Press.

Index

Berlant, Lauren, 169, 273n4

Bharatiya Janata Party (BJP), 11

Boellstorrf, Tom, 71

Bosworth, Kai, 165–66

Bourdieu, Pierre, 54, 176

Brahmins/Brahmanism, 25, 56, 103–4; Brahmanical culture, 200; Brahmanical Hinduism, 195; Brahmin masculinity, 103; Brahmanical patriarchy, 205

Brand India (Kaur), 19

Braverman, Henry, 50

Burroughs Ltd., 17

call centers, 87, 89–90, 152, 177, 180, 185, 187, 265nn18–19, 271n17

capitalism, 4, 171, 178, 259n12; colonial capitalism, 228, 229; global capitalism, 19; racial capitalism, 10, 258–59n9; in the South, 237; techno-capitalism, 64, 96; theories of, 239. *See also* startup capitalism

Capper, Beth, 273n11

Captivate Travels, 13–14, 29, 31, 47–57, 149, 153–54, 158, 161–62, 166–73, 181*fig.*, 205–6, 252, 253, 268–69n1; beginnings of, 48, 61; and breaks from reproductive labor, 178–85; career growth and development of different kinds of workers at, 57; and caste relations, 195–96; categorization of workers at, 57; during the COVID-19 pandemic, 247–48; efforts for automation at, 141, 142; elite workers at, 173–78; embodied exhaustion at, 158–62; emerging middle class at, 60; job cuts at, 224–32, 233; location of, 215*fig.*; nonelite workers at, 152–53; office in Indiranagar,

49–51, 51*fig.*; lounge of, 50*fig.*; and the meanings of work, 154–55; opportunities offered by, 58–59; Rangoli decoration at, 198*fig.*; sales training graph of, 172*fig.*; and the shaping of labor as a form of temporal work at, 213–14; test trips offered by, 59; work environment of, 58; workplace automation at, 225–27. *See also* Captivate Travels, employees of; Lata's story, growing up in the company family; management, at Captivate Travels

Captivate Travels, employees of, 48–49, 57–58; employees at an off-site trip, 223–24, 223*fig.*; employees as "test subjects," 219–21; expatriate employees of, 54–55; food orders for employees, 214, 215*fig.*, 216; investment of in employee lifestyles, 60–61; number of employees in Bangalore, 170; sales team employees of, 61; women employees of ("work family"), 185–92; women employees of supporting guest travel, 55–56

care: care with unruly subjects, 202–4; uneven infrastructures of, 199–202

caste, 87–88, 93, 106, 130, 195–96; caste-based coded work, 100; historical life of caste in Indian technology, 265–66n3; as hypervisibilized, 25; imbrication of, 25; romantic love outside one's caste, 104; urban caste-class landscapes of professional life, 95

Chasing Innovation (Irani), 143

Chatterjee, Partha, 263n6

Chen, Kuan-Tsing, 239–40

citizenship, 24; categories of, 10

class, 28, 93, 95, 106, 130; class mobility, 3, 19, 63, 75, 89, 112, 158, 265n19; flexibility as a performance of class, 145–49; gendered middle class, 82–83; middle-class economy and workers, 57–58; South Indian middle-class ethos, 88; urban caste-class landscapes of professional life, 95

Collier, Jane, 274n17

colonialism, 19, 74, 75, 92, 149, 152, 260n20, 272n4, 272–73n8; legacies of, 228

coolies, 228–29; "cyber coolies," 5, 16, 32, 210, 228

COVID-19 pandemic, 247–48

Dalits, 24–25

Dalla Costa, Maria, 273n11

Das, Sophie, 89

Dasgupta, Simanti, 268n18

Davila, Arlene, 260–61n22

Derné, Steve, 262n1

difference, productive force of, 12

Diwali day, 196, 197, 199, 203

Donner, Henrike, 263n5

"Do What You Love (DWYL)" mantra, 23, 31, 173, 175, 195, 202, 249, 252, 259n13

drag queens, Filipina, 203–4

Dubal, Veena, 258n8, 269n4

Dubovskiy, Vlad, 22, 23

economics, as performative, 11

"ecosystems," 7

Edelman, Lee, 189

El Calafate, 205–6, 207

Elyachar, Julia, 165

"Enlightened Woman," figure of, 74, 75

Enlightenment, the, 6

Enloe, Cynthia, 267n11

entrepreneurialism, 15, 127, 144, 210, 249, 250; current economy of, 70; entrepreneurial American ideal of the "self-made man," 266n6

entrepreneurs, 7, 92, 94, 266n7; aspiring entrepreneurs, 44–45, 108–9; elite entrepreneurs, 4–5; Indian entrepreneurs, 6; masculine figure of internet entrepreneurs, 45, 268n18; peripheral entrepreneurs, 250; startup entrepreneurs, 267n9; startup entrepreneurs in Bangalore, 105, 116; startup entrepreneurs as fetishized figures, 112; startup entrepreneurs and urban publics, 113; technology entrepreneurs, 250; value and startup entrepreneurs, 111; women entrepreneurs, 127–28

entrepreneurship, 26, 130; experimental worlds of, 27; global forms of, 9; Indian entrepreneurship, 19; normative world of, 130; women's participation in, 30–31, 129, 132–33, 262n30

Eva Mall, 83

experimental, the, making of, 219–24

"experimental time," 209–10, 234–36, 248–55; embodying experimental time in uncertain environments, 214, 216–19; zones of, 2

experimentation, 4, 20, 25, 30, 58, 64, 106, 209, 211, 231, 238–41, 249; desire for, 165, 205; gender experimentation, 224; local forms of ("jugaad"), 268n14; in the South, 19, 252–53, 275n2; techno-capitalist experimentation, 205–6;

experimentation (*continued*)

    technological experimentation, 6, 11, 14

family, 274n17; family space, 191; families and care with unruly subjects, 202–4; "Indian family values," 200; Indian enterprise and family networks, 266n4; narratives of company as family, 274n16; queering the family, 189, 204; trope of, 191–92; "work family," 185–92, 202; workplaces as family, 201–2, 274n14. *See also* Lata's story, growing up in the company family

Federici, Silvia, 263n3, 271–72n3, 273n11

femininity, 62; public femininity, 200

feminism, 9–10, 234; and the cultivation of confidence, 263–64n8; of everyday life, 96; feminist analyses of technology, 276n14; feminist evaluation of surrogacy, 273n10; feminist theorists, 61–62. *See also* feminist futures

feminist futures, 15, 26–29, 29–30, 70, 192, 237–41, 239, 240–41, 250–51, 253–54

flexibility, 30, 67, 155, 158, 159, 251–52, 271n15; fantasies of, 31; flexibility approaches to work, 143–44; as freedom, 139–44, 160–61; as a gift and moral obligation, 149–53; global flexible specialization, 264n16; limits of, 163; multiple valences of, 162–63; as a performance of class, 145–49

Flexible Bodies (Martin), 223

Freeman, Carla, 258n4

friction, conceptualization of, 123

Friedman, Thomas, 227–28

futures, 143, 250; feminist futures, 15, 26–29, 29–30, 70, 192, 237–41, 239, 240–41, 250–51, 253–54; coercive futures, 232; entrepreneurial futures, 95; feminist itineraries for, 237–41; linear futures, 29; middle-class futures, 224; the robotic future, 228, 232–34; speculative futures, 106, 122; startup futures, 4, 240; work futures, 248

Gandhi, Indira, 260n18

Gandhi, Mahatma, 76

Gandhi, Rajiv, 16

gender, 9, 24, 26, 61–62, 76, 79, 84, 88, 95, 100, 101, 107, 109, 111, 126, 238, 251, 263n5, 264n10, 268n17, 276n14; gender capital, 106, 111, 266–67n8; gender-coded work, 100; gender experimentation, 224; gender norms, 81, 104, 105; gender purity, 261n23; gendered bodies, 89; gendered bodies in the service of global capital, 85; gendered consumption, 264n11; gendered mobilities, 7, 89; and the labor of producing gender, 127–30; as a system of meaning through which everyday labor is distributed, 90

Gens: A Feminist Manifesto for the Study of Capitalism (Bear, Ho, Tsing, and Yanagisako), 11

Gidwani, Vinay, 27

Gimlet Media, 233

globalization, 4, 90; in India, 83, 228, 242

Global North, 9, 52, 55

Global South, 9

Gopakumar, Govind, 20

governance, techniques of, 151

Graeber, David, 15
Gregg, Melissa, 140, 176–77
Gupta, Akhil, 177, 180

Hasan, Anjum, 89
Held, Virginia, 190
Hinduism/Hindus, 195, 197, 199, 259n11, 266n5
Ho, Karen, 268n15
Hochschild, Arlie, 177, 295n18
home, importance of in reproductive services, 179
Honig, Bonnie, 270n9

identity, the "social" of, 144
India: colonial labor in, 23; "Digital India," 11; economic liberalization in, 16, 17–18, 81–82, 86–87, 260n16, 262n1; embodied middle classness in, 275n6; entrepreneurial economy of, 3; globalization in, 228, 242, 83; historical life of caste in Indian technology, 265–66n3; historiography of, 74; Indian enterprise and family networks, 266n4; middle-class professional work in, 24; new middle class of, 260n18, 260n20, 262n1; postcolonial India, 2
Indian Institute of Management, 127
information technology (IT): infrastructure of, 2; IT professionals, 7–8, 87–88; "IT women," 26; publics of, 88–89. See also information technology enabled services (ITES)
information technology enabled services (ITES), 88
infrastructures: "affective infrastructures," 165–66; "infrastructurescapes,"

20; uneven infrastructures of care, 199–202
Ingole, Anagha, 262n1
INK Talks, 104
innovation: distinction between "jugaad" and "innovation," 266–67n8; technoscientific innovation, 266n5
Irani, Lilly, 24, 143, 228, 230, 266–67n8, 167n10
Islam, Asiya, 29, 261n26
Iyengar, Krishna, 141–42, 153, 225, 226, 227–33, 247

Jameson Company, 104
Jayawardena, Kumari, 76
Jegathesan, Mythri, 229, 272n5
Jobs, Steve, 99
John, Mary, 264n14
"jugaad," 158, 268n14; distinction between "jugaad" and innovation, 266–67n8
"juki girls," 265n19
Jyothi, 51–52, 53–54, 65, 154, 246

Kannada, 16
Kaplan, Caren, 54
Karnataka flag, 17fig.
Kaur, Ravinder, 19, 259n12
Kelty, Christopher, 276n9
Khubchandani, Kareem, 86
Kimmel, Michael, 45
Knowledge Commission, 259n11
Kolar Gold Fields (KGF), 72–73, 75–76
Krishna, S. M., 18, 87

labor, 8, 238, 272n4; back-end tech labor, 2, 3; Black women's labor, 271–72n3;

labor (*continued*)

    categories of, 29; colonial labor, 23; contemporary analyses of, 177–78; as experimental future making, 210–14; feminist futures of, 253–54; "feminized labor," 4, 43, 140, 141, 258n4; gendered labor, 199, 273n10; gendered factory labor in Malaysia and Sri Lanka, 63–64; indentured labor, 269n7; invisibilized labor, 24; labor mobility, 3; as method, 9–15, 30, 64, 239–40; migrant labor, 28; pleasurable breaks from reproductive labor, 178–85; racialized labor, 5, 43, 227, 241, 275n3; "relational labor," 272–73n8; task-based labor, 274n13. *See also* labor, reproductive; work; workers

labor, reproductive, 4, 9, 12, 64, 112, 116, 119, 122, 132, 142, 143, 178, 234, 250–51, 266–67n8, 268n17, 269n8; gendered reproductive labor, 31; heterosexual reproductive labor, 30, 131; invisibilization of, 11. *See also* Captivate Travels, and breaks from reproductive labor

"Ladies Hostels," 38, 39*fig.*

Larsen, Jonas, 59

Lata's story, growing up in the company family, 192–95, 216–18, 247

Latour, Bruno, 46

"leisure money," 63

Linux, 226–27, 230, 276n9

longue durée fieldwork, 246–48

Lukose, Ritty, 200, 273–74n12

Lynch, Caitryn, 63, 258n4

Maharani College, 77–78

Malathi, 109–11, 112–13, 116–17, 118, 122, 131

Mallya, Vijay, 84

management: at Captivate Travels, 14, 19, 51, 55, 61, 63, 67, 140, 151–52, 154, 171, 184, 190, 214, 225, 251–52; celebrity management, 119; development management, 11; global management, 150; product management, 228; risk management, 265n1; total quality management (TQM), 223; tourism management, 155

Manalansan, Martin, 203–4

Mangalore, 155

Mani, Lata, 91–92, 262n1

Mankekar, Purnima, 144–47, 157, 176, 177, 180

Martin, Emily, 223, 271n15

Marxism, queer and trans, 28

masculinity, 6, 107, 108, 114, 140, 269n5; Brahmin masculinity, 103; and circulation, 267n11; hegemonic masculinity, 267n11; middle-class masculinity, 44, 111, 267n12; nationalist masculinity, 111; urban masculinity, 110

Maslow, Abraham, 143

Massey, Doreen, 122–23

Mauss, Marcel, 150

Mazzarella, William, 18

Mehnaz, 125–26; interview with, 124–25

Melamed, Jodi, 258–59n9

Melwani, Ramesh, 83–84

meritocracy, 3, 20, 67, 87; fiction of, 56

Mezzandri, Alessandra, 4, 178, 259–60n15

Mies, Maria, 148

Mirchandani, Kiran, 89, 271nn16–17

mobility, 26, 27, 30, 38, 45, 56, 78, 106, 114, 122, 170, 231, 252, 262n30; class mobility, 3, 19, 63, 75, 89, 112, 158, 265n19; global mobility, 131; labor mobility, 3; post-colonial mobility, 4; professional mobility, 229; regional mobility, 158; social mobility, 167, 261n23; upward mobility, 229–30

modernity, 25, 78, 82, 257–58n3, 262n1, 263n6; anti-imperial modernity, 2; the dream of science as, 2; global modernity, 93; markers of, 74

Modi, Narendra, 10

Mody, Perveez, 46

Mohanty, Chandra, 62

"moral community," 67

Mosse, David, 66–67

Murillo, Luis Felipe, 240

Murphy, Michelle, 127, 202–3

Nadasen, Premila, 271–72n3

Naina, 13, 38–40, 40–43, 67, 128

Nair, Janaki, 75, 80

Nakamura, Lisa, 272n4

Natasha, 161–62

nationalism, 82; Hindu nationalism, 10–11; Indian nationalism, 70; masculine nationalism, 3

National Union for Domestic Labor, 271–72n3

Neff, Gina, 100

Nehru, Jawaharlal, 2

Neilson, Brett, 4, 12, 259–60n15

neoliberalism, 70, 76, 95, 100, 114, 161, 241, 249–50, 265n1; neoliberal economy, 264n14; neoliberal feminism, 268n17; as ideology, 91–92; the neoliberal middle-class city, 93–94

Neti neti (Hasan), 89

New Computer Policy, 16

New Indian Woman, figure of, 82–83

"new tourism," 59

O'Malley, Pat, 265n1

Ong, Aihwa, 28, 63, 258n4

"oudhukum," 273n12

Oza, Rupal, 56, 82

Padios, Jan, 258n4, 272–73n8

Patel, Richa, 26

Petryna, Adriana, 216

philanthropism, 82

Philip, Kavita, 24

politics: "politics of pleasure," 275n20; respectability politics, 275n19

postcolonialism, 264n9; postcolonial aspiration, 3; and the postcolonial robot, 276n10; postcolonial science and technology, 32; postcolonial triumphalism, 19

power geometry, 122–23

"project time," 2

public-private partnerships, 93–94

publics, 250, 263n4; of the 1990s, 83; gendered labor of, 72–76; of IT, 88–89; performative nature of the public self, 270n9; pleasures of, 81; public of the samaj, 76; "recursive publics," 230; urban publics, 113

Puja, Ayudha, 266n5

"Queer Marxist Transfeminism, A" (Raha), 261n27

"Questions of Travel" (Kaplan), 54

race: racial capitalism, 10; racial violence, 10; and startup economies, 5–6. *See also* labor, racialized

Radhakrishnan, Smitha, 26, 88, 185; on the "South Indian ethos," 104

Radhika, 149–50, 157

Rajan, Kaushik Sunder, 267n9

Raju, Sarasvathy, 205–6

Raksha Bandhan festival, 191

Ramamurthy, Priti, 9, 27

Ratna, 71, 73, 74–76; daughters of, 76–77; feminism of, 72

rave parties, raids on, 85–86

Reengineering India (Upadhya), 143–44

Revolution at Point Zero (Federici), 263n3

risk, 30, 105–6, 107, 265n2; fabrication of, 114; production of, 104; risk management, 265n1; risk-taking masculinity, 108, 130–31

Rohit, 120–21, 122

Rosalso, Michelle, 274n17

Rotterberg, Catherine, 268n17

Ruhanna, interview with, 119–20

Sakshi, 221–22

Salzinger, Leslie, 140–41

Sandoval, Chela, 262–63n2

Sanjay, 157–58, 271n16; interview with, 155–57

Sanyal, Kalyan, 235

science and technology studies (STS), 6, 236

search engine optimization (SEO), 154, 173–74

Seizer, Susan, 263n7

Sekharan, Abhishek, 142

sexualization, of the female body, 242

Shankar, Sri Sri Ravi, 227, 231

Shanta, 71, 72, 74, 77, 79–81; samaj of, 95–96

Sharma, Sarah, 75

Shiv Sena, 78

Shonali, 181–83, 247

Simone, Abdoumaliq, 165, 238

Singh, Julietta, 232

Sinha, Mrinalini, 263n5

Sivaramakrishnan, K., 18

Smart India Hackathon, 11

Sneha, 199–201, 203, 241–46

social reproduction, 28, 166, 204

social scientists, 46

Solomon, Harris, 275n2, 276n8

space: distribution of time and space under startup capitalism, 116; scaling/movement across, 114–15

Sri Rama Sene (Army of Lord Rama), 86

Stallman, Richard, 226, 231

Star, Susan Leigh, 201

startup capitalism, 2, 3, 4, 10, 15, 25, 26, 37, 64–65, 98, 105, 114, 233–34, 241, 249, 254; and creative world making, 6; current formation of, 9; dispersed sites of, 40–43; distribution of time and space under, 116; early stages of, 45; male domination of, 127–28; neoliberal startup capitalism, 8; place and spatial imaginary in, 7; racialization of, 4–5; and the undoing of caste, 100–101; and visions of the future, 6–7

startup culture, landscape of, 43–47

Startup Festival, 21–26, 23*fig.*, 33*fig.*, 92–93, 97–98, 101–2, 105, 106–7, 128; graffiti on a wall of, 135*fig.*; itinerary of, 102, 114; participation in, 93–94; pedagogical training of, 107–8; registration requirements of, 43; schedule of, 91*fig.*

"Startup India" program, 10, 259n10

storytelling, 107

Strauss, Anselm, 201

Founded in 1893,
UNIVERSITY OF CALIFORNIA PRESS
publishes bold, progressive books and journals
on topics in the arts, humanities, social sciences,
and natural sciences—with a focus on social
justice issues—that inspire thought and action
among readers worldwide.

The UC PRESS FOUNDATION
raises funds to uphold the press's vital role
as an independent, nonprofit publisher, and
receives philanthropic support from a wide
range of individuals and institutions—and from
committed readers like you. To learn more, visit
ucpress.edu/supportus.

www.ingramcontent.com/pod-product-compliance
Lightning Source LLC
Chambersburg PA
CBHW020824270326
41928CB00006B/433